Translating Great Russian Literature

I0585806

Launched in 1950, Penguin's Russian Classics quickly progressed to include translations of many great works of Russian literature and the series came to be regarded by readers, both academic and general, as the de facto provider of classic Russian literature in English translation, the legacy of which reputation resonates right up to the present day. Through an analysis of the individuals involved, their agendas, and their socio-cultural context, this book, based on extensive original research, examines how Penguin's decisions and practices when translating and publishing the series played a significant role in deciding how Russian literature would be produced and marketed in English translation. As such the book represents a major contribution to Translation Studies, to the study of Russian literature, to book history and to the history of publishing.

Cathy McAteer is a post-doctoral research fellow at Exeter University

BASEES/Routledge Series on Russian and East European Studies

Series editors:

Sociology and anthropology: Judith Pallot (President of BASEES and Chair), University of Oxford
Economics and business: Richard Connolly, University of Birmingham
Media and cultural studies: Birgit Beumers, University of Aberystwyth
Politics and international relations: Andrew Wilson, School of Slavonic and East European Studies, University College London
History: Matt Rendle, University of Exeter

This series is published on behalf of BASEES (the British Association for Slavonic and East European Studies). The series comprises original, high-quality, research-level work by both new and established scholars on all aspects of Russian, Soviet, post-Soviet and East European Studies in humanities and social science subjects.

For a full list of available titles please visit: https://www.routledge.com/BASEES-Routledge-Series-on-Russian-and-East-European-Studies/book-series/BASEES

Translating Great Russian Literature

The Penguin Russian Classics

Cathy McAteer

Routledge
Taylor & Francis Group
LONDON AND NEW YORK

First published 2021
by Routledge
2 Park Square, Milton Park, Abingdon, Oxon OX14 4RN

and by Routledge
605 Third Avenue, New York, NY 10017

Routledge is an imprint of the Taylor & Francis Group, an informa business

British Library Cataloguing-in-Publication Data
A catalogue record for this book is available from the British Library

Library of Congress Cataloging-in-Publication Data
A catalog record has been requested for this book

ISBN: 978-0-367-50348-2 (hbk)
ISBN: 978-1-003-04958-6 (ebk)

Typeset in Times New Roman
by KnowledgeWorks Global Ltd.

Dedication

*I would like to thank the ERC-funded RusTrans project and the
Open Research Team at the University of Exeter for supporting
this publication. During the course of my research, I have received
particular assistance from the following people, whom I would like
especially to acknowledge: Penguin Books for their permission to use
the Penguin Archive; the Magarshack family, for their interest and
memories, as well as their permission to reproduce family photos and
extracts from archived papers; Richard Davies at the Leeds Russian
Archive; Hannah Lowery, Michael Richardson, and the Penguin
Researchers' Network at the Penguin Archive, University of Bristol.*

*I am grateful to the anonymous benefactor of my postgraduate research,
whose generosity funded me throughout my PhD; to my supervisors
Dr Rajendra Chitnis (University of Oxford) and Dr Carol O'Sullivan
(University of Bristol) for their guidance throughout my doctoral
research (the basis for this book); and to my RusTrans colleague Dr
Muireann Maguire at the University of Exeter for providing stimulating
post-doctoral mentorship and research opportunities amidst an
atmosphere of encouragement and good humour. I am also grateful
to my editors at Routledge, and to my external reader, who remains
anonymous, but who kindly gave my manuscript their blessing.*

*I would like to extend a special thank you to all the Penguin
translators and their families, for their service to literature and the
translation profession, for their direct assistance to my project,
for their quirks and their passion for language. Without you, I
would never have fallen in love with the Russian literary canon.*

*Finally, I dedicate this work to my husband, my sons,
and my parents for their unstinting support.*

Contents

List of figures

Preface

The cultural and intellectual achievements associated with Penguin Books, as an instigator of cultural change, apply equally to Penguin's series of Russian Classics in translation, which disseminated Russian novels in Anglophone translation across continents, social strata (from academics to national servicemen), and over several decades. Launched in 1950 with Gilbert Gardiner's translation of Ivan Turgenev's *On the Eve*, Penguin's Russian Classics quickly progressed to include translations of Russian classics such as *Crime and Punishment*, *Anna Karenin*, *War and Peace*, *A Hero of Our Time*, *Oblomov*, *Dead Souls*, and many more. The series came to be regarded by readers – both academic and general – in the mid- to late-twentieth century as the *de facto* provider of classic Russian literature in English translation, the legacy of which reputation resonates right up to the present day. By combining publishing innovation with translations written in good, modern English and aspiring to the first Penguin Classics series editor E.V. Rieu's 'principle of equivalent effect', Penguin brought classic Russian literature into a post-Constance Garnett twentieth-century to suit a self-improving, inquisitive, post-war British reader. This book offers the first analysis of this popular series (from 1950-present day), identifying Penguin's Russian Classics as a modern translation publishing phenomenon.

Through an analysis of the individuals involved, their agendas, and their socio-cultural context, this book demonstrates that Penguin's decisions and practices when translating and publishing the Penguin Classics series played a significant role in deciding how Russian literature would be produced and marketed in English translation today. This series gained a reputation for quality textual content (including informative introductions) targeted at all readers; recognisable branding with global sales; affordable prices offered in accessible outlets. *Translating Great Russian Literature* is the first book-length study of the relationship between Russian-to-English literary translation and a major modern British publisher.

Translating Great Russian Literature uses previously neglected archival sources (reviews, letters, notes, articles), interviews with key figures, and translation analysis to supply lost background information about the translators who formed the first Penguin Russian Classics cohort: Elisaveta Fen,

Gilbert Gardiner, and Rosemary Edmonds (about whom very little has been written). This book additionally provides the first case study of the prominent Russian literary translator David Magarshack. Magarshack regarded himself as a 'gatekeeper' of Russian culture for post-war British readers, a view endorsed not just by general readers but also by figures such as Anthony Powell, Kazuo Ishiguro, and even former British Foreign Secretary and Prime Minister Sir Anthony Eden, who was photographed holding a copy of Magarshack's *Turgenev: A life* on one of his diplomatic missions. Along with Rosemary Edmonds, Magarshack was one of the longest-serving early Penguin Russian translators, only surpassed by Ronald Wilks who came to Penguin later. No other Penguin Russian translator provides detailed archival information specifically about their translation practice, theory and career progression. Magarshack constitutes, therefore, a key point of reference for the translators who preceded him (Garnett), worked alongside him (Edmonds, Fen), and succeeded him (Wilks, David McDuff, Oliver Ready). Magarshack's case study – based on his notes on translation, extensive correspondence for seven large-scale Penguin publications between 1951 and 1964, and an in-depth text-based analysis in Chapter Three of Magarshack's approach to translating Dostoevskii, in particular *Crime and Punishment* – assumes importance for the insight it gives into literary translation and publishing practices (and theories) in the mid-twentieth century. It provides a keyhole view into an era of modern translation publishing characterised by attempts to domesticate Russian names and dialogue; to provide explanatory introductions and few footnotes, uniformity in transliteration, attractive cover designs, high-volume print runs, low prices, and paratextual advertising; to pay translators an advance and royalties. My critical focus on Penguin's first phase of translation publishing provides the basis for extended analysis in Chapter Four of Penguin's post-Magarshack Russian literary translation trends when Penguin embarked on commissions with new translators for works of Soviet literature to satisfy a politically interested target audience.

While some of Magarshack's translations are now regarded as over-Anglicised, in their day they symbolised the Penguin Classics mission of presenting 'the general reader with readable and attractive versions of the great writers' books in modern English, shorn of the […] archaic flavour and the foreign idiom that renders so many existing translations repellent to modern taste' (Rieu, 1946). *Translating Great Russian Literature* utilises a combination of archival and text-based analysis to explore how far Penguin, Magarshack and other translators fulfilled Rieu's Penguin Classic manifesto; the ways in which early Penguin Russian translators, particularly Magarshack, have influenced subsequent translators (McDuff, Pevear and Volokhonskaia, Ready); and the extent to which Penguin's Russian Classics prepared the Anglophone readership for the subsequent arrival of Soviet literature. *Translating Great Russian Literature* will illustrate that this series, which continues to evoke a fondness among the readers who first received them, serves as an essential link between Constance Garnett's earliest translations and twenty-first century literary translation.

The different rationales, motives and operational complexities behind the selection of a foreign text for translation are recurring considerations throughout the course of this book. Questions prevail over who will translate the foreign text; who will write its paratext and with a view to projecting which message; who will publish it and why? Who 'will take some sort of possession of it, and slant it with his own point of view, and explain how it fits into the field of reception' (Bourdieu, 1990, p. 222)? The nineteenth-century Anglo-Russian political climate – framed by 'a ready tradition of native Russophobia' (Bullock, 2009, p. 24) and fuelled by events such as the Great Game, the crushing by the Russians of the Polish rebellion in 1830-31, and the Crimean War – encouraged early translators to play to the British public's anti-Russian sentiment and translations became vehicles for propagandistic purposes. What we now know as Lermontov's *A Hero of Our Time* first appeared in 1853 as *Sketches of Russian Life in the Caucasus*, a title that, from the outset, misleadingly suggested a non-fictional account of life in southern Russia. A carefully chosen cover image also endorsed the impression of factuality and lent a paratextual value which conforms to Genette's description of 'iconic' messaging (1987, p. 265). (Within a century, paratextual value would become a key feature of the Penguin Classics series too.) Lermontov was described on the cover page as 'a Russe many years resident amongst the various tribes' and the translator remained anonymous. In the same way, the first English translation of Gogol's *Dead Souls*, which arrived in Britain one year into the Crimean War in 1854, was inaccurately entitled *Home Life in Russia by a Russian Noble*. This translation was the work of Krystyn Lach-Szyrma, a Polish count, writer, journalist, translator, and political activist based in England. The unnamed editor's carefully crafted paratextual intervention leaves the reader in no doubt about Britain's position in Europe's bellicose landscape. Anti-Russian bias permeates Lach-Szyrma's rendering of the source text: he frequently omitted positive images of Russian life, leaving any existing negative images to stand in high relief. It is clear that Lach-Szyrma's interest was not in consecrating great literature.[1]

As regards the reading of foreign literature, a wider audience[2] was being reached towards the end of the nineteenth century thanks to the introduction in 1870 of the Forster Education Act. Publishers realised that '[w]hen larger numbers could read, there was a larger potential market for publishers to exploit' (Feather, 2006, p. 108). Consequently, foreign literature publications increased through outlets like the Everyman's Library (Feather, 2009, p. 107), The Walter Scott Publishing Company, Vizetelly's 'Du Boisgobey's Sensational Novels' and 'Celebrated Russian Novels' series,[3] George Bell and Sons' 'Bohn's Libraries', and Heinemann's International Library. However, the reaching-out to a wider readership did not come without tensions. In 'The Reader-Brand: Tolstoy in England at the Turn of the Century' (2011), Gwendolyn Blume argues that new access, on a national scale, to literature and learning initiated a schism, a cultural divide between the literary 'elite' and the mass audience. Blume argues that the introduction of Russian literature into Britain's new literary landscape revealed an 'inability of the elite to control access to cultural knowledge' (ibid., p. 322), and, consequently, allowed the circulation of Russian literature across all social strata. To read Russian literature in the original would prove as 'off limits' for much of the literary elite as it would for the everyday reader: a levelling experience, therefore. Writing specifically about Tolstoi's assimilation into the British literary field, Blume remarks that an element of intellectual elitism was sustained for a period by reading Tolstoi's works in French translation (ibid., p. 324). However, spotting an opportunity to sell more books, publishers produced the full series of Tolstoi's works (even the lesser-known ones) (ibid., p. 325), not only accommodating the elitist reader's need to exhibit literary one-upmanship and superior knowledge, but also embracing the new brand of Education-Act reader by making more world literature available in English.

The Surbiton-born, Dresden-educated publisher William Heinemann (1863-1920), who had been trained, like Penguin founder Allen Lane, in every aspect of publishing,[4] had his most successful break in terms of literature in translation with the creation of Heinemann's International Library in 1890 (Rees, 2017, p. 180). This series of foreign literary works was headed by the editor (and translator of Ibsen), Edmund Gosse (1849-1928) (St John, 1990, p. 16) whose editorial attributes – reputed linguistic skills, meticulousness, industriousness and punctuality – were also demonstrated years later by the Penguin Classics editors, Rieu and Glover, and may be suggestive of an editorial type. Heinemann's International Library boasted seventeen foreign language titles by 1894 and became one of the 'cornerstones of Heinemann's prosperity' (St John, 1990, p. 16). This prosperity can be attributed, not just to Heinemann's patronage or to Gosse's editorial talents, but to the services of Constance Garnett. Between 1892 and the mid-1920s, Garnett (1861–1946) translated over seventy volumes of Russian literature, the majority of which were published either by Heinemann or Chatto and Windus (Garnett, 2009, pp. 361–362). Garnett's work has been described as 'prodigious almost beyond belief' (Smith, 2000, p. 85)[5] and continues to receive accolades even now.[6]

When literary commentators discuss her contribution, 'single-handedly' is a word that appears with frequency[7] but, whilst the linguistic achievement was indeed hers, it would be simplistic to suggest that she worked alone in cornering the market. Garnett's professional relationship with Heinemann is scarcely analysed in accounts of her career[8] but is of relevance to our understanding of modern Russian-English literary translation at Penguin. Here is a translation publishing model that allows us to observe how translators and publishers began to collaborate professionally, how they responded to market interest and achieved commercial and personal aims by working together. Arguably, without Heinemann, Garnett might not have become a figurehead of translation; and equally, Heinemann would not have enjoyed financial success or such a pre-eminent position in the field of translated literature.

There were pressures too, though. Commercial decisions and market demands drove Heinemann's decisions at the expense of the translator's rights. Heinemann's biggest bone of contention concerned the author's (and later, the translator's) expectation of receiving a royalty, a development which, as Feather argues, 'created new tensions in the trade' (2006, p. 132). He turned down, or at least deferred, all Garnett's requests for some sort of modest royalty on the sale of her translations (St John, 1990, p. 80). In an effort to balance the cost of producing longer books against the risk that they might not sell (as had been the case with Garnett's Tolstoi translations), Heinemann also cut Garnett's pay (ibid.) from twelve to nine shillings per thousand words. Heinemann's unwillingness to pay Garnett exposes the reality that translators had no representation or power as agents attempting to navigate terms in the literary field. Despite an increase in prestige and visibility as a translator (Deane-Cox, 2014, p. 71), Garnett failed to convince Heinemann to translate her symbolic capital – her linguistic, literary, reputational value – into a comparable economic return. In her last attempt in April 1915 to persuade him to pay her a royalty, she pointed out that she was, in fact, 'being paid less for what I am doing for you now than for the work I did in 1895 when I had no name and no experience' (St John, 1990, p. 80). Heinemann's failure to reward Garnett (financially and reputationally) ultimately rendered their relations untenable. With her next proposal, Garnett found a new publisher, Chatto & Windus (St John, 1990, p. 81), and her collection of Chekhov's short stories was published by them in 1916. Heinemann arguably lost the surest route to continued success in his foreign literature publications. This loss might well have influenced Rieu's decision, fifty or so years later, to settle from the outset financial terms and conditions (advances, royalty percentages, and payouts) with his freelancers and to commission more than one specialist per Penguin Classic language, thereby creating an effective, occasionally essential, safety net, which could allow translators to leave without impacting too significantly on production.[9] Heinemann and Garnett represent a valid reference point, therefore, against which it is possible to compare Penguin's twentieth-century publisher-translator relations.

The practical evidence supporting this monograph relies on a methodology that has emerged from the sociological turn in Translation Studies and has recently been advocated by Jeremy Munday, namely, the deployment of archival sources as a way of understanding translators and their translation decisions. Careful and judicious scrutiny of archival material may be used to build a picture, a microhistory (Munday, 2014, p. 65), of the way in which agents interact and produce texts, which cannot be deduced from study of the primary text alone. Munday argues for the usefulness of a microhistory because 'it links the individual case study with the general socio-historical context' (2014, p. 75). He acknowledges that careful application of a micro-historical approach provides the means to reveal information about socio-logical factors – the agents, the nature of their agency, the climate in which they work – which form an era of translation (like Penguin Classics, for example):

> It behoves us to seek out and preserve such accounts and to relate them to the wider social and cultural conditions in which the individuals lived in order to enhance our understanding of the general history of translation. (Munday, 2014, p. 77)

He continues:

> On the larger scale, the new narratives we construe [...] have the potential to challenge dominant historical discourses of text production (ibid.).

Munday maintains that archives are much under-utilised resources which provide new scope for assessing the individual publisher, editor, and translator in their broader 'socio-historical and cultural contexts' (ibid., p. 65). He argues in favour of using archives 'to excavate and recover details of lives past [...] in order to constitute what I term a "microhistory" of translation and translators' (ibid., p. 64). Munday acknowledges that the term 'microhistory' has its origins in the humanities and is associated with 'historians, social scientists and literary theorists' (ibid.). In an earlier paper, 'The Role of Archival and Manuscript Research in the Investigation of Translator Decision-Making' (2013), Munday notes that the use of archived materials to access 'the creative process that is literary translation' (ibid., p. 126) is 'not a typical form of analysis in translation process research' (ibid.). However, if translation scholars are sufficiently flexible to apply methods and selective terminology from the social sciences, arts and humanities to their own discipline, and they can access material which is 'generally hard to find in many collections and require[s] some excavation' (Munday, 2014, p. 71), then archived documents can prove, according to Munday, 'indispensable' (ibid., p. 64). This is an area of rapidly growing interest in translation research. I have used Munday's framework to interrogate the different motivations behind Penguin's commissions, identifying: the translator's eligibility for a commission; the publisher's/editor's perception of a translator's monetary worth; the translation strategy itself; the way in which a translation is presented and marketed for maximum sales and audience appeal.

I have also adopted some sociological – Bourdieusian – terms at times in my analysis too, in order to deliver a meaningful evaluation of Penguin's corporate and literary position, to interpret the relevance of archived primary material, and then to make visible Penguin's less well-known individuals. Sociological terminology can occasionally be problematic, though, and is often regarded as overly abstract and imprecise, consistent with a research area 'still "in the making"' (Wolf, 2007, p. 31). Bourdieu's own treatment of sociological concepts, habitus, for example, has been described as nebulous (Walther, 2014, p. 22) and, according to translation scholar Reine Meylaerts 'the concept suffers from theoretical abstraction and methodological imprecision' (2006, p. 60). There is a recognition among translation scholars, like Meylaerts, that Bourdieu's vocabulary requires further refinement if it is to serve Translation Studies effectively. In the spirit of ongoing critique, this book incorporates some Bourdieusian terms (such as: 'capital', 'habitus', 'patronage', *'illusio'*) but also contributes to the refinement that Meylaerts seeks by demonstrating that some terms are more useful than others in the context of Penguin and its employees. In the chapters which are dedicated to Magarshack, for example, I argue that the term *'hexis'* is more applicable to exploring the complexities of character and position than the term 'habitus'.

This book seeks to take forward Munday's investigations into agency and, therefore, to advance the sociological turn (Wolf, 2007, p. 6). First, my research does not privilege either the publisher (McCleery (2002), Sapiro (2008)) or the translator (Simeoni (1998), Munday (2013, 2014), Buzelin (2005), Sela-Sheffy (2008)) as independent agents; it forces a finer-grain analysis on each of them but, crucially, as part of a diverse network of collaboration, from those directly involved in the project (the publisher, editors, and translators) to those who are indirectly involved (general readers, reviewers, and academics). In Penguin terms, my analysis starts with the relationships between the founder of Penguin Books, Allen Lane, the series and copy editors Emile Victor Rieu and Alan (A.S.B.) Glover, and the first Russian translators Gardiner, Fen, Edmonds, and Magarshack; and finishes with an analysis of more recent Penguin Russian translators and the arrival of Soviet literature. Reference is also made to target readers (general and academic) and their correspondence with Penguin, as well as reviewers who influenced public opinion paratextually in the national press.

Second, in a departure from the agency-focused sociological turn, I have reintroduced textual analysis, regarding it as an essential component of this study. Daniel Simeoni places methodological emphasis on 'the practices of translating and authoring rather than on texts' (1998, p. 33), which has been interpreted as a privileging of agent/agency analysis over text-based analysis (Meylaerts, 2006, p. 60). There are benefits, however, from an analysis which reunites the agent(s) with their work. An archive-informed analysis of the translated text explains, for example, 'surface manifestations' (Simeoni, 1998, p. 5) of the personal and commercial dynamics behind the literary collaboration, in the translator's chosen strategy, and publisher, editor or translator bias. This combined approach is only possible where archives yield sufficient material; the text-oriented study that features in Chapter Three – specifically of Magarshack's work but with occasional reference to Edmonds too – capitalises on such archival insight as a final way of exploring whether Penguin's aims influenced translation practice and to what extent we can perceive a translator's personal and professional background manifesting itself in the finished text.

In this book, therefore, I have synthesised innovative strands of Translation Studies: socio-historical, archival, and textual analysis in order to explain the rise of Penguin, its Russian classics, and individual agents (most notably Lane, Rieu, and Magarshack) whose collaboration determined success. A combined approach of this nature facilitates a more holistic investigation into agents and their agency, ultimately revealing: dynamics of commercial, literary collaboration; the place of each agent within the collaborative network and, where applicable, in a bigger socio-historical context; how agents' varying cultural influences and aspirations have a noticeable impact on the finished text and, more broadly, on the representation of another nation's literature in English translation. The Penguin Russian commissions may be indicative of the practices employed throughout the early Penguin Classics series and will become all the more interpretable 'in the context of other similar studies which will enable comparisons to be made across translators and projects' (Munday, 2013, p. 137).

My research has centred on the Penguin archive, housed at the University of Bristol. Among the 2,300 boxes that constitute the Penguin archive (Clements, 2009), there are twenty-three Russian Classics folders for the period from 1950-1970, and approximately fifteen files from 1970 to the early 1980s.[10] The rich, albeit fragmentary, mass of material has never been used to analyse the dynamics behind Penguin's relaunch of nineteenth-century Russian literature. I have mainly utilised the folders which specifically concern Russian titles published during the Medallion and Black Cover Titles phases.[11] The Medallion Titles were the earliest incarnation of the Penguin Classics series, which began in 1946 with Rieu's translation *The Odyssey* and lasted until its transition in 1962 to Black Cover Titles.[12] The final chapter of this book extends my analysis to the post-Rieu additions to the Russian Classics titles, which include lesser-known works by key Russian authors, re-translations of some of the very first Russian titles in the series, and also introduces Penguin's move into Soviet literature.

There are a number of reasons behind my decision to focus significant attention on the earliest phases of the Penguin Classics series. The Medallion Titles, so called because of the roundels on their front covers,[13] mark a period of intense activity when ideas and translation commissions flourished. There is substantial correspondence in the archive, perhaps reflecting the fact that questions were being raised for the first time. These enquiries prove most informative about early initiatives. There is valuable consistency to the themes that were discussed, including the selection of titles, the search for eligible translators, translation strategy, terms of employment and pay, the logistics of obtaining source texts, managing deadlines and publishing dates, and negotiating corrections. Correspondence for the early Penguin Russian titles contains most, sometimes all, of these editorial concerns at various times and to varying degrees. The fact that there is thematic consistency in the questions which arise, provides a valuable point of comparison from one commission and translator to another. With translators working to the same corporate terms and conditions (but not necessarily always the same pay), and all handling classic Russian literature to fulfil the same corporate mission, the variables in my archival analysis have centred on the nature of the interactions between agents. Analysis of correspondence and memos exchanged between Penguin editors and translators has allowed me to engage with the personalities and the processes behind commissioning, translating, and publishing a text. Out of a total of 122 Classic titles produced during the first phase of Penguin Classics, these sixteen Russian works represent the most active and productive phase in Penguin's Russian translations. By comparison, the next phase of Penguin Classics, the Black Cover titles, includes only ten Russian titles out of a total of 128 Classics, but represent a period of transition at Penguin, both in terms of the titles being selected for translation with a subtle shift towards Soviet literature, and in terms of editorial staff changes. These titles, therefore, warrant investigation too.

I encountered pitfalls commonly associated with archive usage, as identified in Munday's methodology (2014, p. 69), but also a number of problems that relate specifically to the Penguin archive. Whilst much of the correspondence comes from outside the company, material on the company itself is often corporate in nature and should be used with caution, for example, the in-house publicity booklet *Penguins Progress*, sent free-of-charge to 50,000 readers on request (Yates, 2006, p. 114), advertisements, interviews, memos, readers' reports, etc. In addition, the scale and complexity of the archive, with its multiple classifications by subject, series, date, and name, pose difficulties for the researcher. In 'Penguin Books and the Translation of Spanish and Latin American Poetry' (2016), Tom Boll alludes to complex layers of Penguin history which cloud research. He writes that '[a]ny attempt to establish a coherent narrative trajectory is complicated [...] by the diversity of the cast and the variety of their roles' (p. 29). The archive consists of 500 metres of Penguin titles; it grows by one metre of shelf space every month (Clements, 2009) and has yet to be fully catalogued online. It would be impossible, therefore, within the realistic timescale of a research project, to scour all of its contents and piece together a detailed overview of sales trends, contracts, and the terms and conditions.

Gaps in evidence – which cannot be attributed to Penguin withholding commercially sensitive information but reflect more a general lack of consistent record-keeping in the early years – lead ultimately to unanswered questions. It proved impossible, for example, to find exact details regarding recruitment, since it is generally acknowledged that many of the early decisions at Penguin were brokered over business lunches and details were either only sketchily or, more often, never documented.[14] Similarly, the recording of sales figures is patchy and inconsistent, or otherwise unsystematically filed, making it more difficult to measure Penguin's success in quantitative terms. The archive did not always yield sufficient material – copies of sample translations, readers' reports, and copies of proofs with corrections – on which to build in-depth case studies for all the translators in the cohort, therefore. In the case of Magarshack and Fen, however, I was able to consult their archives at the Leeds Russian archive. For the other early Penguin translators who do not have private archives, I analysed archive-based correspondence about their contributions to Penguin's Russian Classics alongside press reviews from journals at that time and digital archives for *The Times* and *The Times Literary Supplement* in order to consolidate and augment biographical detail.

While researching 'A Conservative Revolution in Publishing', Pierre Bourdieu encountered the 'extremely secretive attitude of a professional milieu that is ill disposed to the prying questions of outsiders and therefore disinclined to disclose either tactical information regarding sales or descriptive information regarding the social characteristics of their executives' (2008, p. 127). Adrienne Mason observes in 'Molière Among the Penguins' (2014) that '[i]t is often difficult to assess the impact of factors such as the publishing house, editorial policy, marketing strategy or commercial viability on the nature and diffusion of a translation because publishers' records are seldom available' (p. 123). As Mason and I have both found to our advantage, however, the existence of such data in the Penguin archive, and the Leeds Russian archive too, no matter how dispersed, is transformative for researchers. The contents of both archives can be utilised effectively to demonstrate how 'interactions govern not only the choice of translator and titles for translation but the way the text is translated' (ibid.).

Useful insights have been gained from the findings of other researchers who have already consulted the Penguin archive. For example, Wootten's and Donaldson's *Reading Penguin: A Critical Anthology* (2013) consists of twelve essays resulting from the AHRC-funded Penguin Archive Project which was based at the University of Bristol between May 2008 and April 2012 (ibid., pp. xiv-xv).[15] Collectively, these essays have provided a signposting service for the interdisciplinary scope and exact location of material stored in the archive. I have used books by Jeremy Lewis (*Penguin Special, The Life and Times of Allen Lane* (2006)) and Steve Hare (*Penguin Portrait, Allen Lane and the Penguin Editors 1935-1970* (1995)), compiled through their own archive-based research, for quick and reliable checking of names, dates and event chronology. Over two hundred Penguin Collectors Society (PCS) contributors (Yates, 2006, p. 7) conduct ongoing research into Penguin and their findings have assisted in this book too.[16] Of particular relevance is their publication *Penguin Classics* (Edwards, Hare and Robinson, 2008). It includes an essay by Bryan Platt on Rieu and his founding of the series; Hare's essay 'A History of Penguin Classics', which juxtaposes the characteristics of Rieu's editorship with Betty Radice's; Rieu's own essay on his translation strategy entitled 'The Faith of a Translator'; Tanya Schmoller's essay 'Roundel Trouble', which explains how Penguin matched the translated text with a front-cover roundel; and a comprehensive list of the first 250 titles included in the series, with names of translators, dates of publication, and issue reference numbers. The information collated in this, the PCS's other reference book, Yates's *The Penguin Companion* (2006), and Henry Eliot's more recent *The Penguin Classics Book* (2018) has provided this book with material specific to the early Classics series and sourced directly from the archive, for which I would otherwise have had to spend considerable time hunting in dispersed locations within the archive.

The opportunities are still considerable for researching and interpreting the translation practices and editorial processes applied to other national literatures represented in the Penguin Classics series. Some research, from a translation perspective, has already been conducted in the French series by Mason, who laments, as I do, that 'the creative and interpretative status of those responsible for a translation is still not universally acknowledged or thought worthy of much critical attention' (2014, p. 123). Sun Kyoung Yoon has conducted research into Rieu's translations of Homer, arguing that his translation practice and ethos can be appreciated as 'egalitarian' (2014, pp. 179–184). For his chapter 'How to Fillet a Penguin' (2012), Rob Crowe researched Penguin's handling of Latin and Greek texts requiring expurgation and I echo his observation that 'A full(er) understanding of what is going on in books, and more precisely why, cannot be achieved without dogged enquiry into the shadowy world of a publication's genesis, and a serious attempt to come to terms with the world into which the book is delivered' (ibid., p. 209). In his study of Penguin's Spanish and Latin American poetry translations, Boll (2016) argues that 'a focus on the social interactions that produced those publications allows an observer to draw contemporary lessons from the Penguin history [...] one can begin to identify how new translation projects might be formulated in the current dispositions of publishing, public funding, research assessment and impact' (ibid., p. 57). In a timely way, therefore, this book draws on socio-historical, archival, and textual approaches to construct the first 'microhistory' of Penguin's Russian Classics: the people, their working relations, their thoughts on translation, and the end products.

The accumulation of David Magarshack's detailed archival material both in the Penguin archive and the Leeds Russian archive reflects his character, his engagement with the literary field (both in the United Kingdom and the Union of Soviet Socialist Republics), his development from translator to translation theorist, and his desire to accrue status. Magarshack's private papers, stored at the Leeds Russian archive, comprise twenty-seven boxes (of texts, correspondence, notes, photographs, articles, reviews, posters, and theatre programmes for productions which used his translations). Whilst Chekhov translator Elisaveta Fen's archive contains valuable correspondence with Rieu relating to her contributions as an advisor assisting with the early selection of translators and assessing sample translations (see Chapter One), it does not contain articles, reviews, advertisements, notes,

or theorising which specifically relate to her translation practice, translation theory, and career progression in the way that Magarshack's does.[17]
Magarshack's Penguin papers, therefore, have yielded the most comprehensive amount of information specifically relevant to this book. The accumulation of this personal material lends new insight into a man who needed
to earn his living, which can be seen as early as 1928 in his letters seeking
employment at the *Manchester Guardian*. Magarshack's desire for status
and professional affirmation is reflected in the papers he saved. The assid-
uous preservation of papers suggests that someone – perhaps Magarshack
himself or his wife, Elsie – believed in the future merit of researchers being
able to access the diverse range of references to his life's work, from fleeting mentions in the local press and a 'Happy New Year' postcard from the
USSR-Great Britain Society, to boxes full of letters (from critics, publishers,
and well-known cultural figures Sir John Gielgud, thanking Magarshack
for his advice on staging Chekhov, and Anthony Powell agreeing to endorse
an effort by English Heritage to honour Magarshack's literary translations
with a blue plaque).[18]

Magarshack's archive contains enough material about his role as an agent
of translation (and translation theory) for a researcher to construct an original microhistory. For this reason, Magarshack features more than any other
translator. In particular, this book examines Magarshack's correspondence,
literary reviews, and his notes on translation strategy, and juxtaposes this
with an analysis of his 1951 Penguin translation of *Crime and Punishment*
(his very first Penguin commission), with a view to finding the extent to
which we can see the context in the publications. *Crime and Punishment* has
been chosen for archival and textual reasons. The Magarshack case study
examines the development of his career from émigré, journalist, novelist,
and biographer to successful literary translator, and analyses the way in
which he utilised personal capital, position in the field, and reputation to
further his career both within and beyond Penguin.

Magarshack's case study – with his notes on translation and extensive correspondence for seven large-scale Penguin publications – therefore, assumes
particular importance for the insight it gives into literary translation and
publishing practices (and theories) in the mid-twentieth century. It has also
been possible to gain more detailed insight into the finer practicalities of
working for a collaboration like Penguin's Russian Classics, specifically by
drawing comparisons between Magarshack's and Rosemary Edmonds's
tenures and practice. Whilst there is a relative paucity of archival material
relating to Edmonds (only the correspondence stored in the Penguin archive
is available), she was also long serving (her first contract agreement is dated
24 July 1950) and was an equally productive Russian translator in the early
corps with seven publications between 1954 and 1966. Further parallels
are made in Chapter Four between Magarshack and his successor Ronald
Wilks, who also translated Gogol, Chekhov, Dostoevskii, among others.
Edmonds's and Wilks's commissions generated detailed exchanges with the

Penguin editorial team and have provided some useful comparisons with Magarshack's Penguin career.

When handling primary sources, gaps emerge in correspondence; exchanges can suddenly tail off or die; there is the potential for ambiguity and subjectivity. During the course of my research, I had the opportunity to interview Magarshack's daughter, Stella, who provided some of the biographical detail that was missing from the Penguin archive. However, where the material is sourced via interviews – or 'oral history' (Munday, 2014, p. 66) – there is a risk that the 'mediation of memory' (ibid.) can result in unreliability. I treat this oral history with some caution, therefore, especially after discovering archived correspondence that suggested an alternative outcome to some of those recollections recorded about Magarshack during my interview with Stella Magarshack.[19] Wherever possible, I have corroborated reminiscences, either referring to other, alternative primary sources or to reliable secondary sources. Access to other archives has not always been possible, however. As Munday recognises, there are 'gatekeepers who control access' (ibid., p. 72). In the case of this project, permission was sought on several occasions, but has not yet been given by Curtis Brown, to explore the Columbia University-held Curtis Brown archive which holds further material relating to Magarshack.[20]

Chapter One analyses the origins of Penguin's Russian Medallion Titles through a microhistorical approach, constructed largely based on correspondence held in the Penguin and Leeds Russian archives. It examines Penguin's early interest in Russia as expressed via *The Penguin Russian Review*; the origins of the Penguin Classics series; the backgrounds, careers, and professional suitability of the editors E.V. Rieu and A.S.B. Glover and of their early freelancing translators, Gardiner, Fen, Edmonds and Magarshack. This chapter explores Penguin's publisher-editor-translator relations by investigating day-to-day commissioning practices, with topics ranging from pay negotiations and royalties to translation style, corrections, and deadlines. Archival material pertaining particularly to Fen, Magarshack, and Edmonds provides historical insight into early Penguin's practical translation publishing concerns.

Chapter Two provides a detailed case study of David Magarshack, who serves as a bridge between pre- and post-Penguin Russian translators, and follows his development as a translator/translation theorist with comparisons to other Russian literary translators as appropriate (for example, Garnett, Edmonds, Fen, Chukovskii, and Nabokov). This chapter uses Magarshack's previously unpublished, and largely unexplored, drafts, lectures, and notes on translation as a means of analysing how Magarshack's professional background (a life spent partly in Russia and a career spent entirely in the United Kingdom) formed the general principles behind his translation practice and a benchmark for subsequent, more recent Dostoevskii translations. It locates Magarshack's views on translation and on his role as a cultural gatekeeper in the context of contemporary Soviet and Western translation scholars, while exploring how Magarshack's personal and professional (Penguin) background was channelled into his final commission, a book on literary translation theory.

Chapter Three evaluates Magarshack's practice in light of his own theorising and seeks textual manifestations of his personal and professional background (as detailed in Chapters One and Two). Archival evidence supports a traditional text-based analysis of Magarshack's 1951 Penguin translation of *Crime and Punishment*, selected because it is the very first translation Magarshack undertook for Penguin and benefits from rich archival documentation. This chapter considers the opinions of reviewers at the time when *Crime and Punishment* was published with a view to assessing how Magarshack's translation strategies were first received, but also compares Magarshack's Dostoevskii translation decisions with those made by his successors, namely David McDuff, Oliver Ready and Nicolas Pasternak Slater.

Chapter Four examines what happened at Penguin's Russian Classics after the departure of Rieu, Magarshack and the earliest cohort, and analyses the series with a focus from 1964 to the mid-1970s. This chapter introduces the next phase of Penguin Russian translators – Ronald Wilks, Ralph Parker, Charles Johnston, Michael Glenny, David Burg, and Lord Nicholas Bethell – and identifies shifts in Penguin's translation interests to suit an audience now more familiar (thanks to the first cohort of series translators) with Russian names, places, and culture-specific references. This chapter tracks Penguin's post-Rieu commissions of lesser-known classic Russian literature alongside re-translations of the key works by Dostoevskii, but also introduces Soviet literature (Solzhenitsyn, in particular).

The **Conclusion** asserts that Penguin's distinctive success lies in sociocultural timeliness, in the shrewd selection of literary/language experts, and the ability of its editors and translators to seize their professional opportunities (and, at times, to challenge the field's status quo). The conclusion explores the extent to which the Anglophone readership has received Penguin's Russian Classics through a specific, yet evolving Penguin filter and argues that Penguin, Magarshack, and his fellow translators left literary legacies for Russian literature in modern English translation.

Notes

1. On a more magnified and modern scale still, the same processes and preoccupations can be found again, just over half a century later, in Gorkii's post-revolutionary Soviet drive (so-called *Vsemirnaia literatura*, his 'World Literature Publishing House', or 'Worldlit' (Leighton, 1991, pp. 6–7)) to translate and publish millions of copies of works of politically-harmonious, state-endorsed world literature. Brian James Baer writes in *Translation and the Making of Modern Russian Literature*, that 'Translation played an important and very visible role within the Soviet empire as reflected in the domestic policy of *druzhba narodov*, or friendship of Soviet peoples, [...] and in the Soviet Union's foreign policy, which sought to establish Moscow as the capital of world communism' (2016, p. 60).

2. As Gwendolyn Blume notes, 'the masterpieces of world literature became a mark of education – or a self-education that could replicate the effects of education' (2011, p. 330).

3. Vizetelly was progressive in terms of applauding and publishing Russian literature. His 'Celebrated Russian Novels' series consisted of ten titles according to Denise Merkle (2009, p. 89), but from my own research, I have found evidence of twelve titles. According to the opening pages of another Vizetelly publication from the French Sensational Novels series, *Where's Zenobia?* (du Boisgobey, 1888) the following eleven Russian titles are advertised in the 'Celebrated Russian Novels' series: Tolstoi's *Anna Karenina, War and Peace, My Husband and I*, and *The Cossacks*; Dostoevskii's *Crime and Punishment, Injury and Insult, The Friend of the Family* and *The Gambler, The Idiot*; Gogol's *Dead Souls, Taras Bulba*; and finally, Lermontov's *A Hero of Our Time* (no translator names are given). The <onlinebooks.library> website shows that one further translation by Whishaw is listed as a Vizetelly publication: *Uncle's Dream; and The Permanent Husband* (1888).

4. Heinemann was apprenticed in 1879 to the German publisher Nicholas Trübner at Longman. Like Lane, Heinemann is described as having '[...] gained practical experience of every phase of publishing from routine selling and publicity to buying paper and dealing with printers' estimates. His interest in and grasp of technical details were to contribute to many of his future successes. He always took meticulous pains over the appearance of his books, over the quality of the paper, typeface and binding, and his brain seemed to be equipped with a built-in computer when calculating production costs' (St John, 1990, p. 6).

5. For a complete list of the stories included in each volume, see the appendix in Richard Garnett's biography (2009, pp. 361-362).

6. See, for example, the online discussions on the Goodreads webpages concerning the 'best' translations of *Anna Karenina* and *The Brothers Karamazov*, respectively: <http://www.goodreads.com/topic/show/826979-which-english-translation-of-anna-karenina-was-the-best> and <https://www.goodreads.com/topic/show/983001-which-translation-is-the-best-translation>.

7. See Smith (2000, p. 85) and Delisle and Woodsworth (2012, p. 146).

8. Heilbrun's Garnett study only makes brief reference to Constance's relations with Heinemann: 'In the beginning Heinemann paid her twelve shillings per thousand words; for the translation of <u>War and Peace</u> she received £300. When she went over to Chatto and Windus, she was better paid. But she only made a financial success at the end of her life when she translated Chekhov's plays' (Heilbrun, 1959, p. 243).

9. Translators who failed to complete their commissions for Rieu were soon found replacements; Magarshack swiftly replaced Seeley for a translation of Dostoevskii's *Prestuplenie i nakazanie*, Edmonds replaced Gardiner for a translation of Turgenev's *Otsy i deti*.

10. According to Henry Eliot, author of *The Penguin Classics Book* (2018), record-keeping became all the more patchy and there were less frequent transferrals to the archive after Betty Radice's death in 1985 (email to CMcAteer, 20 February 2019).

11. Correspondence is filed under the book title and an accompanying Penguin reference, DM1107 (the code for Penguin Classics) and a specific title reference <L+ the publication's numerical position in the series>.

12. See Appendix 1 for a full list of Russian titles.

13. See Edwards, Hare and Robinson (2008, pp. 58-9).

14. '[...] as with many others there was no such thing as a hard and fast job-title or clear definition of duties' (Hare, 1995, p. 124) and, from Rieu's letter to Lane on newly approaching the Penguin Classics series, 'Perhaps you could kindly

ring me up just to confirm the main arrangements, and to make a date (pref-erably for lunch with me at the Athenaeum) when we could get ahead with the scheme' (ibid., p. 186). See also Rieu's letter to Kitto (4 Nov 1944).

15. The book consists of papers presented at the University of Bristol's celebra-tory conference '75 Years of Penguin Books: An International Multidiscipli-nary Conference' from 29 June-1 July 2010. Papers reflect the multidisciplinary nature of the archive and cover, amongst other topics, the *Lady Chatterley's Lover* trial (McCleery), reminiscences of Penguin Books (Cannadine), a broad overview of Penguin Classics (Sanders) and the Penguin English Library (Donaldson), poetry (Wootten), and Puffin Books (Reynolds).

16. The PCS, 'founded in 1974 by a small group of enthusiasts' (Yates, 2006, p. 8), defines itself as an organisation which aims 'to encourage and promote the study, collection and preservation of the works of Allen Lane and Penguin Books, their contributors and contemporaries' (ibid.). Their works include a biannual members' journal *The Penguin Collector* and *The Penguin Compan-ion* (2006) performs the role of a Penguin encyclopaedia (currently in its third edition).

17. Fen's private archive is sizeable, documenting all aspects of her life: official and personal correspondence from Russia; letters regarding UK domestic life, for example, to her hairdresser, Bristol Eye Hospital, libraries, tv licence and tax offices; letters and postcards from friends; travel diaries and holiday bookings; personal diaries and notebooks; and letters to publishers request-ing that they publish her autobiographies. One box of letters (eight folders) concerns her relationship with Penguin – mainly as an occasional (but paid) advisor to Rieu from 1945 until 1951, but also as a translator of Chekhov plays (1951/1954/1959) (see Chapter One) – and proved useful in corroborating cor-respondence in the Penguin archive. Just three of the eight folders relate to the early years of Penguin Classics when she was most actively involved; the remaining five consist largely of royalty and re-print updates.

18. There is still no blue plaque dedicated to Magarshack and his work.

19. For example, according to Magarshack's daughter, Stella (2015), her father never used an agency, and yet Kevin Crossley-Holland's letter of 16 May 1973 (Magarshack, Box 1) which acknowledges termination of Magarshack's Gol-lancz contract is sent to Peter Grose, an employee of the literary agency Curtis Brown who, the letter makes clear, is acting on Magarshack's behalf.

20. The Curtis Brown archive log references Magarshack in Box 285 of Series II: Author Files.

References:

Anon., 2017. Curtis Brown, Ltd. Records 1914-2006, *Columbia University Libraries*, [online] Available at: <http://findingaids.cul.columbia.edu/ead/nnc-rb/ldpd_4079685/dsc/2#subseries5040> [Accessed 07 June 2017].

Baer, B.J., 2016. *Translation and the Making of Modern Russian Literature*. New York and London: Bloomsbury Academic.

Blume, G. J., 2011. The Reader-Brand: Tolstoy in England at the Turn of the Century, *Texas Studies in Literature and Language*, 53(3), (Fall), pp. 320–337.

Boll, T., 2016. Penguin Books and the Translation of Spanish and Latin American Poetry, 1956-1979, *Translation and Literature*, 1, pp. 28–57. DOI: 10.3366/tal.2016.0236.

Bourdieu, P., 1990. *The Logic of Practice*. Translated from French by R. Nice. Stanford, California: Stanford University Press.

— 2008. A Conservative Revolution in Publishing. Translated from French by R. Fraser. *Translation Studies*, 1(2), London: Routledge, pp. 123–153. http://dx.doi.org/10.1080/14781700802113465.

Bullock, P. R., 2009. *Rosa Newmarch and Russian Music in Late Nineteenth and Early-Twentieth Century England*. Farnham: Ashgate, pp.19–37.

Buzelin, H., 2005. Unexpected Allies, *The Translator*, 11(2), pp. 193–218.

Clements, T., 2009. History of Penguin Archive. *The Daily Telegraph*, 19 February, [online] Available at: <http://www.telegraph.co.uk/culture/books/4691018/History-of-Penguin-archive.html> [Accessed 12 December 2016].

Crowe, R., 2012. How to Fillet a Penguin. In: S. Harrison and C. Stray, eds. *Expurgating the Classics, Editing Out in Greek and Latin*. London: Bloomsbury Press, pp. 197–212.

Deane-Cox, S., 2014. *Retranslation: Translation, Literature and Reinterpretation*. London and New York: Bloomsbury Academic.

Dostoevskii, F., 1866. *Crime and Punishment*, Translated from Russian by D. Magarshack., 1951. Harmondsworth: Penguin.

Edwards, R., Hare S., and Robinson, J., eds. 2008. *Penguin Classics*. Revised ed. Exeter: Short Run Press.

Eliot, H., 2018. *The Penguin Classics Book*. London: Particular Books.

— 2019. Private email to C. McAteer, 20 February.

Feather, J., 2006. *A History of British Publishing*. 2nd ed. Abingdon and New York: Routledge.

Garnett, R., 2009. *Constance Garnett – A Heroic Life*. London: Faber and Faber.

Genette, G., 1987. Introduction to the Paratext. Translated from French by M. Maclean., 1991. *New Literary History*, 22(2), pp. 261–272. DOI: 10.2307/469037.

Gielgud, J., 1954. Letter to David Magarshack, 11 May, Magarshack Archive, Box 1.

Hare, S., 1995. *Penguin Portrait: Allen Lane and the Penguin Editors, 1935-1970*. London and New York: Penguin.

Heilbrun, C., 1959. *The Garnett Family, The History of a Literary Family*. [online] Ann Arbor: ProQuest Dissertations Publishing. [Accessed 22 May 2017].

Leighton, L., 1991. *Two Worlds, One Art*. DeKalb, IL: Northern Illinois University Press.

Lermontov, M., 1853. *Sketches of Russian Life in the Caucasus*. London: Ingram, Cooke & Co., [online] HathiTrust Digital Library. Available at: <https://babel.hathitrust.org/cgi/pt?id=hvd.32044025039124;view=1up;seq=9> [Accessed 30 September 2016].

Lewis, J., 2006. *Penguin Special, The Life and Times of Allen Lane*. London: Penguin.

McCleery, A., 2002. The Return of the Publisher to Book History: The Case of Allen Lane, *Book History*, 5, pp. 161–185.

Magarshack, D., 1928. Letter to E.T. Scott, 18 June. Magarshack Letters, GB133 GDN/A/M25. Manchester: University of Manchester Special Collections, The John Rylands Library.

Mason, A., 2014. Molière among the Penguins, John Wood's Translations for the Early Penguin Classics. In: K. Krebs, ed. *Translation and Adaptation in Theatre and Film*. Abingdon and New York: Routledge, pp. 122- 139.

Merkle, D., 2009. Vizetelly and Company as (Ex)Change Agent. In: J. Milton and P. Bandia, eds. *Agents of Translation*. Amsterdam: John Benjamins, pp. 85–105.

Meylaerts, R., 2006. Conceptualizing the Translator as a Historical Subject in Multilingual Environments, A Challenge for Descriptive Translation Studies? In: P. Bandia and G.L. Bastia, eds. *Charting the Future of Translation History*. Ottawa: University of Ottawa Press, pp. 59–79.

Munday, J., 2013. The Role of Archival and Manuscript Research in the Investigation of Translator Decision-Making. *Target*, 25(1), pp. 125–139.

— 2014. Using Primary Sources to Produce a Microhistory of Translation and Translators: Theoretical and Methodological Concerns. *The Translator*, 20(1), pp. 64–80.

Penguin Archive, Bristol University Arts Library, Special Collections.

— Letter from Rieu to Kitto, 4 November 1944, DM1938.

— Contract Agreement Rosemary Edmonds, 24 July 1950, DM1107/L41.

Powell, A., 1992. Letter to Elsie Magarshack, 15 March, Magarshack Archive Box 1.

Rees, K., 2017. The Heinemann International Library, 1890-7, *Translation and Literature*, 26, pp. 162–181. Available at: <http://www.euppublishing.com/doi/pdf-plus/10.3366/tal.2017.0287> [Accessed 08 September 2017].

Rieu, E.V., 1946. The Penguin Classics, *Penguins Progress*. 1 (July).

St. John, J., 1990. *William Heinemann: A Century of Publishing 1890-1990*. London: Heinemann.

Sapiro, G., 2008. Translation and the Field of Publishing, A Commentary on Pierre Bourdieu's "A Conservative Revolution in Publishing", *Translation Studies*, 1(2), pp. 154–166.

Sela-Sheffy, R., 2008. The Translators' Personae: Marketing Translatorial Images as Pursuit of Capital, *Meta: Translators' Journal*, 53(3), pp. 609–622. Available at: <http://id.erudit.org/iderudit/019242ar> [Accessed 26 April 2017].

Simeoni, D., 1998. The Pivotal Status of the Translators' Habitus, *Target*, 10(1), pp. 1–39.

Smith, G. S., 2000. *D.S. Mirsky: A Russian-English Life, 1890-1930*. Oxford: Oxford University Press.

Walther, M., 2014. *Repatriation to France and Germany: A Comparative Study Based on Bourdieu's Theory of Practice*. Wiesbaden: Springer Gabler.

Wolf, M., 2007. Introduction: The Emergence of a Sociology of Translation. In: *Constructing a Sociology of Translation*. Amsterdam and Philadelphia: John Benjamins. Available through: <https://www.dawsonera.com/abstract/9789027292063> [Accessed 10 October 2016].

Wootten, W. and Donaldson, G. eds., 2013. *Reading Penguin, A Critical Anthology*. Newcastle upon Tyne: Cambridge Scholars Publishing.

Yates, M. ed., 2006. *The Penguin Companion*. Chippenham: Octoprint.

Yoon, S.K., 2014. Popularising Homer: E.V. Rieu's English Prose Translations, *The Translator*, 20(2), pp. 178–193.

Acknowledgements

I would like to confirm that every effort has been made to contact the estates of all individuals cited in this book. I would like to thank everyone who granted me permission to reproduce citations from their correspondence, including: the Magarshack family; Professor Pamela Davidson of UCL; Peters Fraser & Dunlop for allowing me to reproduce an extract (56 words in total) from a letter Ronald Hingley wrote to Allen Lane on 14 December 1962 (Ref.: DM1107/2053) reprinted by permission of Peters Fraser & Dunlop (www.petersfraserdunlop.com) on behalf of the Estate of Ronald Hingley; The Aleksandr Solzhenitsyn Center.

I would also like to thank Penguin Books Ltd. for their generosity in granting me access to the archive and in agreeing to the publication of the following extracts, which are reproduced by permission of Penguin Books Ltd: Seventy-three (73) words from Letter from Lane to Benckendorff, 24 January 1946, DM1819/11/7; Eighty-five (85) words from Letter from Rieu to Kitto, 21 October 1944, DM1938; One hundred and fifty-one (151) words from Letter from Rieu to Kitto, 4 November 1944, DM1938; Three (3) words from Letter from Glover to Rieu, 30 July 1946, DM1107/L4; Eighty-four (84) words from Letter from Glover to Rieu, 30 July 1946, DM1107/L4; Sixty (60) words from Letter from Rieu to Elisaveta Fen, 18 March 1946, MS1394/6550 (Fen archive, Leeds Russian Archive); Fifty-six (56) words from Letter from Rieu to Elisaveta Fen, 9 November 1946, MS1394/6561 (Fen archive, Leeds Russian Archive); Nineteen (19) words from Letter from Rieu to Elisaveta Fen, 22 July 1950, MS1394/6591 (Fen archive, Leeds Russian Archive); Six (6) words from Letter from Rieu to Elisaveta Fen, 20 March 1950, MS1394/6588 (Fen archive, Leeds Russian Archive); Seven (7) words from Letter from Rieu to Elisaveta Fen, 1 May 1950, MS1394 (Fen archive, Leeds Russian Archive); Forty (40) words from Letter from Rieu to Elisaveta Fen, 22 May 1950, MS1394/6589 (Fen archive, Leeds Russian Archive); Nineteen (19) words from Letter from Rieu to Elisaveta Fen, 26 March 1957, MS1394/6753 (Fen archive, Leeds Russian Archive); Sixty-one (61) words from Letter from Rieu to Elisaveta Fen, 10 September 1957, MS1394/6754 (Fen archive, Leeds Russian Archive); Nine (9) words from Letter from Will Sulkin to Gardiner, 5 May 1976, DM1107/L9; Ten (10) words from Letter from Glover to F.F.

Seeley, 13 March 1947, DM1107/L23; Sixty-eight (68) words from Letter from Glover to F.F. Seeley, 13 March 1947, DM1107/L23; Forty-one (41) words from Letter from Rieu to Glover, 8 October 1949, DM1107/L23; Twenty-one (21) words from Letter from Glover to Nitya Nand Tiwari Kasayap, 22 August 1956, DM1107/L23; Twenty-four (24) words from Letter from Cochrane to Richard D. Mical, 13 January 1966, DM1107/L23; Seventy-seven (77) Letter from Will Sulkin (Penguin) to Grant Wallace, Victoria, 18 August 1978, DM1107/L23; Fifty-nine (59) words from Letter from Glover to Rieu, 17 June 1952, DM1107/L35; Twenty-one (21) words from Letter from Cochrane to Miss Atkins, 13 January 1966, DM1107/L35; Forty (40) words from Letter from Glover to Magarshack, 26 March 1954, DM1107/L40; Forty (40) words from Letter from Rieu to Glover, 8 September 1952, DM1107/L41; Thirty-three (33) words from Letter from Glover to Rieu, 10 September 1952, DM1107/L41; Six (6) words from Letter from James Cochrane to Mrs Joan Miller, 5 July 1972, DM1107/L41; Thirty-three (33) words from Letter from Glover to Macy, 9 March 1955, DM1107/L54; Fifty-four (54) words from Letter from Glover to Magarshack, 20 May 1955, DM1107/L54; Sixty-one (61) words from Letter from Magarshack to Glover, 25 May 1955, DM1107/L54; Thirty-nine (39) words from Letter from Glover to Macy, 20 May 1955, DM1107/L54; Twenty-one (21) words from Letter from Miss Cookman to Elisaveta Fen, 14 February 1969, DM1107/L96; Forty-five (45) words from Letter from Miss Jean Ollington to Rosemary Edmonds, 1 August 1961, DM1107/L119; Twelve (12) words from Memo Rieu, 8 August 1959, DM1107/L139; Eight (8) words from Memo Rieu, 23 July 1959, DM1107/L139; Forty-one (41) words from Memo Rieu to DLD [Duguid], 11 August 1959, DM1107/L139; Eleven (11) words from Letter from Baldick to Mr. Duguid, 21 November 1963, DM1107/L143; Seventy-two (72) words from Letter from Cochrane to Duguid, 24 January 1964, DM1107/L143; Fifty-two (52) words from Letter from Cochrane to Duguid, 24 January 1964, DM1107/L143; Eighteen (18) words from Telex from Sulkin to Dick Seaver at Viking Penguin, 17 February 1978, DM1107/L151; Seventy-two (72) words from Telex from Will Sulkin to Sue Zuckermann at Viking Penguin, 28 February 1978, DM1107/L151; Twenty (20) words from Letter Sulkin to Elizabeth Sifton, Viking Penguin, 6 March 1978, DM1107/L151; Sixty-seven (67) words from Letter from Michael Loeb to John Rolfe (Penguin UK), 4 May 1979, DM1107/L151; Forty-three (43) words from Letter from Michael Loeb to John Rolfe (Penguin UK), 4 May 1979, DM1107/L151; Twenty-three (23) words from Letter from Cochrane to Foote, 17 June 1964, DM1107/L176; Ten (10) words from Memo from Jim C to AG, 14 May 1965, DM1107/L176; Seven (7) words from Letter from Will Sulkin to University of Nottingham, 20 March 1974, DM1107/L176; Seventy-three (73) words from Letter from Baldick to Cochrane, 7 June 1966, DM1107/L184; Thirty-six (36) words from Memo from Cochrane to Fred Plaat, 8 May 1972, DM1952/330/044/L291; Fifty-eight (58) words from Letter from Sulkin to Wilks, 4 May 1976, DM1952/331/044.3029; Sixty-four (64) words from Memo from Tony

Godwin to Lane, 31 January 1963, DM1107/2053; Sixty-six (66) words from Memo from AL to AG, 4 February 1963, DM1107/2053; Twenty-eight (28) words from Letter from Penguin to Mrs J. M Addington, 12 December 1974, DM1107/2053; Twelve (12) words from Letter from Oliver Caldecott to Julia Rollason, Collins, n.d., DM1952/676; Thirty-seven (37) words from Memo from Judith Burnley to Tony Mott, 12 January 1974, DM1107/2053. Copyright © Penguin Books.

1   Creating Penguin's Russian Classics

Introduction

This chapter examines how Allen Lane, his editors, and Penguin's commissioned freelancers created the Penguin Russian Classics series. I will first explore critical developments such as: Lane's (and Penguin's) interest in Russia and Russian literature as expressed in the early periodical *The Penguin Russian Review*; Lane's acknowledgment of Rieu's background as an experienced editor and translator; and his confidence in handing the series over to such an expert. This chapter will then examine more closely the Penguin Classics editors – Emile Victor Rieu and Alan Glover, with occasional reference to their successors Betty Radice and Robert Baldick (see also Chapter Four) – and the early corps of Penguin's Russian Classics translators, including Gilbert Gardiner, Elisaveta Fen, Rosemary Edmonds, and David Magarshack.

The key reference point for this chapter is archival primary material, particularly the first fourteen Penguin archive folders (see Appendix 1) which relate to the earliest phase of Penguin's Russian Classics (from 1950–1962), the Medallion Titles, and to the correspondence found in Magarshack's and Fen's papers at the Leeds Russian archive. The contents of the Penguin folders document the working relations between these editors and translators, they identify who was hired by Rieu in his role as inaugural Penguin Classics series editor. Many of these folders contain a large quantity of letters and memoranda on subjects ranging from negotiations over royalties, to day-to-day comments on corporate and personal housekeeping. Translators even occasionally revealed their need for a holiday or to pay household bills. Some folders are scant in both volume and informational content. In nearly every case, the earliest, precise details of how Rieu met and commissioned a new translator are absent (lost, it seems, in a blur of sociable lunch and dinner dates that were never officially recorded).[1] Nevertheless, the folders provide valuable insight into the field of twentieth-century Russian-English literary translation and publishing. Following Munday's work on microhistories and his insistence that 'by focusing on the "little facts" of everyday lives [...] a picture can be built up of the specific interaction between a translator and other individuals, groups, institutions and power structures' (2014, p. 77), the archival study of correspondence exchanged between Penguin editors and freelancers reveals the sociological side to translation publishing. Research into translation publishing has previously often overlooked personalities, work dynamics, and professional pressures (deadlines, corrections, turnaround times, royalties). This chapter demonstrates that publishing and translation agents do not work in isolation; they are inextricably linked, each with their own expectations, aspirations, motives, and constraints. The result is an enlightening case study of Penguin agency, which begins (as Boll (2016) suggests from his own research into Penguin's Spanish and Latin American translations) to inform our understanding of the route Russian literature took in the mid-twentieth century in order to arrive at current translation publishing practices.

Penguin promotes Anglo-Russian relations

Before appointing E.V. Rieu as the Penguin Classics series editor, Lane had already liaised with two émigré Russians, Samuel S. Kotelianskii and Sergei Konovalov, about the prospects of publishing Russian literature in translation. He exchanged ideas during the late 1930s and early 1940s with Kotelianskii (1880–1955), who worked alongside Virginia Woolf on collaborative translations from Russian for Hogarth Press (Beasley, 2013, p. 1). Kotelianskii's *Three Plays of Chehov* [sic] was published by Penguin in 1940, followed by his edited volume *Russian Short Stories* (1941). Penguin also corresponded with the Oxford scholar Konovalov (1899–1982), who declared that 'we would all welcome a further selection [of stories] covering the Soviet period' (20 November 1945). Both Kotelianskii and Konovalov provided Penguin with names of translators (some better qualified than others) who might have been interested in contributing to short-story collections: John Middleton Murry, D.H. Lawrence and Mrs N. Duddington, Miss E. Kutaisov, Mr du Bray, and Mr F. Friedeberg Seeley. Kotelianskii volunteered the authors Kuprin and Bunin as being worthy of translation, but he dismissed Zoshchenko on the grounds that 'there are more worthwhile Russian writers than Zoshchenko to be published by you' (24 November 1940). (Zoshchenko made a brief Penguin appearance in a one-off parallel-text edition *Soviet Short Stories/Sovetskie Rasskazi* (1968), but he did not return again until the 2005 Penguin anthology *Russian Short Stories from Buida to Pushkin*.)[2]

In his letters to Eunice Frost, Lane's secretary at that time, Kotelianskii alluded to the saleability (or otherwise) of Russian literature at key stages in Anglo-Russian relations. For example, in his letter of 29 April 1941, Kotelianskii noted optimistically that his *Russian Short Stories* 'should sell very well at present'; however, just over a year later, his letter of 1 July 1942 acknowledges that the opposite may be the case 'in view of the Anglo-Russian relations at the moment'. Penguin's Russian titles only moved beyond tentative discussions after the war, at which point, as Lygo notes, '[...] Soviet culture became a matter of interest to a much broader section of the British public [...]. The public mood was pro-Soviet' (2013, p. 24). A certain sense of post-war euphoria prompted Lane to commission four editions of *The Penguin Russian Review* (launched in September 1945 and the last one produced in January 1948),[3] under the joint editorship, initially, of Count Constantine [Conny] Benckendorff and Moura Budberg.[4] After three issues, handicapped by disjointed editorship and mismanaged budgets, the role of editor passed to Colonel Edward Crankshaw, British 'writer and commentator on Soviet affairs' (Oxford DNB, 2004). No other post-war nation qualified for similar Penguin Review[5] treatment. The extent of Penguin's preoccupation with Russia is even more evident from the *Reviews'* paratextual advertisements for Penguin's other Russian/Soviet publications, for example: W.E.D. Allen's and Paul Muratoff's *The Russian Campaigns of 1941–1943* and *The Russian Campaigns of 1944–1945*, James S. Gregory's and J.F. Horrabin's *An Atlas of the U.S.S.R*, James S. Gregory's *Land of the Soviets*, and Eric Ashby's *Scientist in Russia*. Prior to the *Russian Review*, Penguin also published '[t]opical books, mainly on contemporary political and social issues' (Yates, 2006, p. 143), the so-called Penguin Specials, which ran from 1937–1989. According to Nicholas Joicey, these Specials were 'marketed as a truthful alternative to an accepted orthodoxy. D.N. Pritt's *Light on Moscow* (October 1939) was sold as an assessment of "the blame for the failure of negotiations with Moscow", despite being an obvious apologia for the Soviets' (1993, p. 34). Maintaining this pro-Soviet tone, each *Russian Review* contains contributions on subjects specifically relating to Russia and the Union of Soviet Socialist Republics, including Soviet economics, classic Russian and Soviet literature, geography, art, history, and agriculture. Contributors included Russophiles and specialists, some of them well known and some with pro-Soviet associations; amongst them (in addition to Edward Crankshaw) were, for example, Paul Winterton, Andrew Guershoon Colin, George Reavey, and Sir Robert Bruce Lockhart.

The first issue opens with a lengthy, reflective composition, 'Moscow – Winter 1944' by Paul Winterton (1908–2001), the Moscow correspondent for *News Chronicle* during the Second World War, a crime novelist (under the *noms de plume* Paul Somers and Andrew Garve) and a founder of the Crime Writers' Association (*The Times*, 2001). Winterton's contribution – informed by his own experiences and observations of living and working in Russia – set out in his own words to 'describe, as factually as I can, the circumstances of life as it is led to-day by the ordinary person in Moscow' (p. 7). In this issue, his self-imposed task takes on the role of an editorial commentary. What follows is a sympathetic, largely apolitical description of all areas of everyday Muscovite life, from public transport to city architecture and accommodation, childcare to education, meal habits to recreation ('The ballet is outstanding in every way and almost certainly has no equal anywhere in the world' (p. 17)). Winterton's only (and fleeting) allusion to politics occurs when he extols the successes of the Russian health service, a socially-astute remark considering that Britain's National Health Service would not be inaugurated for another three years. In his conclusion, he tries to normalise Anglo-Russian relations at grassroots level:

> But the point I am trying to make is that the British working man could always meet the Russian working man on plenty of common ground. If they could mix enough, they wouldn't long feel strangers with each other. They would soon understand and be interested in each other's way of life. That is a fact of supreme importance in the future develop-ment of Anglo-Russian friendship. (1945, pp. 19–20)

While Winterton's exhortations for mutual understanding are self-explanatory, an even clearer explanation of the rationale behind *The Penguin Russian Review* appeared in the second issue, published in March 1946. Penguin stated its mission in an anonymous note to 'The Reader' at the end of the publication, a message which serves, in fact, as a precursor to Rieu's Penguin Classics endeavour, but which resonates especially with the Russian titles later selected for the series:

> The purpose of this review, which dedicates itself to the general reader, is nothing less than to contribute to the initiation of the stranger to Russia into the spirit of the Russian people as it is embodied in their history and literature, their arts and sciences, their philosophy, their aspiration, and their economic life. We believe that one of the greatest impediments to a true understanding of Russia's aims and problems has been an over-simplification of the complex nature of her attain-ments and the innumerable cross-currents of her life and thought. In this Review we shall seek to combat this tendency by bringing together articles and essays on the multitudinous aspects of Russian life and by allowing Russia herself to speak through her imaginative writers and poets. (1946, pp. 138–139)

As ambitious as Penguin was in offering this compelling counter-message to growing Anglo-Russian hostilities, their efforts failed to make sufficient impact. A letter from Lane to Benckendorff on 24 January 1946 reveals the idealistic, rather than profiteering, rationale behind the *Penguin Review*, but also expresses Penguin's growing doubts about the viability of the venture:

> As I think you know, we went into this on a somewhat idealistic basis without thoughts of making enormous profits, but even bearing this in mind, the results are pretty catastrophic. As a matter of interest, our cost of production on the first issue came to something in excess of the price received from the booksellers, [...]. To date, out of our first print-ing of 25,000 copies, we have received back over 4,000.

By the third *Review*, the editorial commentary had moved to the opening pages and the message is increasingly defeatist; the anonymous editor admits that progress on the *Russian Review* mission has been hampered 'as a result of war-time publishing difficulties [...] and the intervals between the first three numbers have been longer than was contemplated. World events, on the other hand, have moved more swiftly. There is no hope now of preventing disillusionment: the best that can be done is to soften the effects' (p. 7). Again, as if looking ahead to Penguin's Russian Classics, the editor concludes his commentary to the third issue with a note of attempted optimism:

> [...] these pages, [which] will more than fulfil their intention if they arouse in the reader a desire to go more deeply in the literature and history of Russia. (p. 11)

The opening editorial commentary (Crankshaw's) in the fourth and final issue of *The Penguin Russian Review* (published five months before the Berlin Airlift in 1948) reverts to pessimism, however, admitting a state of near-deadlocked post-war Anglo-Russian relations. Crankshaw does not attempt to apportion blame for failed relations, nor does he applaud Soviet foreign policy; instead, he appeals for future, bilateral harmony and volunteers Penguin as the ideal vehicle for fostering such a hope:

> What we are trying to do is to present Russians in the round – to provide, as it were, the raw material for a practical political understanding at some future date, to remind our readers perpetually that the Russians are *people* with lives, traditions and outlooks of their own. (1948, p. 8)

In spite of this aspiration, Penguin discontinued *The Penguin Russian Review* that same year. As Rieu's successor, Betty Radice, later observed about discontinued imprints, 'these are our mistakes or failures to estimate public interest' (1984, p. 17). Penguin's subsequent efforts to promote an acceptable version of Russia were henceforward channelled into the translation of Russian classics rather than commissioning new reports about the region. Rieu's intention was to offer Penguin readers *belles-lettres* – 'to select works that have a perennial value' (Rieu, October 1944) – rather than a politically-charged message only pertinent to a particular period. This intention carried its own cultural significance and acted as a counterweight to political concerns. The Penguin Classics were designed to 'help us [...] to appreciate and understand the essential differences that divide us, as much as the universal truths that bind us together [...] Their value is incalculable, and their loss or destruction would diminish us all' (Hare, 2008, p. 31). In essence, therefore, Rieu's Penguin Russian Classics would fulfil the same aim of Anglo-Russian mutual understanding to which *The Penguin Russian Review* aspired, but more subtly.

Lane, Rieu and the Penguin Classics mission

For a future publisher, the young Lane left little, if any, evidence of a genuine interest in literature, even though he trained from 1919, aged sixteen, in all areas of the publishing industry at his uncle John Lane's business, The Bodley Head. Although he lacked formal academic qualifications, Lane excelled in non-literary, purely entrepreneurial ability to evaluate risks and spot and seize opportunities, no matter how uncertain success might initially appear.[6] Lane possessed an enquiring intellect (Lewis, 2006, p. 225), an affinity with literature for the masses (if not necessarily for literature itself), ruthlessness and commercial acumen (McCleery, 2002, p. 179), including an ability to spot opportunities, possibilities, and connections all around (Lewis, 2006, p. 4). He was also astute enough to recognise his own limitations.[7] He generally accepted the academic and professional capital represented by approved advisors and scholars,[8] who could confidently select books for translation in the Penguin Classics series and who could assess, for example, the quality of a translator's work in a way that he would not have been able to do. After the failure of the 1938 Illustrated Classics series (ibid., p. 143), Lane might well have heeded the advice of his colleagues and his brother Richard, and decided not to publish any further series dedicated to the classics on the grounds that 'there was already a glut of translations on the market' (ibid., p. 251). The consensus among his advisors was that any effort at publishing paperback classics would 'lead to commercial disaster' (Edwards, Hare, Robinson, 2008, p. 8). But, when Lane was approached by Rieu (1887–1972) – managing director for Methuen Books in Britain between 1923 and 1936 – with his own new translation of Homer's *Odyssey*, Lane dismissed the advice he had received and proceeded to publish it regardless.[9]

During his Methuen period, Rieu had rediscovered his enjoyment of classical scholarship, re-reading the *Odyssey*, translating and sharing his own version with his wife, Nelly.[10] What began as an evening pastime assumed written form and, by the end of the Second World War, Rieu had offered his translation to Lane. On the basis of the first two chapters, Lane authorised the publication of Penguin's first classic translation (Platt, 2008, p. 8). It is this book which became the figurehead of the Penguin Classics series and which would re-awaken British interest in the international literary canon.[11] In terms of professional positioning, with his past in editorship and current translation activity, Rieu represented a reliable figure whom Lane could trust. But, as Mason notes in 'Molière among the Penguins', Rieu 'took a fairly cavalier attitude to the depth of a translator's first-hand knowledge of the source language or culture' (2014, p. 127). As will be shown in this chapter, Rieu relied on Fen's knowledge during the early years of Penguin's Russian Classics. By delegating power to Rieu, however, Lane allowed him the autonomy to create a business venture of his own. Rieu could follow his own ideas, although guided by his copyeditor A.S.B. Glover, and remaining under the auspices of the Penguin organisation.

On 19 October 1944, Rieu informed Lane that he would be able to devote one day a week to the role of General Editor 'of your new Translation Series from the Greek, Latin and other classics' (Hare, 1995, p. 186). The letter radiates anticipatory enthusiasm. Ahead of his 1 November start date, Rieu revealed that he had already compiled a list of Greek and Roman authors to be included in the series, that he had plans for a similar list of French authors, and was ready to set 'one or two Scandinavian translations afoot' (ibid.). Explaining that he might consult friends over which books should feature on the French list, Rieu revealed his own wish for a network of advisors. His letter just two days later to Kitto (Humphrey Davy Findley Kitto, Professor of Greek at the University of Bristol) testifies as much:

> Any comments you may care to make on my lists will be most welcome, and I shall be particularly grateful for any help you can give me in finding first-class men (possibly among the younger scholars not yet clear of the war) who are likely to be fired with the idea. What a chance! (21 October 1944)

The unprecedented success of Rieu's own translation[12] not only provided the impetus for an expanded Penguin Classics series, but also marked Rieu out as an ideal in-house reviewer for the Penguin Classics translations. His personal criteria would become identified with general Penguin translation practice. He elucidates some of his key considerations in his early correspondence with Kitto, whom Rieu commissioned to translate Greek classics. In his letter of 21 October 1944, Rieu restricts himself to just one point, that Kitto (and all other Penguin-commissioned translators) use 'the bare minimum of footnotes, if any', adding:

> I think I can say without immodesty that, in my Homer, I have succeeded in telling them all they need to know in my fairly long introduction. It is the translator's job to make the text explain itself, remembering always that it is not erudition we want to teach but appreciation.

Rieu expands further in his next letter to Kitto of 4 November 1944:

> In the past there has been too much translation by scholars for scholars, resulting in a weird kind of Greek-English (Butcher and Lang is an excellent text-book of Homeric idiom and syntax). The principle was not accepted that it is a translator's duty not only to render the words of his original but also, where they are recalcitrant, the syntax and idiom. If he fails here, he defeats his own purpose and creates an impression which was not created on the readers or audience of the Greek.

Rieu's initial expectations for his Penguin Classics translation were outlined more publicly in July 1946 in a copy of the *Penguins Progress*. The extract announces the arrival of the Penguin Classics series, not without a momentous air: the July issue marks Penguin's relaunch of *Penguins Progress* after a six-year absence necessitated by paper rationing during the Second World War:

> The first volume of our new Classics series, the editor's translation of *The Odyssey*, appeared in January. The series is to be composed of original translations from the Greek, Latin and later European classics, and it is the editor's intention to commission translators who could emulate his own example and present the general reader with readable and attractive versions of the great writers' books in good modern English, shorn of the unnecessary difficulties and erudition, the archaic flavour and the foreign idiom that renders so many existing translations repellent to modern taste. (1946, p. 48)

Ever committed to the aspiration of 'good, modern English', Rieu reiterates more developed views on the translator's priorities in his next *Penguins Progress* contribution, 'Translating the Classics', in October 1946. During this short article, he introduces the one general principle which he has 'hammered out' (p. 37) and to which 'I pin my faith and from which I deduce all minor rules and decisions' (ibid.), namely the principle of equivalent effect. In another *Penguins Progress* essay, 'The Faith of a Translator' (1950), Rieu (a harbinger of Eugene Nida, who was beginning his translation career around this time) returns to discuss the significance of his translation theory on his practice. He admits that:

> [...] when I had finished the work [Homer's *Iliad*] and came to revise it, I found that there had once more fallen on my shoulders, I will not say the mantle of Lang, Leaf and Myers,[13] but at least its shadow; and I had to rewrite the first few books in what I trust is English and not Greek.

Rieu expressed his principles succinctly in a 1953 BBC interview with his co-translator, J.B. Phillips. Regarding Penguin's publication of his translation *The Four Gospels*, Rieu was asked whether, during the course of his project, he had 'worked out careful principles of translation?' (Rieu and Phillips, 1955, p. 153). In his response, Rieu identifies only one, the 'principle of equivalent effect', which he defined as the 'lodestar of the translator's art' (ibid.). Rieu explained that 'the translation is the best which comes nearest to giving its modern audience the same effect as the original had on its first audiences'.[14] He cites an example where, to translate literally the French endearment *mon chou* as 'my cabbage' (ibid.), fails entirely in producing an equivalent effect on the target reader. Throughout his career, Rieu was consistent in his view that literal translation disadvantages equivalence, resulting (in the case of Ancient Greek literature, at least) in an overly Homeric idiom and syntax. While he treated paraphrasing as an acceptable, and often desirable, means to achieve equivalence, he categorically insisted that the text should not be reduced to a 'lower standard of English in order to make things crystal clear', otherwise 'we're going beyond our jobs as translators' (ibid., p. 154). Rieu's perception of the 'good', archetypically 'Penguin' translation struck a reliable balance between accuracy, authenticity, and accessibility. Its nearest parallel, and likely ancestor, in translation history is John Dryden's recommendation for paraphrases where 'the author is kept in view by the Translator, so as never to be lost, but his words are not so strictly follow'd as his sense, and that too is admitted to be amplified, but not alter'd' (1680, p. 38).

It is clear from Rieu's *Penguins Progress* announcement that, by 1946, Lane's and Rieu's joint venture was well under way; the extract concludes by listing authors who would be included in future volumes of the series (Homer, Xenophon, Ibsen, Chekhov, Ovid, Voltaire, Turgenev, Gorky, Maupassant) (1946, p. 48) as well as those already commissioned (such as Sayers's translation of Dante's *Inferno* (1949) and Watling's translation of Sophocles's *Theban Plays* (1947)). Rieu's Medallion Titles were dominated by translations from Greek and French literature (twenty-nine and twenty-eight translations respectively), followed by Latin and Russian literature, each with sixteen translations. It is striking (but not, perhaps, altogether surprising given Penguin's earlier promotion of the *Russian Review*) that Russian literature commanded such a high position in the early hierarchy of the Penguin Classics publications. We can list several commercial, professional, and socio-cultural factors likely to have contributed subsequently to Penguin's robust Russian representation. These include Rieu's awareness that the average translation has a limited shelf-life, hence acknowledging that Garnett's versions were long overdue a revision; Rieu's (or perhaps his advisor Fen's) recognition of Russia's own high regard for its nineteenth-century classics;[15] a corporate, competitive awareness of which classic titles were being tackled by other publishers[16] (for example, J.M. Dent's Everyman Library series included Russian titles and Magarshack also published his translations with Faber and Faber, Allen and Unwin, and Secker and Warburg); and Lane's own, alleged inclination towards left-leaning politics and culture (Yates, 2006, p. 133).

The list was supplemented with further translations from Italian (eight), Early English (six), German (four), Middle Eastern (four), Scandinavian (four), Spanish (three), Far Eastern (three), and Portuguese (one), but these remained significantly fewer in number than translations from Greek, French, Latin, and Russian. Each language was given its own colour code (ibid., p. 58). Translations of Russian literature were identified by red borders on the cover and spine (see Figure 1.1) and the front cover of each novel in the series sported a unique, black-and-white illustrated roundel, or medallion, the subject of which was intended to whet the reader's literary

Figure 1.1 David Magarshack's 1951 translation of Dostoevskii's *Crime and Punishment* [digital photograph] (author's private collection)

appetite by intimating a significant point in the plot or depicting a key character from the novel. Roundels were often discussed in advance with the translator. Magarshack, for example, offered a roundel for *Oblomov* which had been specially designed by his art-student daughter Stella, but which was not used, and Edmonds specifically requested a say over the *War and Peace* roundel designs after disapproving of the *Anna Karenin* roundel (see Rosemary Edmonds section in this chapter).

Whereas some of the first Penguin Books (Agatha Christie, for example) enjoyed popular, rather than 'quality' literary appeal, the Penguin Classics series strove to deliver both in the same volume. In selecting texts for the series, Rieu was able (as Lane was not) to combine popularity and quality, packaged at an affordable price, in a format which appealed to the post-war mood of 'pleasure, expansion and reconstruction' (Radice and Reynolds, 1987, p. 14). Texts were presented with 'rather cosy introductions' (ibid.) but, in terms of a corporate translation style, no specific document setting out clear, in-house translation guidelines has been discovered in the

Penguin archive. Rieu, nevertheless, set his own unambiguous standard for translators:

> Dr Rieu's object was to break away from that academic idiom in which so many of the world's classics have been put before the general reader, and to present them in contemporary English without any transgressions of scholarship or textual accuracy. (Williams, 1956, p. 19)

Translators may have been clear about the aesthetic requirements for Penguin Classics, but some of them remained uncertain about how to approach Penguin's introductions, which they were expected to write. Paul Foote, translator of Lermontov's *A Hero of Our Time*, asked exactly this question of editor James Cochrane in June 1964. Cochrane's comprehensive reply not only outlined all the ingredients for the ideal Penguin introduction, but also identified Penguin's typical target reader. Cochrane advised Foote to assume a target reader who knows nothing about the source author, or the book itself, and very little about Russian literature in general. Foote should convince the reader as to 'why he ought to get to know this book' and why the experience will be 'pleasant and profitable'; he should position Lermontov and his novels within the broader context of European literature. Cochrane instructed Foote to 'sell' the book, to make 'the highest possible claims for it'. Penguin introductions were intended to imbue the target reader (described by Cochrane as an 'intelligent and sophisticated adult') with authoritative knowledge and enthusiasm. Hence, the introduction should focus on providing literary context, preparing an inquisitive but uninitiated reader for a new, cultural experience.

In the field of literary production, the translator is generally regarded as ideally placed to provide essential cross-cultural insight: who else could be more skilfully equipped than the translator at handling culture-specific detail while also offering lexical and literary context? (As far as the Russian Classics are concerned, there is evidence in Penguin's archived correspondence that some of the translators offered the benefit of their expertise – meanwhile reiterating and confirming their professional credentials – by volunteering suggestions and encouraging, even, it seems, expecting, Penguin to publish further Russian titles.)[17] Translating and/or writing the preface for a new translation gave a translator or scholar a chance to define a text's place in world literature (strangely, Constance Garnett is known to have declined the opportunity to pen introductions to her translations, relying instead on her husband Edward[18] and, later, on their son David to do so). Yet linguistic analysis of the original work rarely formed part of the introductory paratext. Seldom does a pre-1962 Penguin Russian Classic introduction discuss either semantic or linguistic peculiarities of the source text or extrapolate on the solutions found by the translator. It is possible that the translators themselves veered away from such discussion, keen to hide their stratagems from a critically enquiring public who might quibble with lexical or grammatical decisions or doubt the translator's judgment. However, insights into the art of translation would probably have seemed irrelevant to both readers and editors during the early Penguin Classics years, when more interest was generated simply by the (re)discovery of the Russian literary canon at affordable prices.

As the bridging agent between translator and publisher, Rieu acted as a negotiator, matching the novel to be translated with the 'right' sort of translator. For Rieu, this meant someone with proven skill and expertise, preferably with a flair for literary translation, and a professional bent towards Penguin's (and his own) benchmarks of readability and equivalent effect.[19] Although as a translator himself, Rieu must have been aware of the commitment and sacrifices necessary to complete a project and satisfy a client, Rieu was also a publisher and thus affiliated to the commercial side of the business. These contradictory roles sometimes caused him to act in a way that privileged commercial or corporate considerations over the translator's requirements. Rieu demonstrates both savviness and company loyalty during his negotiations, as with the translation commission, for example, of Dostoevskii's *Crime and Punishment*. Rieu first introduced the Penguin Classics copyeditor, A.S.B. Glover, to the existence of Russian-English translator David Magarshack when he wrote hopefully on 20 January 1949 that Magarshack would replace Seeley, who had initially been commissioned for the job of translating *Crime and Punishment* in 1946.[20] Rieu stated his certainty that Magarshack will 'give us an excellent and most readable Penguin Classic, better in fact than Seeley's would have turned out. He knows exactly what is wanted'. It comes as a surprise then to read in the same letter that for such excellence and, presumably, a speedy replacement translation, Rieu offered Magarshack 'less than we offerred [sic] Seeley', namely £200 in advance. Rieu continues by highlighting to Glover that Magarshack was receiving generous royalties from other publishers at that time, but that their own, less-than-generous royalty – seven-and-a-half per cent, compared to Magarshack's usual fifteen per cent from one (unidentified) publisher – will be 'compensated for by larger sales', which Magarshack accepted. On balance, though, Rieu's offer suggests that Magarshack was short-changed. Magarshack's own readiness to settle for less-than-generous terms draws a historical parallel with his literary inspiration Dostoevskii, who also made financial compromises over *Crime and Punishment*. According to Joseph Frank, Dostoevskii offered his editor Mikhail Katkov the 'modest' rate of 'one hundred and twenty-five rubles per folio sheet, although it was well-known that writers like Turgenev and Tolstoy received a good deal more' (2010, p. 461).

A.S.B. Glover: unconventional and undervalued

Another key figure in the Penguin Classics network is Alan McDougall,[21] better known to Penguin as Alan Samuel Boots (A.S.B.) Glover (1895–1966), who joined the company in 1944[22] to work alongside Rieu as a copyeditor. Just as Lane and his background were relatively atypical among his peers in the British publishing industry, Glover too stands out as an unconventional figure. Glover never went to university, something which 'inflamed his urge to omniscience' (Lewis, 2006, p. 237). A pacifist and First World War 'absolutist', Glover was jailed for four years for conscientious objection, preferring prison rather than to offer any contribution to the war effort (Hare, 1995, p. 128). It was during his time in prison that he furthered his education.[23] Glover was nearly fifty (ibid., p. 121) when he arrived at Penguin Books and, like Rieu, was not new to the publishing industry; he had already worked for Burns & Oates, Routledge & Kegan Paul, Odhams and *Reader's Digest,* and mixed in publisher circles, counting among his acquaintances Francis Meynell, the publisher of Nonesuch Press (Lewis, 2006, p. 242). Unlike Rieu (and later, Radice), whose Oxford and *Athenæum* credentials may well have fast-tracked his recruitment to Penguin, Glover's arrival was more circuitous and less routine: having taken it upon himself over the course of nine years to notify Penguin of all typographical and factual errors, Glover was eventually invited by Lane to join the company, partly in a bid to stem the flow of critical correspondence, but also to exploit his eye for detail to Penguin's advantage. Lane wrote about this decision in Glover's obituary, published in the *Times* on 8 January 1966:

> My own acquaintance with him goes back to 1944 when I invited him to join Penguin Books so that he could apply his exceptional gifts as a scholarly reader to manuscripts rather than published books on which, as a member of our public, he used to send in detailed lists of factual errors and misprints, usually saying these had not spoiled his enjoyment of books as such. (p. 10)

Glover's tenure at Penguin began modestly, by reading proofs. His position evolved in the same way as did other early Penguin employees' posts: quickly and organically, and in the 'Penguin way', according to Hare (1995, p. 129). Glover 'soon became a vital part of the Penguin editorial team – sharing responsibilities and duties with Eunice Frost across the Penguin list' (ibid.), with particular influence over the Pelican and Penguin Classics series but with no specific job title. J.E. Morpurgo, Lane's General Editor for Pelican Histories and Lane's biographer, identifies Glover as the head of a two-man copy-editing department (consisting of Glover and his secretary-assistant) (Morpurgo, 1979, p. 192), and notes that, had Glover aspired to become Lane's successor, he would have had the credentials (ibid.). Glover did not however possess this ambition; he chose to channel his energies into his work and rarely joined Lane for the frequent sessions of sociable, after-work drinks (ibid., pp. 193–194).

   Glover's symbolic capital was rooted in his ability to expose the factual and typographical failings of a text,[24] as well as in his erudition, making him 'more often than not the only member of the senior staff competent to conduct informed discussion with the authors of the many abstruse books on the list' (Morpurgo, 1979, p. 192). He also demonstrated a great respect for the text; when Glover received a letter from Nitya Nand Tiwari Kasayap, an Indian translator, on 21 August 1956, requesting permission to render Magarshack's translation of Dostoevskii's *Crime and Punishment* into Hindi, Glover's reply politely probed whether 'a Hindi translation of Dostoyevsky [should] be made rather from the original Russian than through the medium of an English version?'

Central to the desirability and demand for Glover's capital within Penguin is the fact that Lane (and his advisors) lacked Glover's skills. Glover's impressive intellect, though, may explain the reportedly difficult relationship Lane had with Glover. Although Lane avoided socialising with university-bred academics and expressed a preference for left-leaning, philanthropic politics – common attitudes which might, in fact, have brought him and Glover closer together – Lane could not feel comfortable in Glover's socially unconventional company, referring to him as, 'Oh that old Buddhist!' (Lewis, 2006, p. 240). Morpurgo provides his own analysis of their relationship:

> Allen could never establish a comfortable relationship with Glover. As with Pevsner, so with Glover he was awed by the other man's learning. Unlike Pevsner, Glover had no proud university title to substantiate his scholarship; he was instead almost entirely dependent on Allen for such dignities as might be granted him. Awed, suspicious, embarrassed, uncomprehending: the confusion of contradictory sentiments set Allen apart from Glover. (1979, p. 193)

To the comparatively conservative, image-conscious Lane ('a famously natty dresser, never appearing in public without a tie' (Lewis, 2006, p. 10)), Glover's extensively tattooed appearance (ibid., p. 237) must have represented radical eccentricity. Whilst their relationship floundered from the mismatch of appearances and intellectual achievements, it is allegedly Glover's unsolicited outspokenness and candour regarding the pay and conditions of fellow staff that served as a persistent and no doubt uncomfortable reminder to Lane of his moral responsibility as patron:

> For younger editorial members of staff, many of whom had joined the firm straight from university, Glover was a mentor and a spokesman. Though overworked and underpaid himself, he wrote long memos to Lane on behalf of his younger colleagues, urging him not to take their good will for granted, and to provide longer holidays and better pay [...] they should, he suggested, 'be recompensed for their work with something more concrete than kind words and smiles'. (Ibid., p. 240)

Glover served as the key interface between the in-house Penguin Classics advisory hierarchy and the external mechanism of freelance translators. His role was that of intermediary, with all the challenges one might expect when trying to satisfy both upper and lower echelons in a corporate hierarchical structure. Like Rieu, Glover, a translator from medieval Latin (Thomas Aquinas) and French (Harries, 2013, p. 560) also conducted his role of commissioner with an awareness of the textual, temporal, and financial challenges facing the translator. He coupled his practical knowledge with awareness of in-house expectations, thus placing himself in the awkward position of a mediator; he fielded and pacified complaints from all angles, internal and external, while remaining professionally polite and obliging.

One example of this tension can be seen in Glover's handling of the bill incurred by Magarshack for page-proof corrections of his translation *Oblomov*. Glover sent warning letters on both 26 and 31 March 1954 stressing the Penguin policy that 'corrections in page proofs are expensive and we do not like feeling obliged to call into operation the clause in our contracts which enables us to charge authors corrections to the author if they exceed 10% of the composition cost'. In his 'endeavour to get closer to the original text', however, Magarshack's corrections ultimately resulted in a bill for £104.19.6 (equating to £2,556.66 in today's money). Ever-patient, no doubt attempting to soften the blow, Glover informed Magarshack by letter on 26 May 1954 that Penguin would not take full advantage of Penguin's correction costs policy, and proposed instead that Magarshack pay half, i.e. £52.9.9, out of his royalties. Even with such assistance, there is no disguising the dismay in Magarshack's response:

> Your news about the cost of the corrections is terrible. This has never happened to me before. [...] I disagree with your point about the difference between an original work and a translation. It is just a translation that requires a great deal more changing. [...] I wonder if you could spread out my share of the cost corrections over two or three six-monthly periods. Otherwise I am not likely to get any royalties for a year or more. (27 May 1954)[25]

Ultimately, it was Glover's service as a bridge between Lane and the junior in-house staff and the dynamics of this difficult relationship that led to Glover's resignation in 1958. Glover is described as having been 'undervalued by the Penguin hierarchy' (Yates, 2006, p. 61), a claim supported not only by Lane's failure to offer Glover an official job title and his reactions to Glover's head-on challenges over general working conditions, but also by Glover's low pay and long hours. Glover's resignation letter in 1958 suggests ignorance on Lane's part for failing to recognise the work and joint effort required by Glover and his team to produce a successful series like the Penguin Classics.

Public-facing Penguin

With their professional accomplishments and literary experience, Penguin's editors formed a vital link between Lane and Penguin's external agents (for example, advisors, translators, and critical readers). As the archived correspondence for Penguin's Russian Classics shows, the Penguin Classics editors also had to manage inquisitive, often concerned, academics from all over the world. Some academics penned letters lobbying for withdrawn works to be reinstated (Lermontov's *A Hero of Our Time*), while others sent censorious notes requesting detailed justifications for omissions (Dostoevskii's *Crime and Punishment* and *The Devils*),[26] and undeclared abridgements (Turgenev's *Sketches from a Hunter's Album*).[27] Letters did not just come from academics; general readers also shared their thoughts and book evaluations with Penguin, often including praise of the range, presentation, and price of titles included in Penguin's Russian Classics. Miss P. A. Ford from Blackpool, for example, wrote to Penguin in April 1966 in order to point out a printing error in her copy of *The Idiot*, but concluding:

> I write merely to ensure that the same mistake does not occur again should the book go for a further impression, and not for complaint. After all, who is going to complain about having great novels brought within reach of the average pocket? For that, I say many thanks.

Similarly, Mr Richard D. Mical from Massachusetts wrote 'to congratulate Penguin Books and the person responsible for the very striking front cover photograph of the 1964 edition of <u>Crime and Punishment</u>. The purple and black tones with the photograph from Chenal's film is quite striking indeed'. Miss L. A. Atkins wrote from London to say that she was reading Magarshack's translation of *The Devils*, but that 'My enjoyment of this book has been marred by the fact that, though the main translation is excellent one keeps tripping over phrases, not to say paragraphs in French'. (Although fairly frequent, instances of French in *The Devils* rarely extend beyond fragmentary sentences; Miss Atkins's observation, however, still finds expression now in discussions on websites like Reddit and in Amazon book reviews.) In addition, there are criticisms of the translations themselves. One example came from Miss Margaret Walsh in Leeds, who wrote that 'It is my duty [...] as a lover of poetry to express extreme dissatisfaction with the translation of the poetry of Yvegeni Yeshtuskenko [sic] by Robin Milner-Gulland + Peter Levi S.J. in your Penguin Edition'. She criticises their 'clumsiness of style and the obvious lack of the poet [sic]'. Other readers expressed disappointment regarding title translation: Mrs Joan Miller called the title *Anna Karenin* an act of 'impudence and vandalism' by Rosemary Edmonds. Readers noted typing and printing errors, and even the *over*-readability of translations for the benefit of a general audience. Jerome Minot, for example, wrote on 25 January 1969 regarding Fen's translation of Chekhov's *Plays*, 'If your justification is that this sort of translation is necessary to "popularize" the work, then I can only say that it is impossible to prostitute literature, just so that it can be understood by people without literary knowledge'. In nearly all cases, a courteous reply was sent to each correspondent, usually after contact had been made with the translator to verify the validity of a reader's query. The exception is Minot's letter, which in fact received no reply, as will be seen in the section later in this chapter dedicated to Fen.

Though not necessarily sought by Penguin, the regular input from both academics and readers formed an informal quality assurance mechanism, notifying Penguin editors regularly about what was being done well and what was not. I would argue that these groups formed an unofficial but invaluable external advisory network of their own for Penguin, which eventually exercised some degree of influence over the formation of the Russian classics in the Penguin series. Take, for example, Lermontov's *A Hero of Our Time*, which was first printed in 1966 but soon withdrawn as 'the sales did not justify a re-print' (Sulkin, 1974). Paul Foote's translation was successfully reinstated after four years and five requests by different academics, from an initial enquiry in January 1971 through to D. Herring's letter of 6 January 1975, to which Penguin replied on 31 January 1975 that Foote's translation of *A Hero of Our Time* would be re-printed that very week.

The corps of Penguin's Russian translators

> Translation demands an exceptional self-discipline. There can be no 'perfect' translation, even if such positive qualities required could be defined. Negative qualities are more simple to settle. But it was in these areas of fine distinction that Rieu proved to be so remarkable an editor [...]. His ability to single out appropriate books from his wide knowledge of early and foreign literature, and to contact the most suitable translators to carry out each task, was almost unique. (Edwards et al, 2008, p. 12)

As already seen from Rieu's correspondence with Kitto, Rieu used his network of acquaintances to source possible translators. He initially gave Oxbridge dons an opportunity to submit sample translations, but later he famously rejected their efforts on the grounds that 'very few of them could write decent English, and most were enslaved by the idiom of the original language' (ibid., p. 26). Nevertheless, this was not the case with all, and archived correspondence indicates that some translator-graduates were sourced through Oxford University, perhaps through Rieu's contact with Baldick (himself an Oxford-based French scholar and translator). It is equally likely, however, that translators sought out Rieu independently, responding positively to the invitation in the final line of his announcement in the July 1946 edition of *Penguins Progress*: 'Translations are being sought out for many other volumes covering a wide variety of literature ranging from the literature of Ancient Egypt to the closing years of the nineteenth century' (p. 48).

When Penguin launched Rieu's *The Odyssey* translation, British readers were still largely reliant on Garnett's renderings of the Russian literary canon. Hence while Rieu could easily make a case for re-translating the Russian classics, he did not have a wide choice of experienced Russian-English literary translators at his disposal. Since the era of vocational training in literary translation had not yet arrived, anyone with knowledge of translation theory would have been self-taught. Those commissioned by Rieu probably possessed intuitive translational talent and a feel for writing, or else aspired to develop both. Penguin's early Russian classics translators might have acquired and used their language skills in different settings, both professional and personal, but without exception their backgrounds reflect the lived experience of a Europe in transition. Fen and Magarshack immigrated to the United Kingdom from turbulent, post-revolutionary Russia; Edmonds had worked as a senior wartime translator; Foote studied Russian on the inter-service Joint Services School of Linguists (JSSL)[28] course at Cambridge before working as an interpreter in Potsdam in 1946 (Meier, 2011); and Richard Freeborn had worked in the Royal Air Force and post-war Potsdam, before finally moving to the British Embassy in Moscow (Dynasty Press, n.d.). With background details such as these, it is not surprising that these individuals eventually found work which transposed their language skills to the field of translation in peace-time Britain. Where better to do this than Penguin Classics, the publisher of the moment? For Penguin's Russian Classics to succeed in disseminating Russia's literary canon, specialised and seemingly rare language skills would be required. In turn, the prospect of modern patronage, of a career riding a potential wave of Penguin commissions, would have appealed to every literary translator seeking regular and potentially lucrative work. As Rieu wrote in his letter to Kitto, 'What a chance!'. The parameters of mutual dependency (and success) were set.

In order to construct a deeper appreciation of their agency and their contributions, I turn now to relevant microhistorical details of the earliest translators and their contractual arrangements with Penguin. Aside from a brief biographical résumé in the front pages of a Penguin Classic translation (and even then, biographies only began to be included once the series was well established),[29] the Penguin Russian translators remain relatively hidden, and some are, by now, almost forgotten. They are described as 'vital, but often underappreciated' (Yates, 2006, p. 149), validating Theo Hermans's statement that translators are 'hidden, out of view, transparent, incorporeal, disembodied and disenfranchised' (2000, p. 7). The extent of documentation for each Penguin Russian translator varies but tends to be scant, with the exceptions of Magarshack and Fen and, to a lesser extent, Edmonds, all of whom compensate for the dearth of material elsewhere. My aim in the rest of this chapter, therefore, is to make 'corporeal'[30] these previously hidden early Penguin translators and through their experiences, be better able to 'understand the complex intercultural process which is translation' (Munday, 2017, p. 3).

Gilbert Gardiner

There are no records of how Rieu and Gardiner became acquainted, nor are there any details of how they negotiated the first Russian commissions. But if Rieu's letter to Kitto is representative of these early discussions (as is very likely), they would have met over lunch, possibly at Rieu's club.[31] Gardiner is the first Russian translator to be commissioned by Penguin; fittingly, he would enjoy an untroubled correspondence with the Penguin editors. He raised no concerns and accepted all terms regarding his translation of Turgenev's *On The Eve* (1950). On paper, his commission was uncomplicated. Gardiner's letter to Penguin from 21 April 1976, twenty-six years after the initial release of his translation, in which he claimed to have missed royalties for the entire period since 1951, is a surprise development, therefore.[32] With 40,000 copies sold during this time, Gardiner was owed a sizeable £633.48.[33]

I suggest two possible interpretations of Gardiner's twenty-six year restraint. First, his patience implies that he was not in urgent need of this money and that translation was not his sole means of income; and also, that Penguin's accounts department did not rush to despatch royalties until directly requested.[34] According to the British Library catalogue, Gardiner translated only three books: Turgenev (for Penguin), and two books translated from German into English and published (one of them by Routledge) in 1935 on Russia and socialism. This suggests that Gardiner translated for intellectual, rather than financial, reasons. I identify Gardiner, therefore, as a perfect counter-example to Magarshack, who, as we will see, persistently reminded the Penguin staff that translation *was* his primary source of income and that his accounts must be settled urgently. Where Gardiner neither sought nor provided a counterweight to the commissioning process, Magarshack, on monetary matters, more than compensates, and, in contrast to Gardiner, never failed to chase his payments.[35]

Elisaveta Fen

Belorussian-born Lidia Vitalievna Zhiburtovich (1899–1983) studied Russian Language and Literature at Leningrad University before immigrating to Britain in 1925. She became Lydia Jackson after marrying a British citizen, Meredith Jackson, in 1929. She established a career for herself in child psychology during the 1930s, gaining a doctorate in psychology from Oxford University in 1949. In addition to her work in child psychology, Jackson supplemented her career writing novels, biographies, Russian-language teaching material (*A Beginner's Russian Reader* (1942) and *A Beginner's Russian Conversation* (1944), published by Methuen), and translating Russian literature. For her literary work, she adopted the pen name Elisaveta Fen. Although

Figure 1.2 Elisaveta Fen, Photographic portrait (Gerson, 1962)

her first Penguin translation appeared in 1951 (a compilation of Chekhov plays including *The Cherry Orchard*; *Three Sisters*; and *Ivanov*), correspondence in the Penguin and Fen archives demonstrates that Fen (see Figure 1.2) was acquainted with Rieu in an advisory capacity from as early as 1945. At Rieu's request (16 September 1945), she evaluated sample translations by a Mrs Scott (Rieu divulges no further details) for a collection of Tolstoi's short stories, also commenting on the suitability of such stories for Penguin Classics. Fen also positively assessed F. F. Seeley's sample translation of a chapter of *Crime and Punishment*. Rieu wrote to her again on 9 November 1946 to ask:

> May I consult you? We have the offer from Chatto and Windus of the Constance Garnett translation of <u>Dead Souls</u> for my Series. Do you know this, and do you think it is so good as to make it not worth while to try for a new one?

Fen's reply is thorough. She summarises Garnett's translation as 'very uneven, in parts quite good, but mostly only fair, and frequently far too literal, while in details it is often grossly inaccurate' (19 January 1947), citing eleven relevant examples. Her verdict, reached with Gardiner's help,[36] was that *Dead Souls* be either 'carefully revised [...] or the novel translated anew' (ibid.).

Rieu also asked Fen 'whether you think that Goncharov deserves a place in our list and would go down with the Penguin public' (22 July 1950). He sought her opinion on the quality of sample translations by James Hogarth for *Oblomov*, Rosemary Edmonds for *Anna Karenin* (24 February 1950), and M. Whittoch for Lermontov's *A Hero of Our Time* (15 December 1950). Fen was critical of Hogarth's and Whittoch's submissions, which were not commissioned, but we may deduce that she was undecided about Edmonds. Her report is not included in the Penguin archive or her private archive, but Rieu took Fen's advice to 'get her [Edmonds] to do another passage' (20 March 1950), which Fen also assessed. Rieu asked her specifically to check 'the scholarship and style of the work' (1 May 1950). Satisfied that Fen had 'told me just what I wished to know', Rieu sent Fen a cheque for £2.0.0. and concluded 'I propose to make an agreement with Mrs. Edmonds, after pointing out to her the slight blemishes that still occur in her work. I agree with you in thinking it most readable' (22 May 1950).

In his assessment of Fen's own sample translation of an act from Chekhov's *Ivanov*, Rieu was an exacting editor. He agreed with 'a competent English scholar' that 'there remains too much that is not convincing as English idiom', adding:

> I know that Chehov [sic] [...] makes his characters say things that English people don't, and that it would be a great mistake on a translator's part to try to turn Russians into Englishmen, but I still contend that the best way to get the characters across is to make them say everything they have to say in the most English way, however foreign the <u>sentiment</u> may be to us. (8 December 1945)

Rieu's dissatisfaction continued even after further attempts by Fen to Anglicise Chekhov's idioms. He observed that:

> [...] your main weakness lies in the finer shades of English idiom. As it is exactly in this respect that we have an opportunity of doing better than anyone who has already translated Chehov [sic], I attach the greatest importance to perfection in this respect [...]. May I suggest that you should do the work in collaboration with a first-class English scholar? (18 March 1946)

Although Fen translated other Russian authors, Zoshchenko, Bondariev and Shvarts for other publishing houses, she translated only Chekhov's plays for Penguin, adding four more plays (*The Seagull, The Bear, The Proposal, A Jubilee*) to a new 1954 edition, and a final edition in 1959. Correspondence reveals that Rieu declined Fen's offer to translate Chekhov's short stories for Penguin. Rieu informed her that 'We are going slow on Russian works, apart from the 2 great works of Tolstoy and 4 of Dostoievsky's' (26 March 1957). Just six months later, however, Fen received confirmation of Penguin's decision to commission a different Chekhov translator (Magarshack) instead:

> I think it only fair to let you know now that we have just decided to place the work in the hands of another translator. I am afraid this news may be a disappointment to you, but you will remember that we and our advisors had something to say in criticism of the English style in which the samples were submitted. (Rieu, 1957)

It seems, therefore, that Fen's most significant contribution to Penguin's Russian Classics was her early consultative role. Subsequent correspondence with Penguin (up to 1983) chiefly concerns payment of royalties, proposed re-prints of her Chekhov plays, and clarification of readers' queries over her renderings. Penguin's new generation of editorial staff wrote, for example, to ask for her comments after receiving a letter from the reader mentioned above, Jerome Minot. Minot, who described himself as having 'done a considerable amount of translating', wrote of Fen's translation of Chekhov's plays that 'there are certain things in this book which seem to me <u>inexcusable</u>'. He contests Fen's lexical choices (it should be 'estate' and not 'plantation'), transliteration ('Elena' instead of her 'Yeliena'), meaning ('What on earth does "looking out" a book mean?'), and over-domestication ('Why is the nurse called Nanny, when every literate person knows what a Nanya or Nania is?'). Minot accused Fen (and therefore, by association, Penguin too) of justifying 'sloppy translation' in order to 'popularize' Chekhov 'so it can be understood by people without literary knowledge' (25 January 1969). His evaluation of both Fen's work and, apparently, Penguin's broader mission was scathing. As editor at the time, James Cochrane (via his secretary Miss Cookman) invited Fen to comment. Fen offered concise justifications for her decisions, saving her most vigorous defence for her conclusion in order to deflect attention away from the finer points of her translation method:

> The rest of his letter is just muddle-headed ravings. From all this I cannot but conclude that your correspondent [...] belongs to a fairly common category of cranks who like to pose as experts. (11 February 1969)

Minot's delivery may have been boorish, but his interrogation of the Penguin translation process fulfils the role of external 'quality control' discussed above in *Public-facing Penguin*. It is commendable that Cochrane took Minot seriously and directed the challenge back to Fen. However, Fen's dismissive reply is a reminder of the capital which endured in her reputation as one of Rieu's earliest advisors. Her prior connection to the company trumps all of Minot's comments. Cookman replied to Fen, 'In view of what you have said I don't think that we shall find it necessary to reply to the critic!'

Rosemary Edmonds

Rosemary Edmonds (1905–1998) worked as a translator to General de Gaulle at the Fighting France Headquarters in London, and on liberation in Paris. Having been funded by de Gaulle to study Russian at the Sorbonne after the war (Hahn, 2004), she was 'recruited' by Rieu (the details of their first meeting are not recorded) after submitting sample translations. She translated works by Tolstoi, starting with *Anna Karenin* (1954), the first re-translation in the United Kingdom since the Maudes' version in the 1920s. Like Garnett before her, Edmonds embarked on a career in Russian literary translation without ever having been to Russia; in the same year that her translation of *War and Peace* was published, Edmonds informed Penguin (4 May 1957) that she had been invited to Russia for the first time.

Edmonds's lack of direct experience of Russia might explain Rieu's evaluation of her first typescript. In a letter to Glover on the typescript of *Anna Karenin*, Rieu discussed the improvements she had made to the text at his suggestion (such as reading her 'stuff aloud' and consulting with native Russians). He remarks that, 'I have examined the text carefully and found it good, though I do not think she is one of our A+ translators. I have also read the introduction which is, in my opinion, a bit feeble, but not altogether rotten' (8 September 1952). Defending her translation style, she later explained that she didn't 'like tidying Tolstoy up too much' (3 June 1960); some of her introductions are conspicuously telegraphic, though, and structurally disjointed (those to *Anna Karenin* and *The Death of Ivan Illyich* [sic] *And Other Stories* in particular), especially when compared to the coherent and cohesive introductions offered by translators such as Fen and Freeborn.

Edmonds was, however, alert to issues which might directly influence her book sales. She requested the opportunity to discuss the medallion image for the cover of *War and Peace*, declaring the roundel on *Anna Karenin* 'a disaster', possibly on account of the quality and style of the drawing.[37] She expressed an eagerness for Penguin to coordinate publication of her *War and Peace* translation with the 1956 film release featuring Audrey Hepburn, an obvious opportunity for Edmonds to maximise book sales. She also pointed out that there were fewer sales of *War and Peace* Volume II, compared to Volume I. Her remark to Penguin that 'I don't like the conclusion I come to about the different figures for the two volumes of War and Peace' (27 May 1966), pre-empted Penguin's commercial decision later, in 1982, to re-issue the novel in one volume. In this respect, Edmonds was as commercially astute as Fen and Magarshack, who also tracked book sales and requested regular royalty updates from the Penguin editors.

One feature of Edmonds's first Penguin translation which elicited an altogether more positive response from the editors was her decision to use the Anglicised form of Tolstoi's eponymous character Anna Karenin, rather than the Russian form, Anna Karenina, adopted by previous translators Nathan Haskell Dole and the Maudes. Edmonds's approach was applauded by Glover, who noted that 'if the wife of the Russian gentleman whose name you may know, had occasion to be referred to frequently in the English press, she would be called Madame Stalin and not Madame Stalin*a*' (10 September 1952).[38] Reading Edmonds's archived correspondence, there is a sense overall that, even had the editors disagreed with her preference for Anna Karenin, she would have doggedly stood her ground. Edmonds justified her decisions with conviction, a forcefulness which is apparent, for example, in correspondence regarding the galleys for *The Queen of Spades and Other Stories*:

> When I sent my typescript I attached a note requesting that my punctuation should not be altered. But not only punctuation but paragraphing, too, has been re-arranged; and someone has had the impertinence to 'correct' my choice of words and even delete a word here and there. [...] changes which destroy flavour and balance. (20 July 1961)

The tensions which arose repeatedly for Edmonds during her time with Penguin concern 'unauthorised' changes to her text: spellings, punctuation, deletions. (As we will see in Chapter Three, Edmonds was not alone in expressing concern over alterations; Magarshack also questioned the editor's right to make changes to his text.) Presumably conscious of looming publishing deadlines, Edmonds chose this moment to exert some of her own professional power over Penguin's treatment of her work. She concludes her above letter to Miss Jean Ollington with the following demand:

> Of course it may be argued that my text has been improved for me; but when my i.e. and cf. become I.e. and Cf. in work for which I am responsible it is too much to bear silently. So can you tell me that this will never happen again?

Edmonds eventually had a specific clause written into her contract of 1 February 1966, which stated that 'some commas may be altered but no dashes'; however, her tenure with Penguin terminated in 1966. Then, according to exchanges in the archive, editors Baldick and Cochrane concurred that the quality of her translation for a sample manuscript of Tolstoi's *The Kreutzer Sonata* had fallen below the required standard. (The sample manuscript is not included in the archive in order to judge how fair Baldick and Cochrane were in their opinion.) In his letter to Cochrane on 7 June 1966, Baldick sounds fatigued from sustained correspondence with Edmonds:

> I have just had the enclosed piece from Rosemary Edmonds, which I fear is as stiff and stilted as we thought it would be. I cannot believe that this is all Tolstoy's fault. I have written to tell her that I will be sending it on to you: perhaps you could look at it and tell her what you decide. I really do not feel up to writing yet another letter to her.

While Edmonds's pertinacity over translation and punctuation decisions may have been justified by improved outcomes, Baldick's letter indicates that she had exhausted the goodwill usually expressed by the Penguin Classic editors. By 1966, the editors had no more energy to challenge her grievances; no further Penguin commissions from Edmonds were made. Edmonds's tenure at Penguin was terminated in a way that echoes the termination of Magarshack's tenure two years earlier. The editors' letters from this period indicate that Edmonds and Magarshack both represented an old guard who had dogmatically upheld their translation decisions, eventually relying in each case on an over-idiosyncratic translation style and outmoded idiom.

Edmonds and Magarshack were of the same generation, both having made their careers out of their skill with words, both sufficiently forceful personalities to defend their positions as translators (as their correspondence shows); and they both associated with the 'heavy-weights' of Russian literature, Tolstoi and Dostoevskii. As we will see in Chapter Three, both Edmonds and Magarshack developed similar approaches to characterising dialect; they both insisted on retaining their own punctuation. They even made largely the same decision to Anglicise Russian naming conventions. For Edmonds, challenges to her translation practice followed her from the outset, with regular queries over punctuation, dissatisfaction with her introduction-writing and hybrid portrayal of dialect, and later, criticism of stilted syntax. One would expect Magarshack's archive to contain a comparable volume of queries over the course of his seven large commissions and yet, it was not until his final Penguin commission that a critical reader's report challenged his practice. Given the era when they lived, one wonders if Magarshack's practice was queried less by editorial staff, and Edmonds's was queried considerably more, because of gender expectations at the time. (Edmonds is the only long-serving female translator in the series; Fen only translated Chekhov's plays, and other female translators of the Russian Classics – Babette Deutsch, joint translator with Avrahm Yarmolinskii of *Eugene Onegin* (1964), Moura Budberg, translator of Gorkii's *Fragments From my Diary* (1972), Jessie Coulson, translator of Dostoevskii's *The Gambler* (1966) and *Notes from Underground* (1972), and later, Jane Kentish, translator of Dostoevskii's *Netochka Nezvanova* (1985) – completed just a handful of commissions between them.)

Despite Rieu's initial assessment of her work, he referred to Edmonds in a letter to her in 1966 as 'one of "my" translators who never gave me any trouble or a moment's anxiety'.[39] Perhaps Rieu sent such warm sentiments as a gesture of sympathy to Edmonds knowing that her tenure at Penguin had finished (or would soon finish); or he may simply have been looking back over his own tenure at Penguin from the nostalgic perspective of retirement. Rieu's (long-awaited) praise is not an isolated case, however. Henry Gifford also offered a positive verdict of Edmonds's work in his essay 'On Translating Tolstoy' (1978). He remarks that, whilst 'Miss Edmonds is sometimes lax about detail':

[...] her work is readable and it moves lightly and freely; the dialogue in particular is much more convincing than that contrived by the Maudes. (pp. 22–23)

Apparently 'no seeker of public recognition' (*The Telegraph*, 1998), Edmonds was awarded the Freedom of the City of London in March 1979, but it is the endurance of her translations which best contests Rieu's early view that she was not an 'A+ translator'. Penguin published a new translation of *Anna Karenina* only as recently as 2000, forty-six years after Edmonds's version and her 1958/1962 translation of Pushkin's *The Queen of Spades and Other Stories* is still being used by Penguin, reprinted in 1968, 1978, and as an e-book in 2004.

David Magarshack

David Magarshack's personal archive at the University of Leeds, along with the seven folders of correspondence in the Penguin archive and a handful of letters held in the Special Collections archive at the University of Manchester, has provided a surprising amount of material with which to work. A hoarder of letters, reviews, notes, photographs, theatre programmes, and articles, Magarshack left behind a range of professional markers which show him to have been a man of talent, consciously drawing on his capital and contacts to ensure success. Through Magarshack, and to a lesser extent the other early translators, it has been possible to analyse closely the dynamics of a freelance translator's relationship with Penguin and to demonstrate 'the types of collaborations and frictions in the translation process' (Munday, 2017, p. 3). Magarshack's archive provides evidence of the influences over his agency – habitus, a complex set of personal dispositions, capital, and patronage – when producing a commissioned work.

Magarshack (see Figure 1.3) was born in Riga in 1899 and he died from lymphoma in 1977 after a period of ill health (Magarshack, 2015). He was educated at a Russian secondary school, immigrated to England in 1920 and was naturalised as a British citizen in 1931. As a Jew, Magarshack faced repressive anti-Jewish education regulations which were imposed on students at that time in Russia and which would have prevented him from pursuing higher education there. Magarshack's prime motivation for leaving Russia, therefore, was to advance his education. When he arrived in the United Kingdom, he undertook an evening course in English Language and Literature at University College London, from where, four years later, he graduated with a second-class honours degree on 22 October 1924. On graduation, Magarshack 'traveled a few blocks to Fleet street [sic] and there learned the trades of English journalism, as reporter and subeditor' (*Chicago Tribune*, 1963). Magarshack summarised his journalistic credentials in detail in three letters, sent between June 1928 and November 1929, when seeking full-time employment at the *Manchester Guardian*.[40] As the

Figure 1.3 David Magarshack, (n.d.)

letters confirm, his English was of a suitably high standard to be able to make a career from writing:

> My journalistic career has now stretched over a period of seven years, during which time I worked on the staff of a London News Agency, was Literary Editor of an English daily published overseas, was contributor of articles to the American press, was Editor of 'Foreign Affairs', in full charge of the paper, and am now under an agreement to write bi-weekly editorials for the Christian Science Monitor [...]. (12 November 1929)

Decades later, *John O'London's Weekly* returned to the subject of Magarshack's language skills, 'For many years he has written as fluently in English as in Russian, though he still speaks with a slight accent' (22 February 1952), and 'Now, Mr Magarshack is very Russian as well - by birth and upbringing, and yet thoroughly adept at writing clear and cogent English' (14 March 1953).

Magarshack wrote three crime novels in English, published in the 1930s by Constable & Co. Ltd.: *Big Ben Strikes Eleven* (1934); *Death Cuts a Caper* (1935); *Three Dead* (1937). Attempts to echo Dostoevskii's style – in terms of theme and also description – are recognisable in Magarshack's narrative. They indicate his self-perception as not just a crime-writer, but one with literary aspirations firmly localised in the United Kingdom. There are significant plot references to overdue rent (*Death Cuts a Caper*), Porfiry Petrovich-inspired Superintendents (after the Columbo-like police officer who manipulates Raskolnikov in Dostoevskii's novel), and in the first novel, *Big Ben Strikes Eleven*, there are even detailed Dostoevskian discussions of characters blessed and burdened with genius:

> Every genius was no doubt self-centred, every genius was in the first place a sublime genius, especially where his own work was concerned, but while civilisation could and should put up with the small annoyances and provocations of its men of genius for the great benefactions which they conferred on the whole human race, could it afford to tolerate a genius whose egotism was so all-embracing, whose appetite was so all-devouring, that he needed the whole of humanity to appease his hunger? (1934, p. 29)

In terms of descriptive style, Dostoevskii's influence can also be detected in the opening line of the same book:

> The discovery of Sir Robert Boniface's body on the floor of his blue limousine was made quite accidentally *on a sultry Friday evening towards the end of June*. (p. 1) (my italics)

Compare with the opening line of *Crime and Punishment*, with the source text of which Magarshack would have been familiar, and which he himself later translated for Penguin as:

> *On a very hot evening at the beginning of July* a young man left his little room at the top of a house in Carpenter Lane, went out into the street, and, as though unable to make up his mind, walked slowly in the direction of Kokushkin Bridge. (1951, p. 1) (my italics)

Much to his disappointment (Magarshack, 2015), despite all his stylistic and thematic nods to Dostoevskii and a positive review from Dorothy L. Sayers[41] ('This is really a very jolly book, with sound plot, some good characterisation, a number of thrills, and everything handsome about it.'),[42] Magarshack's career as a novelist did not take off. The literary and financial capital which he had anticipated failed to materialise. His novel-writing presented an opportunity, though, for him to explore and fine-tune the interplay of British dialects and the application of idiomatic turns of phrase, fixed expressions, and proverbs, which he recorded and practised in notebooks included in his personal archive. Financial need provided the greatest motivation for him to shift his focus towards translation.[43] Magarshack's professional relationship with Rieu began in 1949 with his first Penguin commission, Dostoevskii's *Crime and Punishment*. It is unclear how they met; one might speculate that they were introduced by Sayers, who was both the first Penguin translator of Dante's *Inferno* (1949) and reviewer of Magarshack's *Big Ben Strikes Eleven*.

It is evident from the assertive tone adopted in his letters that, from the outset, Magarshack's relationship with Penguin was one of clearly delineated mutual dependency. He was no subservient operative; he stood his ground and exerted symbolic power whenever required. Whereas Edmonds exerted *linguistic* power over the Penguin editors, insisting that she knew best when it came to the text, there is no evidence to suggest that she ever called into question her terms and conditions. By contrast, Magarshack regularly challenged Rieu and Glover over both payment and, to a lesser extent, textual matters. In Rieu's introductory letter to Glover of 20 January 1949, he explains that Magarshack 'lives by his translations', adding, with a suggestion of caution, that he 'has published translations from the Russian with other publishers and has several new ones in the hands of various firms (Faber's, Lehman, etc [sic]). They deal generously with him'. We may presume from this that, in their initial meeting, Magarshack offered Rieu this information himself in a bid to increase his negotiating power, a position which is reiterated in Magarshack's first letter to Glover. Dissatisfied that Glover appeared to be reneging on Rieu's terms, Magarshack spelled out his views:

> There is no question of approval at all. I am not an amateur, and my books have been published and are due to be published by well-known publishing houses including Allen & Unwin, Faber & Faber, and John Lehmann. Penguin Books, too, will be publishing a long contribution by me in the next issue of New Writing. Mr Rieu was in complete agreement with me about this question of approval. [...] I hope to hear from you without delay, as, following Mr Rieu's assurances, I have already begun the preliminary work on the book. (3 March 1949)

Magarshack's overriding message is that it would take little for him to take his talents elsewhere, where they (and he) will be properly appreciated. Aware of Seeley's terminated contract, which would already have put Magarshack in a powerful negotiating position, this tactic of showing demand for his translation skills played to Magarshack's strengths. Given how few UK-based Russian-English linguists there were, Magarshack's credentials were ideal for Penguin to keep commissioning him, thereby extending their repertoire of Russian classics and increasing their financial capital. Knowledge of this position clearly did not escape Magarshack, who hints at his cultural, symbolic power – along with his position and ability to play one publisher off against another – throughout his correspondence with the Penguin editors.

Magarshack's drive to assert his position is particularly evident in his letter to Glover of 18 June 1952. Having submitted the typescript for Dostoevskii's *The Devils*, Magarshack requested his final advance of £50 for the typescript, as well as an advance on royalties from sales of *Crime and Punishment*; this time his tone is insistent. At some length – and it is clear from the chronology of correspondence that he has already discussed this request – Magarshack reiterates all the reasons why he *must* break with Penguin's set terms and receive his royalties before the designated annual pay-out. The careful construction of his argument is worth quoting at length; it reveals the multiple angles of persuasion at Magarshack's disposal which he employed in order to endorse his claim and reinforce his position:

> You say you are always willing to stretch a point, and it seems to me that in the circumstances you could stretch another point for me, especially if all I ask for is to let me have some of the royalties already received. If there are no royalties, then there is nothing to be done about it.
>
> I have now to sit down to do a translation of OBLOMOV, which is one of the greatest works of art in Russian literature and is written in a style that is not as slapdash as Dostoyevsky's. It will require a tremendous lot of concentration and careful adaptation of an appropriate English style. I told you in my last letter that I feel that before I sit down to it I simply must have a decent holiday. It is therefore in your interest as well as mine to make things easier for me.

Magarshack's letter concludes with an addendum expressing concern about the absence of copies of *Crime and Punishment* in his local bookshop, Wilson's in Hampstead, and the impact upon his royalties. Although always impeccably polite to his clients, Glover vented his personal frustrations in a letter on this subject to Rieu. He wrote that Magarshack 'is in a frantic hurry for money and wants to get the balance of the advance payable of which he has already had more than he is entitled to' (17 June 1952). He continues in his understated way, 'I am getting very tired of Mr Magarshack. I know it is my duty as a Buddhist to help the needy, but he seems so very needy all the time'. Magarshack's persistence worked however, and Penguin obligingly met him part way with a promise to advance an approximation of his dues by the end of July. In contrast to Gardiner, Magarshack's business acumen was ever present. As he made quite clear, he could not afford to be obediently subservient. Magarshack's habitus – the turn-of-the-century Russian immigrant turned professional writer and translator, with a family to support – determined the tone, the expectations, and the boundaries of his agency. He repeatedly shows signs of pushing back at the commissioner, of turning cultural and linguistic capital into economic and symbolic capital.

Nor did Magarshack restrict his sphere of influence simply to the United Kingdom. It is of particular interest that – at a time when East-West relations were becoming increasingly polarised – Magarshack increased his chances of success by keeping one foot in the West, and the other in Russia.[44] The contents of Magarshack's archive offer none of his political views on the Cold War (according to his daughter Stella, Magarshack was areligious and, it would seem, apolitical too). They do, however, reveal that he actively sought and cultivated a relationship with the Soviet Union's literati and enjoyed the praise and acknowledgement he received from his former countrymen, affirmation by literary peers from across a difficult political divide.[45] Regularly reminded – professionally and personally – of his foreignness here in the West, it seems hardly surprising that Magarshack strove for some recognition from his native land. It is surprising, given the Soviet government's official disapproval of exiles, that Magarshack received due acknowledgement. Magarshack did not just receive affirmation from Professor Morozov at the All-Russia Theatre Society conference on 10 November 1944[46] for his translations into English of Ostrovskii, he also received printed praise and publicity from within the Union of Soviet Socialist Republics in articles published in *Komsomol'skaia pravda*, *Izvestiia*,[47] and *Literaturnaia gazeta*, years before he attracted any such interest or recognition by the British media.

Coming from a respected figure in the Soviet literary and academic circuit, Morozov's positive review provided Magarshack with a tangible benchmark for his work and, no doubt, an appreciated boost to his sense of self-worth. It is telling, however, that Morozov described Magarshack as the '*talantlivyi angliiskii pisatel*' ('the talented English writer'), deliberately overlooking or genuinely failing to realise Magarshack's Russian birth (this seems unlikely, however, given Magarshack's easily identifiable Russo-Jewish surname). By identifying Magarshack as English, Morozov was confirming to Magarshack that his career and reputation were British, not Soviet. Arguably, however, by courting the commercial West and the Soviet East, Magarshack captured the best of both worlds for his career, that is, as a Russian literary translator making a living and forging a reputation in the West, whilst maintaining contact with and kudos within the Union of Soviet Socialist Republics. He was able, therefore, to secure a steady flow of repeat business at Penguin with none of the spectre of Soviet censorship or possible punishment.

His last Penguin translation was Chekhov's *Lady with Lapdog and Other Stories*, published in 1964. It was initially commissioned on the assumption that it would be the first of three volumes of Chekhov short stories. However, completion of Magarshack's final commission coincided with the era immediately preceding Rieu's retirement from Penguin Classics, and his manuscript was handled rather differently by Robert Baldick in his role as Advisory Editor. A reader's review was supplied for the *Lady with Lapdog* typescript, the only one to be found in Magarshack's folders in the

Penguin archive. In the anonymous reader's comments, eight pages of hand-written questions are produced concerning Magarshack's style and accuracy, ranging from awkward syntax to 'stilted, unnatural speech', tautology and lexical selection, transposition of phrases, tenses and adjectives, and most frequently of all, mis-conveyed sense. Baldick's summary to Penguin colleague David Duguid of the reader's points, having checked them with Magarshack, also alludes to Magarshack's reaction. The delay in checking the typescript was partly because 'it has been difficult to get a reply out of Magarshack' (21 November 1963). Baldick's choice of language thereafter intimates the awkwardness of his exchange with Magarshack, who had replied 'with great indignation', was 'very indignant' and even (Baldick wrote) "retort[ed]" abrasively to one of their queries.

It comes as no real surprise to learn that further volumes of Chekhov were not commissioned, as Cochrane's follow up letter to Duguid confirms:

> Chekhov: Selected Tales
> I have sent the manuscript of this Classic through to Production with the above provisional title. I have marked it provisional because it would probably give rise to difficulties if a second or third volume was produced. (There was no contract for another volume with Magarshack. It was assumed when the first contract was made that he would do another volume but he has since fallen out of favour). [sic] (24 January 1964)

Magarshack's relationship with Penguin thus came to a close – a casualty perhaps of Rieu's retirement in the same year and of the new, more academic rigour of Baldick's and Radice's Penguin Classics. Magarshack's career, however, continued. Instead of retirement, Magarshack's post-Penguin years represent a transition from translator and biographer to translation theorist, a shift I will address in the next chapter.

Conclusion

This chapter has demonstrated how the field of translation and publishing in the mid-twentieth century progressed from the era of Heinemann and Garnett. Literature in translation gathered new momentum since the launch of the Penguin Classics series with Rieu's *The Odyssey*. Even more importantly for my study, Russian literature gained significance within that series, building on lessons learned from the unsuccessful *Russian Review* initiative. This chapter has outlined how the corporate structure of Penguin's publishing house organised itself operationally, introducing the necessary institutional frameworks in order to approach the Penguin Classics series in a strategic and considered way. Whereas its early interest in promoting Russian literature in translation was dependent largely on the dedication of individuals or fortuitous partnerships, during this period Penguin actively introduced well-supported mechanisms of delegation and autonomy (from Lane's choice of editors to the editors' selection of suitably skilled translators and advisors) to ensure that some of the best expertise and knowledge facilitated the creation of a broad, commercially attractive library of classics.

Through my historical approach (recommended by Munday as a way of investigating the sociological factors behind agency such as the 'conditions, working practices and [the] identity of translators and [...] their interaction with other participants in the translation process' (2014, p. 64)), the Penguin archive's Russian folders and private papers in the Leeds Russian archive – specifically the content which relates to the individual motivations, backgrounds, and expectations of those producing the Penguin Classics series – reveal a surprising degree of autonomy in the Penguin Classics microcosm, which Rieu, in particular, enjoyed during his editorship. Lane's trust in Rieu's proven capabilities – as a commercially-minded editor and a translator – enabled Lane to delegate the Penguin Classics series to Rieu, a move which was liberating not only for Lane, but for the future of the series too. Unlike Lane's early, failed, attempt at producing the Illustrated Classics series, the Penguin Classics series flourished under Rieu's expertise and network of specialist connections.

Penguin's era of Russian classics represents the sort of success which can be achieved through balanced collaboration, where compromises are made on both sides, by the editor and by the translator, for their mutual benefit and the success of the project. Whilst driving a hard, commercial deal (as with Magarshack's *Crime and Punishment* contract, for example), Rieu's consistent professionalism, his careful commitment to a target text, and his impeccable politeness earned him the greatest respect. Glover matched a critical eye for errors and inconsistencies with an impressive capacity to understand the translator's need for deadline flexibility, the translator's desire to produce a perfect text even at the risk of crippling correction costs, and the translator's difficulties with cash flow while waiting on royalties. These editors' ability, born out of first-hand experience, to relate to the translator's world, generated not just appreciation, but immense loyalty to the series amongst the early Russian Classics freelancers.

For the freelancers, especially the energetic and engaged ones like Magarshack and Edmonds, Penguin represented a reliable employer with dynamic prospects for individual and corporate achievement. In contrast to Garnett, who seems to have lacked the leverage to convert her literary and linguistic capital into satisfactory economic capital, the Penguin freelancers were also considerably more involved and, in some cases, quite forceful in their contractual negotiations (payment of advances and royalties, deadlines, corrections). By the mid-twentieth century it has become clear that freelancers were able to make Penguin work for them and their interests (such as flexible, home working; employment allowing application of their specialist language skills; the prospect of repeat business) to at least the same degree that Penguin gained from them. By commissioning members of this group of freelancers to translate a variety of different Russian authors, the Penguin Classics editors were also able to secure certain flexibilities: they could manage production time and the flow of publications; they could offer interrupted and/or terminated contracts to other freelancers for completion;[48] they could call on translators to peer review typescripts. From their editorial remove, Rieu and Glover were able to oversee in-house stylistic requirements of translation equivalence, accessibility, and readability, thus completing their final act of agency: the bridge between Penguin the publisher and the paying customer, the outside reader.

Notes

1. In 'History of Penguin archive' (*Telegraph*, 2009), Toby Clements identifies Lane's early staff as 'mostly maverick autodidacts who met for planning dinners that lasted long into the night in a Spanish restaurant in Soho'.
2. Fen identified Zoshchenko as a worthy addition to the series in her early correspondence with Rieu, but Penguin presumably respected Kotelianskii's opinion above Fen's on this matter.
3. Lane courted speculation throughout his career about having left-leaning political tendencies, maybe even Communist (an opinion assisted by his visit to Moscow in 1957). According to Steve Hare, 'It was inevitable that a certain logic would dictate that since Penguin published books that inclined towards the Left, then its editors and owners must be similarly inclined' (1995, p. 71).
4. Count Constantine "Conny" Benckendorff, the son of the Russian ambassador to London (1900–1917), emigrated from Russia to the UK in 1924 after suffering repeated arrests and imprisonment by the Cheka (Minshall, 1954, p. 355). Budberg, also a Slavic émigrée, is described in her obituary as an 'author, translator, production adviser on plays, films and television programmes, [...], publishers' reader of manuscripts in five languages' (*The Times*, 1974). Budberg aroused interest for having enjoyed relationships with H.G. Wells, Sir Robert Bruce Lockhart, and Maxim Gorkii, but also attracted speculation that she might be a Soviet spy (McDonald and Dronfield, 2016).
5. During 1943–1946, Penguin produced thirty-four monthly issues of a periodical called *Transatlantic*, the aim of which was 'to assist the British and American peoples to walk together in majesty and peace' (Yates, 2006, p. 149). The periodical became a casualty of paper-rationing, however, and Lane 'sold the title and goodwill for a nominal five shillings to Transatlantic Books Ltd' (ibid.).
6. On launching his first Penguin list he is remembered as having said (presumably not seriously), 'Of one thing I'm sure; there's no money in it for anybody' (Lewis, 2006, p. 110).
7. Lane recognised the need for expert advice after his first attempt to introduce Illustrated Classics, just one year before the outbreak of the Second World War, was a failure. The series, published in May 1938, consisted of ten titles, including Jane Austen's *Pride and Prejudice*, Laurence Sterne's *A Sentimental Journey* and Herman Melville's *Typee*. The books were diminished by Penguin's use of 'indifferent paper' and a smaller format, 'too cramped to carry illustration' (Morpurgo, 1979, p. 143). The series was swiftly discontinued and Lane subsequently sought opinions to ensure careful "publishable" decisions.

8. Morpurgo believed it was particularly important for Lane to receive his honorary degrees (1979, p. 226). Newly-bestowed academic status provided Lane with an opportunity to close intellectual gaps between him and his agents and to achieve at least the semblance of an equal footing with editor-advisors. His difficult relationship with the erudite, self-taught A.S.B. Glover is perhaps the only exception.

9. Russell Edwards (Penguin Collector's Society) argues that Lane's apparent rashness 'added piquancy to the series [...], with Allen Lane flying in the face of the advice of the literary and commercial experts and backing his own judgment – with triumphant success' (2008, p. 141).

10. Rieu studied classics at Balliol College, Oxford (Connell, 2004), but according to his obituary in *The Times*, 'His career at Oxford did not, however, end with academic distinction of the kind confidently expected of him though he obtained a First in Honour Mods. He suffered a breakdown of health and left the university at the end of his seventh term without a degree'.

11. Platt is more effusive still about the impact on the general readership of Rieu's *The Odyssey* translation and the Penguin Classics series: '[...] he [Rieu] made possible wondrous voyages, far more extensive than those of Odysseus with whom Rieu's name will for ever be linked' (2008, p. 9). Effusions like this nurture the 'legendary' aspect of the Penguin Classics series' reputation.

12. According to Platt, 'over three million copies were sold', and the book 'remained Penguin's best seller for 16 years until Lady Chatterley's Lover appeared in 1960' (2008, p. 9).

13. Andrew Lang, Walter Leaf and Ernest Myers were translators of Homer's *Odyssey* and *Iliad* during the late nineteenth century.

14. Whilst the nature of the principle of equivalent effect is problematic (see, for example, Munday, 2008, p. 52), many of the Russian works which were being translated at the time of Penguin were still less than one hundred years old. The original audience, therefore, might be considered close enough in time for their translator to be able to anticipate their first reactions.

15. Contemporary Russia and Russian culture were not entirely perceived at second hand by Rieu; an article in the *Times* written on the occasion of Rieu's retirement describes a journey he took on the Trans-Siberian Railway at the start of the twentieth century, which included 'gate-crashing the Kremlin and catching glimpse of the Tsar' (8 January 1964).

16. Rieu noted to Glover (29 July 1946), for example, that both *Candide* and *Madame Bovary* featured on Hamish Hamilton's list of 6/ translations. Hamish Hamilton also published some Turgenev classics and Gogol's *Dead Souls* in the late 1940s-early 1950s. Glover replied that he was keen to 'get ahead' of Hamish Hamilton (30 July 1946).

17. Magarshack prepared over a thousand pages of a book on the history of nineteenth-century Russian literature, which Penguin considered publishing as a Pelican but which ultimately never appeared. Apparently sensing that her support at Penguin was on the wane (a realisation which Baldick himself spotted and commented on in his letter to Cochrane of 7 June 1966), Edmonds suggested rounding off Penguin's Tolstoi series with the controversial play *Power of Darkness* in the hope of gaining another commission. Penguin did not commission her, or any other freelancer, to translate *Power of Darkness*.

18. Garnett's husband Edward was well-positioned in the literary field as a publisher's reader and able therefore to promote his wife's work. He penned the introductions and biographical sketches which Heinemann felt were a necessary supplement to Constance's works, but which she felt were beyond her. According to David Garnett, 'Constance "found it an agony to write anything original"' (Garnett, 2009, pp. 306–307).

19. See Rieu's statement in the July 1946 *Penguins Progress* announcement, 'it is the editor's intention to commission translators who could emulate his own example' (p. 48).
20. Three years on from initially agreeing the Seeley contract, Penguin still had nothing to show for the time they had invested. No reason is provided in the archive, but the contract was, seemingly, terminated at Seeley's instigation.
21. Biography references to Glover present general inconsistency over the spelling of his Christian name, at times 'Allan', at others 'Alan', a fact which is consistent with the notion that he cultivated an air of enigma about his former life (see Morpurgo, 1979, p. 192).
22. The exact date is unclear but his tenure began in the same year as Rieu's (Yates, 2006, p. 61).
23. According to correspondence he exchanged with T.C.N. Gibbens, Pelican author of the (unpublished) *Crime and Criminals*, this period of Glover's life was divided between Exeter, Pentonville, Durham, Wormwood Scrubs and Winchester prisons. Prison provided an opportunity for him to commit the *Encyclopaedia Britannica* to memory and to edit the prison newspaper, which was written on lavatory paper. His photographic memory and breadth of knowledge also spanned *Wisden Cricketers' Almanack*, Bradshaw's railway guide, Greek and Hebrew literatures, he was a formidable scholar of Jung and psycho-analysis, and had an ongoing interest in religion, from Quakerism to Catholicism, before he settled on Buddhism (Hare, 1995, pp. 128–130).
24. He is noted for 'amiably and abundantly pointing out errors and misprints' (Yates, 2006, p. 61).
25. Magarshack's response puts into rare context the finely-balanced realities of the freelance world, where the royalty pipeline is an essential feature and must be carefully maintained in order to survive the long wait between manuscript submission and actual publication (sometimes as long as two years, or more, much to Magarshack's and other Penguin freelancers' annoyance).
26. Letter from Mr Grant Wallace, Heywood High School, Victoria, 4 August 1978, regarding the omission of two lines concerning Lazarus from *Crime and Punishment*, perceived as crucial to the spiritual understanding of the novel. Letter from Dr Edward D Sullivan, Princeton University, 28 December 1954, regarding the omission of Stavrogin's confession from *The Devils*.
27. Having ordered 150 copies for use in the Dept. of Slavic Languages and Literatures, Northwestern University, an anonymous academic declared that 'such a publishing procedure [the abridgements] is perilously close to intentional fraud' (22 October 1974). There was also considerable discussion at Penguin over which title to use, the faithful rendering of *A Sportsman's Notebook* being deemed too off-putting to the reader (see correspondence between James Cochrane and translator Richard Freeborn, 12 June and 5 July 1964). By contrast, *Fathers and Sons* remained the title of Turgenev's novel, *Otsy i deti*, even though Gardiner, the initial translator, noted, as did some readers, that *Fathers and Children* would have been more accurate. Gardiner's translation was never used and Rosemary Edmonds was commissioned instead, keeping the slightly inaccurate title.
28. Geoffrey Elliott and Harold Shukman define the JSSL training programme as 'a key Cold War initiative in which over 5,000 men were secretly pushed through intensive training in Russian.' (2011, p. 11).
29. I have only been able to locate brief translator biographies in editions from the Black Cover series, which emerged from the Medallion Series and ran from 1963–c.1970.

30. This research aim was explored across languages at the British Library conference *The Translator Made Corporeal: Translation History in the Archive* in 2017, at which a version of this chapter was presented as a paper.
31. 'On the matter of translation I only wish we could meet. Mattingly and I thrashed it out at my club the other day over a protracted lunch and he went away keen as mustard' (Rieu, 4 November 1944).
32. The reason cited for non-payment is 'because our Royalties Department did not have [your] address' (Sulkin, 1976).
33. A sum which was worth £3983.64 in 1976.
34. This incident is reminiscent of Agatha Christie's occasional quizzing of Lane, '"Allen, isn't it about a year since I had any royalties from you?" she would ask from time to time: "I wondered whether you'd notice," he'd reply looking "half-guilty, half-mischievous"' (Lewis, 2006, p. 33).
35. See, for example, Magarshack's letter to Glover: 'I expect to hear from you soon about the query in my letter of January 2nd. I should like to know the total sales [sic] my two Dostoevsky books in the U.S.A., the price at which they are sold, and the accruing royalties which I do not seem to have yet received' (5 January 1954).
36. Fen continued to correspond regularly with Gardiner until his death in 1981.
37. The *Anna Karenin* roundel image features in *Penguin Classics* (Edwards et al, 2008, p. 71).
38. Nearly twenty years later, Edmonds's and Penguin's decision to use the Anglicised form provoked a quite different response from the aforementioned reader Mrs Joan Miller. Miller decried Edmonds's naming strategy in emphatic terms ('impudence and vandalism'), an accusation which Cochrane described as 'at the very least an over-statement' (5 July 1972).
39. The original letter cannot be located but the passage is cited in Edmonds's obituary in *The Telegraph*, 1998.
40. Magarshack submitted articles but never worked as an editor for the *Manchester Guardian*.
41. Sayers wrote twelve detective novels (all but one featuring the aristocratic, amateur sleuth Lord Peter Wimsey) and presided over *The Detection Club* in London from 1949–1957 (Symons, 1979).
42. Sayers's review of *Big Ben Strikes Eleven* appears on the blurb of Magarshack's second novel, *Death Cuts a Caper* (1935).
43. Money was scarce for Magarshack (he was married with four children by now). He and his wife, Elsie Duella, received little support from relatives (Magarshack, 2015). Magarshack's own parents had no further contact with him once he had emigrated and, from the outset, he was regarded by Elsie's parents as an undesirable match (ibid.). Howarth-born, grammar-school educated Elsie (1899–1999) won a scholarship to read English at Cambridge University. She met Magarshack at a 'students' Christian meeting club' in London, and they shared a passion for English (a factor in their relationship which later became crucial to Magarshack's literary success). When she married the man her parents called 'the foreigner' (ibid.), Elsie's parents were greatly disappointed; they never accepted their son-in-law 'because he never earned any money' (Magarshack, 2014). In a letter seeking employment at the *Manchester Guardian*, he described himself as being 'glad of anything at present, for I am rather in a tight corner' (12 September 1928). Elsie earned some money by home-coaching students for university and David worked from home but 'earned nothing until the end of the war when he started translating Russian literature which he loved' (Magarshack, 2014).

44. At the very start of his translating career in 1944, Magarshack sent the USSR Society for Cultural Relations with Foreign Countries and Professor Morozov, the renowned Soviet scholar of Shakespeare, his translation of Ostrovskii's comedies for their evaluation. The translations were positively received. Morozov wrote a review which was published in *Literaturnaia gazeta* (No. 6) on 9 December 1944 under the heading, *P'esi Ostrovskogo v Anglii* ('Ostrovskii's Plays in England'), where he wrote of Magarshack's work, '*Ego perevody napisany iasnym i zhivym iazykom, iazykom pisatelya, a ne filologa*' ('His translations are written in a language that is clear and alive, the language of a writer, not that of a grammarian') (My translation). Later correspondence reveals that Magarshack maintained contact with the USSR in the fifteen years after his Ostrovskii translations. In a letter to Mr Rosenthal, Magarshack quotes correspondence from 24 February 1960 in which Pasternak praised him for the skilful translation *I Remember: Sketch for an Autobiography* (1959): 'Please convey to Mr. Magarshack my admiration for his masterly translation, his profound, informative Introduction, his unerring, shrewd judgment, and his quite astonishing knowledge which surpasses even mine' (29 April 1971).
45. The Soviet definition of émigré writers was, however, categorical: 'a traitor or an ideological (class) enemy, hence a threat to the Soviet way of thinking and therefore was deemed unacceptable for the Soviet public' (Dienes, 2009, pp. x-xi). In practical terms, this meant that, 'Throughout the Soviet period the Russian émigré writer found it well-nigh impossible even to return home for a visit. Not only could his books not be sold in Russia, but it was a crime to possess or conspire to possess them, to circulate, import, or even make a longhand copy of them. The only acknowledgement the writer could expect if he returned home was a prison sentence ... or worse' (Glad, 1999, p. 297).
46. See letter from Kislova, 10 February 1945.
47. (Ibid.).
48. For example, Seeley's terminated *Crime and Punishment* contract was offered to Magarshack. The contract for a translation of Turgenev's *Fathers and Sons* was first given to Gardiner but, after three years, Edmonds was commissioned instead. There is no correspondence in the Penguin archive detailing reasons for the change of translator.

References

Anon., n.d. Richard Freeborn, *Dynasty Press*, [online] Available at: <http://www.dynastypress.co.uk/richard-freeborn.html> [Accessed 29 January 2020].
Anon., 1972. Obituary, Dr E.V. Rieu Best-selling editor of paper-back classics, 13 May [online] Available at: *The Times Digital Archive*, [Accessed 23 May 2019].
Anon., 1974. Obituary, Baroness Budberg Hostess and intellectual leader, 2 November [online] Available at: *The Times Digital Archive*, [Accessed 27 June 2019].
Anon., 1998. Obituary, Rosemary Edmonds, 21 August [online] Available at: *The Telegraph Historical Archive*, [Accessed 16 March 2018].
Anon., 2001. Obituary. Paul Winterton, 14 February [online] Available at: *The Times Digital Archive*, [Accessed 14 June 2019].
Anon., 2004. Crankshaw, Edward (1909–1984), *Oxford Dictionary of National Biography*. https://doi.org/10.1093/ref:odnb/30979.
Anon., 2014. Question regarding the gratuitous French in Dostoevsky's The Devils, [online] Available at: <https://www.reddit.com/r/literature/comments/1dhdn6/question_regarding_the_gratuitous_french_in/> [Accessed 02 March 2020].

Beasley, R., 2013. On Not Knowing Russian: The Translations of Virginia Woolf and S.S. Kotelianskii, *The Modern Language Review*, 108(1), (January), pp. 1–29.

Boll, T., 2016. Penguin Books and the Translation of Spanish and Latin American Poetry, 1956–1979, *Translation and Literature*, 1, pp. 28–57. DOI: 10.3366/tal.2016.0236.

Clements, T., 2009. History of Penguin Archive. *The Daily Telegraph*, 19 February, [online] Available at: <http://www.telegraph.co.uk/culture/books/4691018/History-of-Penguin-archive.html> [Accessed 12 December 2016].

Connell, P.J., 2004. Rieu, Emile Victor (1887–1972), *Oxford Dictionary of National Biography*, [online] Available at: <http://www.oxforddnb.com/view/article/31609> [Accessed 04 October 2016].

Dienes, L., 2009. Introduction: On Gazdanov and His Novel Night Roads. In: *G. Gazdanov, Night Roads. Translated from Russian by J. Doherty*. Evanston, IL: Northwestern University Press.

Dryden, J., 1680. From the Preface to *Ovid*'s Epistles. In: L. Venuti, ed. 2004. *The Translation Studies Reader*. Abingdon and New York: Routledge. pp. 38–42.

Edwards, R., 2008. Afterword. In: R. Edwards, S. Hare, and J. Robinson, eds. 2008. *Penguin Classics*. Revised ed. Exeter: Short Run Press.

Edwards, R., Hare, S., and Robinson, J., ed.2008. *Penguin Classics*. Revised ed. Exeter: Short Run Press.

Elliott, G., and Shukman., H. 2011. *Secret Classrooms, An Untold Story of the Cold War*. London: Faber & Faber.

Fen Archive, MS1394. Leeds: Leeds University Special Collections, Russian Archive.

- Letter Fen to Rieu, 16 September 1945, MS1394/6540.
- Letter Fen to Rieu, 17 September 1945, MS1394/6542.
- Letter Rieu to Fen, 8 December 1945, MS1394/6546.
- Letter Rieu to Fen, 18 March 1946, MS1394/6550.
- Letter Fen to Rieu, 19 January 1947, MS1394/6550.
- Letter Rieu to Fen, 24 February 1950, MS1394/6578.
- Letter Rieu to Fen, 20 March 1950, MS1394/6588.
- Letter Rieu to Fen, 22 May 1950, MS1394/6589.
- Letter Rieu to Fen, 9 November 1946, MS1394/6561.
- Letter Rieu to Fen, 22 July 1950, MS1394/6591.
- Letter Rieu to Fen, 15 December 1950, MS1394/6616.
- Letter Rieu to Fen, 10 September 1957, MS1394/6754.
- Letter Fen to Phyllis Gardiner, 1981, MS1394/3966.

Frank, J., 2010. *Dostoevsky: A Writer in His Time*. Princeton, NJ: Princeton University Press.

Garnett, R., 2009. *Constance Garnett – A Heroic Life*. London: Faber and Faber.

Gerson, M., 1962. *Elisaveta Fen (neé Lydia Jackson Jiburtovich)*. [photograph] (London: National Portrait Gallery).

Gifford, H., 1978. On Translating Tolstoy. In: M. Jones, ed. *New Essays on Tolstoy*. Cambridge: Cambridge University Press.

Glad, J., 1999. *Russia Abroad: Writers, History, Politics*. Washington and Tenafly, NJ: Birchbark Press and Hermitage Publishers.

Hahn, D., 2004. Edmonds, Rosemary Lilian (1905–1998), *Oxford Dictionary of National Biography*, [online] Available at: <http://www.oxforddnb.com/view/article/62696> [Accessed 04 October 2016].

Hare, S., 1995. *Penguin Portrait: Allen Lane and the Penguin.* Editors, *1935–1970.* London and New York: Penguin.

- 2008. A History of Penguin Classics. In: R. Edwards, S. Hare, and J. Robinson, eds. 2008. *Penguin Classics.* Revised ed. Exeter: Short Run Press.

Harries, S., 2013. *Niklaus Pevsner: The Life.* London: Pimlico.

Hermans, T., 2000. Shall I Apologize Translation? [pdf] Available at: <http://discovery. ucl.ac.uk/516/1/Ep_Apologizetrans.pdf> [Accessed 26 January 2020].

Joicey, N., 1993. A Paperback Guide to Progress: Penguin Books 1935–c.1951, *Twentieth Century British History*, 4(1).

Lane, A., 1966. A.S.B. Glover, *The Times*, 8 January, p. 10. [online] Available at: *The Times Digital Archive* [Accessed 23 May 2017].

Lewis, J., 2006. *Penguin Special, The Life and Times of Allen Lane.* London: Penguin.

Lygo, E., 2013. Promoting Soviet Culture in Britain: The History of the Society for Cultural Relations between the Peoples of the British Commonwealth and the USSR, 1924–1945, *Modern Language Review,* 108(2), pp. 571–596. <https://doi.org/ 10.5699/modelangrevi.108.2.0571> [Accessed 19 June 2019].

McCleery, A., 2002. The Return of the Publisher to Book History: The Case of Allen Lane, *Book History,* 5, pp. 161–185.

McDonald, D., and Dronfield, J., 2016. *A Very Dangerous Woman: The Lives, Loves and Lies of Russia's Most Seductive Spy.* London: Oneworld Publications.

Magarshack, D., 1934. *Big Ben Strikes Eleven, A Murder Story for Grown Up People.* London: Constable and Co. Ltd.

- 1935. Death Cuts a Caper. London: Constable and Co. Ltd.
- 1937. Three Dead. London: Constable and Co. Ltd.

Magarshack Archive, MS1397. Leeds: Leeds University Special Collections, Russian Archive.

- Anon., 1952. 'More About Chekhov'. [Review] *John O'London's Weekly*, 22 February, Box 25. Degree certificate, 22 October 1924, Box 23.
- Dent, A., 1953. 'Chekhov's Sad Gaiety'. [review] *John O'London's Weekly*, 14 March, Box 25.
- Igoe, W.J., 1963. 'The Gift of Tongues'. [article] *The Chicago Tribune*, 20 October, Box 11.
- Kislova L., 1945. Letter to David Magarshack, 10 February, Box 1.
- Magarshack, D., 1971, Letter to Mr Rosenthal, 29 April, Box 1.

Magarshack Letters, GB133 GDN/A/M25. Manchester: University of Manchester Special Collections, The John Rylands Library.

- Letter Magarshack to Mr Hobson, 12 September 1928.
- Letter Magarshack to Mr Bone, 12 November 1929.

Magarshack, S., 2014. Letter to C McAteer, 19 December 2014.

- 2015. Interview with C McAteer, Camden, London, 20 February 2015.
- n.d., David Magarshack [photograph] (Magarshack Family Private Collection).

Mason, A., 2014. Molière among the Penguins, John Wood's Translations for the Early Penguin Classics. In: K. Krebs, ed. *Translation and Adaptation in Theatre and Film.* Abingdon and New York: Routledge, pp. 122–139.

Meier, A., 2011. Paul Foote Obituary, *The Guardian*, 5 April, [online] Available at: <http://www.theguardian.com/books/2011/apr/05/paul-foote-obituary> [Accessed 16 January 2020].

Minshall, T., 1954. Reviewed Work: *Half a Life: The Reminiscences of a Russian Gentleman* by Constantine Benckendorff, *International Affairs*, 30(3), p. 355.

Morozov, M., 1944. P'esi Ostrovskogo v Anglii (o perevodakh D. Magarshacka), *Literaturnaia gazeta*. 6, 9 December.

Morpurgo, J.E., 1979. *Allen Lane: King Penguin*. London: Hutchinson & Co.

Munday, J., 2008. *Introducing Translation Studies, Theories and Applications*. 2nd ed. London and New York: Routledge.

- 2014. Using Primary Sources to Produce a Microhistory of Translation and Translators: Theoretical and Methodological Concerns. *The Translator*, 20(1), pp. 64–80.
- 2017. Keynote: Excavating the Unexpected? *British Library* (The Translator Made Corporeal: Translation History in the Archive), p. 3.

Penguin Archive, Bristol: Bristol University Arts Library, Special Collections.

- Anon., 1964. Master of Paper-back Classics in English, *The Times*, DM1187/3.
- Letters Koteliansky to Miss [Eunice] Frost, 28 December 1940, DM1107/333.9.

  - 24 November 1940.
  - 29 April 1941.
  - 1 July 1942.

- Letters Rieu to Kitto, 21 October 1944, DM1938.

  - 4 November 1944, DM1938.

- Letter Konovalov to Glover, 20 November 1945, DM1107/1/4/333
- Letter Lane to Benckendorff, 24 January 1946, DM1819/11/7.
- Letter Rieu to Glover, 29 July 1946, DM1107/L4.
- Letter Glover to Rieu, 30 July 1946, DM1107/L4.
- Letter Gardiner to Penguin, 21 April 1976, DM1107/L9.
- Letter Sulkin to Gardiner, 5 May 1976, DM1107/L9.
- Letter Rieu to Lane, 12 February 1946, DM1107/L23.
- Letter Rieu to Glover, 20 January 1949, DM1107/L23.
- Letter Magarshack to Glover, 3 March 1949, DM1107/L23.
- Letter Nitya Nand Tiwari Kasayap to Penguin, 21 August 1956, DM1107/L23.
- Letter Glover to Mr Nitya Nand Tiwari Kasayap, 22 August 1956, DM1107/L23.
- Letter Richard D. Mical to Gentleman, 19 November 1965, DM1107/L23.
- Letter Mr Grant Wallace to Penguin, 4 August 1978, DM1107/L23.
- Letter Glover to Rieu, 17 June 1952, DM1107/L35.
- Letters Magarshack to Glover, 18 June 1952, DM1107/L35.

  - 5 January 1954, DM1107/L35.

- Letter Dr Edward D Sullivan to Penguin, 28 December 1954, DM1107/L35.
- Letter Miss L.A. Atkins to Penguin, 29 December 1965, DM1107/L35.
- Letters Glover to Magarshack, 2 September 1953, DM1107/L40.

  - 26 March 1954.
  - 31 March 1954.

- Letter Magarshack to Glover, 27 May 1954, DM1107/L40.
- Letter Rieu to Glover, 8 September 1952, DM1107/L41.
- Letter Glover to Rieu, 10 September 1952, DM1107/L41.
- Letter Mrs Joan Miller to Penguin, 5 July 1972, DM1107/L41.
- Letter Cochrane regarding Joan Miller, 5 July 1972, DM1107/L41.
- Letter Glover to Magarshack, 7 October 1953, DM1107/L54.
- Letter Miss P.A. Ford to Penguin, 19 April 1966, DM1107/L54.
- Letter Rosemary Edmonds, 27 May 1966, DM1107/L62–63.
- Letter Jerome Minot to Penguin, 25 January 1969, DM1107/L96.
- Letter Sylvia Cookman to Fen, 5 February 1969, DM1107/L96.
- Letter Fen to Miss Cookman, 11 February 1969, DM1107/L96.
- Letter Sylvia Cookman to Fen, 14 February 1969, DM1107/L96.
- Letter Edmonds to Duguid, 3 June 1960, DM1107/L109.
- Letter Edmonds to Miss Jean Ollington, 20 July 1961, DM1107/L119.
- Letter Baldick to Duguid, 21 November 1963, DM1107/L143.
- Letter Cochrane to Duguid, 24 January 1964, DM1107/L143.
- Letter Cochrane to Foote, 17 June 1964, Ref.: DM1107/L176.
- Letter Sulkin to University of Nottingham, 20 March 1974, DM1107/L176.
- Letter Penguin to D. Herring, 31 January 1975, DM1107/L176.
- Letter Edmonds to Penguin, 1 February 1966, DM1107/L184.
- Letter Baldick to Cochrane, 7 June 1966, DM1107/L184.
- Letter Cochrane to Mr Freeborn, 12 June 1964, DM1107/L186.
- Letter Freeborn to Cochrane, 5 July 1964, DM1107/L186.
- Letter Northwestern University to Penguin, 22 October 1974, DM1107/L186.
- Letter Miss Margaret Walsh to Penguin, 29 December 1962, DM1107/D69.
- Radice, B., 1984. A Classic Education, *The Times Higher Education Supplement*, 19 October 1984, DM1187/3.

Penguin Russian Review (The), 1945–48. Vols 1,3,4. Harmondsworth: Penguin Books.

Platt, B., 2008. Founding Father: E.V. Rieu. In: R. Edwards, S. Hare, J. Robinson, eds. 2008. *Penguin Classics*. Revised ed. Exeter: Short Run Press, pp. 815.

Radice, W., and Reynolds, B. eds., 1987. *The Translator's Art*. Harmondsworth: Penguin Books.

Rieu, E.V., 1946. The Penguin Classics, *Penguins Progress*. 1 (July).

- 1946. Translating the Classics, *Penguins Progress*. 2 (October).
- 1950. The Faith of a Translator, *Penguins Progress*. 10.

Rieu, E.V., and Phillips, J.B., 1953. Translating the Gospels. *The Bible Translator*, 6(4) (October 1955), pp. 150–159.

Symons, J., 1979. The Detection Club. *The New York Times*, 30 September [online] Available at: <https://www.nytimes.com/1979/09/30/archives/the-detection-club-detection.html> [Accessed 07 January 2020]

Williams, W.E., 1956. *The Penguin Story*. Aylesbury: Hunt, Barnard & Co. Ltd.

Winterton, P. 1945. Moscow-Winter 1944. In: *The Penguin Russian Review*. Harmondsworth: Penguin Books, pp. 7–21.

Yates, M. ed., 2006. *The Penguin Companion*. Chippenham: Octoprint.

2 David Magarshack: Penguin translator becomes translation theorist

Introduction

The next two chapters utilise more detailed archival source material in order to offer a closer analysis of David Magarshack and his work, with occasional reference to Rosemary Edmonds and, to a lesser extent, Fen. (As an equally productive translator in the early Penguin Russian corps, Edmonds is the best placed to provide further comparative insight both into translation practice and Penguin relations.) Translation scholars (Simeoni (1998) and Meylaerts (2006)) have appealed for more of this approach – sociologically-informed archival analysis – in order to 'investigate how translators, as historical subjects translating for other historical subjects, are implicated in this history [of translation]' (ibid.). The following case study applies a sociological approach to Magarshack's archival material, therefore, analysing the intellectual background to his habitus and the *dispositions* (Meylaerts, 2006, pp. 60–61) that might have influenced his views on translation and shaped his practical approach to translation at Penguin.

Translation scholar Reine Meylaerts (following Bourdieu) defines habitus as an internalised system of social structures in the form of dispositions. She writes:

> The inculcation of social structures is a lifelong process of interactions between structure and agency through various and variable individual and collective experiences. Dispositions engender practices, perceptions, and attitudes [...]. Under the influence of its social position and its individual and collective past, every cultural actor thus develops (and continues to develop) a social identity: a certain representation of the world and of his position therein. (Ibid., p. 60)

This chapter investigates Magarshack's 'social identity', exploring his position in the field of translation both as a practitioner and, latterly, as a theorist. It analyses his dispositions: intellectual and emotional responses to the ambiguities presented by émigré life and language; his sense of entitlement to translate the Russian classics and his annoyance at Garnett for pre-empting him in this field; his criticism of her language abilities; and the manifestations of these dispositions in his translation theory. Magarshack's personal circumstances are, I contend, relevant to his theory of transla- tion. I have been granted access both to Magarshack's personal reflections on translation and to his translated texts. The natural progression from analysing his 'mental apparatus' in this chapter is, therefore, to conduct a traditional textual analysis in the next chapter (Chapter Three), which will enable me to investigate these 'surface manifestations' (textual indi- cators of Magarshack's habitus, intellectual preoccupations, and commit- ment to Penguin's institutional aspirations). Chapter Three capitalises on details extracted from archives in order to facilitate an holistic (agent- *and* text-based) analysis of Magarshack's first Penguin translation, his 1951 version of Dostoevskii's *Crime and Punishment*.

A man of contrasts and contradictions

The close study in this chapter of Magarshack's private papers locates him and his achievements in a European translatorial landscape, which included theorists such as Theodore Savory, Jean-Paul Vinay and Jean Darbelnet, Roman Jakobson, and Eugene Nida during the 1950s–60s. Bourdieu rec- ommends a similar contextualising approach in his analysis of Flaubert's contribution to France's literary field, namely that 'one can only understand what happens there if one locates each agent [...] in the relationships with all the others' (1993, p. 181). Even though Magarshack's theoretical work went unpublished, it was the result of decades of professional practice and is, therefore, an informed reflection of their context. In addition to estab- lishing the extent to which Magarshack conformed to and deviated from translation norms, I will use this chapter to validate his reputation as a man of multiple talents who stood out from his peers, not just as a translator of note, but as a cross-cultural translation theorist and a keen advocate for raising the literary translator's status.

For many readers throughout the second half of the twentieth century, Magarshack's translations were synonymous with canonical, readable Russian classics. Inspiring as he did not only generations of Anglophone lay readers, but also Russian undergraduates in English-speaking univer- sities and even national servicemen on the JSSL Russian programme,[1] it is surprising that Magarshack has, on the whole, attracted little recogni- tion or discussion in literary reviews, criticisms, and handbooks of Russian literature in translation. Positive endorsements of his Penguin translations exist, which hint at his cultural importance. For example, Anthony Powell wrote in *Punch* that 'David Magarshack has revolutionised the reading of Dostoyevsky's novels in English by his translations that have appeared dur- ing the last few years... for years I was rather an anti-Dostoyevsky man, owing to the badness of the translations, but now there is an excellent trans- lator in Magarshack' (*Punch*, 2 April 1958). Magarshack's archive includes cuttings from many articles reviewing his work. The following extracts (located in Box 17 of his personal collection) show a cross-section of reviews; it should be noted, however, that Magarshack may have been selective about the cuttings he kept, preserving only the positive ones (negative reviews did exist, as will be discussed in Chapter Three, but these are conspicuously absent from his papers):

> The editor of Penguin Classics is to be congratulated on having chosen Mr. Magharshack [sic] as the translator of 'Crime and Punishment'. Mr. Magharshack is well known as the translator of Dostoyevsky's minor works, and, if his latest version is more colloquial than those of the standard translations in which we first read this electrifying, titanic, novel, it will help materially to convince new readers of Dostoyevsky that he did not write for highbrows but that he is as homely as Dickens, with whom he has striking affinities. Mr Magharshack makes his translation easier for the ordinary reader by simplifying the names of the characters so that we recognise Mrs. and Miss. Marmelador [sic] much more readily than if, as previous translations did, he had called them Catherine Ivanovna and Sophia Semenovna. *Yorkshire Observer* (Bradford), 13 Dec 1951
>
> But now that a dramatised version of Oblomov has been broadcast, there should be a demand for the Penguin translation of Goncharov's novel of that name. It is by David Magarshack. The present generation is to be accounted fortunate in having so good a translator of Russian and in being able to buy a book like this for 3s 6d. *The Scotsman*, 14 October 1954
>
> With the publication of his Brothers Karamazov (Penguin, 2 vols. 12s) Mr. Magarshack completes his translation of Dostoevsky's four major novels and puts into the hands of English readers a workmanlike version of Dostoevsky's most celebrated production. The publication of Constance Garnett's version of the novel in 1912 was a landmark in the assimilation of Russian culture in England, heralding a decade in which the English vogue for Russian literature soared to a high level of hysteria. With all its faults this translation has maintained itself in public esteem for forty-six years. Mr. Magarshack's version is unlikely to cause a similar furore, but there seems no good reason why, in its turn, it should be superseded before the year 2004. *The Listener*, 20 Mar 1958

The BBC Genome project database[2] shows the extent to which Magarshack's translations were used by the BBC (in both television and radio): a total of forty-nine broadcasts between 1952 and as recently as 1998, compared to nineteen for Fen between 1943 and 1992, and ten for Edmonds between 1957 and 1974.[3] Theatre programmes found in Magarshack's archive show that his theatre translations were performed for decades. In a more academic context, Carl Proffer concluded his 1964 scholarly evaluation of different translations of Gogol's *Dead Souls* by recommending Magarshack's version to students (1964, p. 431) and, more recently, Kazuo Ishiguro singled Magarshack out as 'the favourite translator of Russian writers in the 1970s' (Walkowitz, 2007, p. 221). The majority of references to Magarshack's work in the sphere of literary criticism, however, are cursory. More recently, these tend to be neutral or negative, suggesting that while his reputation at the time was high, his translations have since fallen from favour. More recent translators are predictably critical. In their interview for *the Paris Review* (2015), translators Richard Pevear and Larissa Volokhonskaia express their disappointment at reading Magarshack's translation of *The Brothers Karamazov*; in which, they claim, blandness, 'something tame' replaces the style, tone, and humour of Dostoevskii's original. Style, however, is a subjective quality. For Gary S. Morson, Pevear and Volokhonskaia are 'Potemkin translators' whose efforts at translating he describes as 'flat and fake' (2010); in their hands, he claims, great Russian literature 'has been stripped bare of its solemn mystery'.

Magarshack elicits particular interest here as the only Russian translator of the early Penguin Classics corps to have recorded extensively his thoughts and observations regarding translation and the way in which the translator exists and functions in the literary field. Analysis of Magarshack's personal archive (including notes, drafts, letters, and reviews) reveals a complex man who embodied contrasts and contradictions in both outlook and practice. He was, for example, under financial pressure to complete commissions swiftly (Magarshack, 2015) and dealt with his editors assertively, and yet he was unable to resist fine-tuning his target texts in order to pursue the "perfect" rendering, a trait which ultimately cost him time and money in his *Oblomov* translation. Translation scholar Rakefet Sela-Sheffy (2008) finds in her analysis, conducted between 1999–2004, that those translators (like Magarshack) who 'glorify translation as a "vocation" rather than just a means of earning a living' (p. 611) seek two main sources of prestige, one which 'emanates from their acting as cultural custodian' and the other, which 'derives from their acting as *men of art*, endowed with artistic creativity' (ibid). Sela-Sheffy's focus on the translator's more ego-oriented dispositions anticipates translation scholar David Charlston's preference for the 'less familiar Bourdieusian term *hexis*', which embodies the translator's 'defiant, honour-seeking attitude' (Charlston, 2013, p. 55). Magarshack was a translator who craved such recognition for his work – he was ego-oriented and, as we will see later in this chapter, his notes show that he was honour-seeking – but he was bound to commissioners and their terms for his means of earning a living. His reputation as a man of art depended on reviewers' verdicts. He was, therefore, sensitive to criticism of his own translations and yet critical of others' efforts (in particular Garnett's). He opted to legitimise his residency in the United Kingdom and yet continued to seek affirmation from the Union of Soviet Socialist Republics, a geographical focus that permeated the foundation of his translation strategy too.

Unusually for the time, his theoretical contributions combined Western and Soviet translation traditions. He argued in his general statements of best practice (see Appendix 2) for the translator's worth, calling for the literary translator to receive national recognition in the form of prizes[4] and be hailed as a creative specialist; and he attempted to set out plans for future generations of translators. On a personal level and for personal reasons, Magarshack courted a reputation both in the West and in the Union of Soviet Socialist Republics. Magarshack's work with Penguin (and that of his other fellow Penguin Russian translators) projected a cultural rather than political image of Russia abroad and it becomes clear from his notes that he viewed his translation work as an opportunity to re-draw previously constructed, misleading images of Russia abroad. Fen shared the same aspiration in her translations of Chekhov, whom she regarded as the embodiment of pre-revolutionary Russia (Chekhov, 1954, p. 16 and p. 30) and as a counter-force to Bolshevism.[5]

Magarshack offered some succinct insight into his practice in an interview with the *Chicago Tribune* at the height of his Penguin years. His methodology is summarised neatly, but with some originality:[6]

> Translation is an art in itself: one must transpose the life, the emotional significance of a book in detail. My test is that if I can translate my translation back to Russian quickly – then it is a bad translation. It has not been Englished as a work of imagination. (20 October 1963)

Magarshack does not draw on a sophisticated brand of translation theory here in order to justify the rationale behind a career of translation decisions, nor is there a complicated account of the practical strategies he implemented to fulfil his Penguin commissions. Magarshack appears to suggest that his translations are the result of experienced intuition rather than science. Towards the end of his career, however, Magarshack moved away from the intuitive position demonstrated here and in other interviews in the 1950s–60s.[7] Instead, he underwent a conscious shift from translator to theorist, drawing on a detailed examination of British and Soviet Translation Studies in order to explain his past practice.

A commission ahead of its time

The catalyst for Magarshack to document his views on translation theory was a commission from Victor Gollancz, in the late 1960s, to produce a book entitled *The Principles of Translation*. For Gollancz and the wider field of literary and translation publishing, there were numerous selling points for a book like Magarshack's. The commission seemingly emerged out of Gollancz's[8] interest in Anglo-Soviet relations, an interest which, it was assumed, others would share.[9] In the same way that British interest in Russia spiked during the Crimean War, May maintains that 'At that time, because of the Cold War and the "thaw" in Russian culture, there was an enormous increase in academic interest in Russia in the United States and Britain' (2000, p. 1207). May does not specify which Cold War events captured the nation's interest, but the era witnessed the Hungarian revolution in 1956, the Cuban missile crisis in 1962, the Soviet invasion of Czechoslovakia in 1968, and high-profile cultural and political defections: Rudolph Nureyev (1961), Svetlana Alliluyeva (1967), Natalia Makarova (1970). Later came Mikhail Baryshnikov (1974), Georgii Markov (poisoned in London in 1978), and Oleg Gordievskii (1985).

When Gollancz commissioned Magarshack to produce *The Principles of Translation*, it is plausible to deduce that he expected Magarshack's widely recognisable name to generate ready sales interest. Book markets lacked a study of Russian-English literary translation; and Magarshack was a reputable practitioner with over twenty years' experience – including thirty-five translations by this stage and six biographies – and a connection with the big paperback publisher of the day. Aside from any potential economic gain, Gollancz's commission also presented an opportunity for Magarshack to consolidate his own brand (once and for all) and, 'being well-situated' (Bourdieu, 1993, p. 184), to metamorphose from successful émigré translator to distinguished translation theorist.

According to the synopsis (n.d., Box 13) that Magarshack wrote, he intended his manuscript to serve as a handbook to Russian-English literary translation in which he would analyse grammatical and lexical equivalence, and the translator's loyalty to artistic workmanship and to the source author. On these grounds, his book would have been of interest to translation theorists, literary/language enthusiasts, and other translators including Penguin newcomers like Joshua Cooper (translator of Penguin's *Four Russian Plays* (1972)), for example. From 2 February 1970 to 15 January 1971, Cooper, the Penguin Classics editor James Cochrane, and the reader and translator Paul Foote exchanged twenty-five detailed pages debating the very themes that Magarshack's book intended to address: how best to handle Russian names; how to avoid over-literal renderings; how to capture idioms; how to ensure the English is not dated or odd 'in the mouth of a Russian character'.[10] Had Magarshack been able to see his Gollancz commission through, Cooper would have had a published guide, as well as in-house help, for opinions about such fundamental literary translation questions.

Box number 20 in Magarshack's personal collection at the Leeds Russian archive includes the first six copies of *Delos*, the translation-oriented journals produced by University of Austin, Texas from 1968–1971. This publication represented the leading edge of translation theory at that time. Magarshack annotated many of the articles in his copies and incorporated some of their content in the notes he made for his Gollancz commission. Box number 13 in his collection consists of these preparatory notes:

- Notes and drafts for the book's synopsis, which he appeared to re-name *The Art of Translation* (n.d.)

- A four-page taxonomy (entitled 'General') for best translation practice (n.d.)
- Two lengthy lectures ('General Principles of Translation from the Russian' (n.d.) and 'Notes on the Translation of Chekhov' (n.d.)) based, it seems, on chapters he intended to include in his book[11]

Even though Magarshack's commission ended in termination in 1973[12] – a decision which may have been driven by ill-health – there is evidence to confirm that Magarshack took the project seriously. Fifteen years ahead of its time, Magarshack's commission anticipated André Lefevere's later call for a book to inspire and fill the gap in literary translators' practical aids. In 'Translated Literature: Towards an Integrated Theory' (1981), Lefevere laments the 'rather limited nature of much theoretical writing on translation' (p. 68) and asserts that most of the models designed to 'be put to practical use either in the training of translators' (p. 69) are 'anything but complete, in that they purposefully ignore literary translation' (p. 70). Lefevere concludes:

> The study of existing translations of literature may well, in the end, result in a kind of historical grammar (of the taxonomic type) of translation. It will be able to show how others have managed to solve certain problems, why they decided to try it this or that way, and with what results. (Ibid., p. 78)

Magarshack's synopsis and accompanying notes and lectures present a scholarly yet practical approach and offer the inspiration and guidance that Lefevere was still awaiting years later. Moreover, Magarshack's move into translation theory lends a welcome dimension to a debate that divides the field of translation even today, namely whether and to what extent translation theory is useful for translation practice.[13]

In order to appreciate fully the significance and timeliness of Magarshack's project, it is necessary first to locate Magarshack in two contexts: the era of Western Translation Studies in the 1950s–60s, the period which framed Magarshack's Penguin career and is itself worthy of further scrutiny for its subsequent influence over modern translation theory; and the context of Soviet Translation Studies, to which Magarshack makes frequent reference at a time when Western translators and theorists had little awareness of the debates taking place in the Soviet Union.[14] I will, therefore, first examine the translation debates that formed a background to Magarshack's translation practice, and then analyse Magarshack's own position in that debate.

Western translation theory in the 1950s and 1960s

Magarshack's commission arrived at a point when the Western discipline of Translation Studies had not yet been established but views and discussions were increasingly being explored, documented, and developed. John Percival Postgate's *Translation and Translations, Theory and Practice* (1922) examines contemporary translation practice through an analysis of translation traditions. He argues in favour of translations that retain the 'pleasant piquancy' (1922, p. 33) of foreign suggestion; that an 'English translator has the same rights as an English author' (ibid.); and that the translator is an etcher who 'spares no touch or stroke that brings the copy nearer to the exemplar' (ibid., p. 39). Postgate also pre-empted the principle of equivalent effect, which attracted deeper analysis in the 1950s–60s. He argues that 'a translation from French into English should produce upon an Englishman an impression as far as possible similar to that which the French original produces upon a Frenchman' (ibid., p. 19). In the 1950s–60s, the key writers and critics to pick up on the sorts of themes that Postgate had previously examined were: Rieu and Rev. J.B. Phillips ('Translating the Gospels', 1953); Savory (*The Art of Translation*, 1957, revised edition 1968); Vinay and Darbelnet ('Stylistique comparée du français et de l'anglais', 1958, but only appearing in English translation in 1995); the contributors to Reuben Brower's 1959 anthology, *On Translation* (Justin O'Brien, Willard V. Quine, Douglas Knight, Renato Poggioli); Vladimir Nabokov ('Problems of Translation: *Onegin* in English', 1955; 'The Servile Path', 1959); Jakobson ('On Linguistic Aspects of Translation', 1959); Nida ('Principles of Correspondence', 1964); and Paul Selver's *The Art of Translating Poetry* (1966). Magarshack's 1968 commission was cancelled in 1973, just before the publication of George Steiner's *After Babel* (1975).

Western books on translation in the 1950s exposed the low status of translation at that time; they tried to re-position their subject as a creative act worthy of discussion. In *The Art of Translation*, Savory wrote that the problems of translation have yet to find 'any final and universally accepted solutions' (1968, p. 9) and he notes a dearth of commentary on translation practice:

> When I began to consider these things I was surprised by the comparatively small amount of critical attention they [problems of translation] have received. Translations are many, almost beyond the counting, but appraisals of the art of the translator are in proportion fewer. (Ibid.)

In the United States, Brower wrote:

> [...] the question is often asked (I can hear some readers asking it now), 'Why a book on translation?' A book on intercultural relations, on linguistics, even on comparative literature, certainly, but on *translation*, the horror of the classroom, the waif of Grub Street, the unacknowledged half-sister of 'true' literature? (1959, p.4)

In developmental terms, theorists in the 1950s pushed the debate beyond the binary (literal vs. free) perspective in which translation had traditionally been viewed. Savory's taxonomy, a list of points through which he attempted to summarise the essence of translatorial practice, brings out the contradictions resulting from a binary translation perspective:

1 A translation must give the words of the original
2 A translation must give the ideas of the original
3 A translation should read like an original work
4 A translation should read like a translation
5 A translation should reflect the style of the original
6 A translation should possess the style of the translator
7 A translation should read as a contemporary of the original
8 A translation should read as a contemporary of the translator
9 A translation may add to or omit from the original
10 A translation may never add to or omit from the original
11 A translation of verse should be in prose
12 A translation of verse should be in verse (1968, p. 50)

Savory placed renewed emphasis on sense-for-sense, citing Postgate's preference for faithfulness over literal translation (ibid., p. 54) and Rieu's views on equivalence (ibid., p. 55), whom he echoes in his own position on translating into modern English:

> [...] in most cases a reader is justified in expecting to find the kind of English that he is accustomed to use. If a function of translation is to produce in the minds of its readers the same emotions as those produced by the original in the minds of its readers, the answer is clear. (Ibid., p. 57)

The translatability of a text is determined by the translator who strives for equivalence and adopts appropriate linguistic procedures in order to achieve this equivalence. It was Rieu and Phillips whom Nida credited in 1964 with coining the term the 'principle of equivalent effect', which first appears in their interview 'Translating the Gospels' (conducted on 3 December 1953, but not published until October 1955 in *The Bible Translator*). For Rieu, equivalence is the phenomenon that renders a text accessible to the target reader, generating the same response as the original text generated in the source reader. The target reader was not only commercially significant to ventures like Penguin Classics; they were epistemologically significant to theorists like Nida, who cemented Penguin's, and specifically Rieu's principle, in theoretical terms in his 'Principles of Correspondence' (1964).

At around the same time, Vinay's and Darbelnet's methodology (1958/1995), based on a contrastive analysis between French and English, recognised similar binary delineations to those outlined in Savory's taxonomy and attempted to identify separate procedures for both literal and free translation. They aligned the following procedures to direct (literal) translation: borrowing; calque; and literal translation. Oblique (free) translation included: transposition; modulation; and adaptation (1995, pp. 128–137). What their methodology achieved was a relatively narrow, prescriptive framework of approaches, which would prove highly influential in translation training courses. Jakobson (1959, pp. 138–143) and Quine (1959, pp. 148–172), on the other hand, couched the discussion in broader linguistic terms: lexical equivalence, gender, syntax, semiotics, register. They explain how words might not necessarily relate directly to their foreign equivalent. Jakobson and Quine each explored the difficulties of simple words such as 'cheese' and 'bachelor'. Their discussions analyse practical solutions to the pursuit of equivalence: synonymy, circumlocution, idiomatic phrase-word, entire message (Jakobson, 1959, p. 139). Jakobson declared equivalence 'the cardinal problem of language and the pivotal concern of linguistics [...] Any comparison of two languages implies an examination of their mutual translatability' (ibid.). The one literary form which eludes full equivalence and translatability for Jakobson, but also Rieu, and Nabokov, is poetry. Jakobson declared it untranslatable, citing the juxtaposition of 'verbal equations', 'syntactic and morphological categories', and 'paronomasia' (ibid., pp. 142–3) as reasons for his verdict. In 'Problems of Translation: *Onegin* in English', Nabokov (1955, p. 118) cites specific complexities of the Russian language[15] compared to English as a justification for never rendering the original through 'free translation' (ibid., p. 115). He argued that it is impossible to keep a poem's rhythmic form while achieving 'absolute exactitude of the whole text' (ibid., p. 121) and lamented the abilities of ignorant 'would-be translators' (ibid., p. 122). Nabokov's 'would-be translators' need flawless knowledge of the source language and culture if they are to succeed:

> Anyone who wishes to attempt a translation of Onegin should acquire exact information [...], such as the Fables of Krilov, Byron's works, French poets [...], banking games, Russian songs [...], Russian military ranks [...], the difference between cranberry and lingonberry, [...] and the Russian language. (Ibid.)

What becomes apparent by its frequent mention among translator-theorists in the 1950s, though, is the shortage of available, reliable, quality language resources, including even source texts. An example of such a resource deficit at Penguin is Seeley's difficulty in obtaining a copy of the source text of Dostoevskii's *Crime and Punishment* [*Prestuplenie i nakazanie*]; even though the translation contract was settled as early as February 1946, Glover wrote to Seeley over a year later, on 13 March 1947, to confirm finally that 'We have managed to track one down, which we shall be receiving in a few days, and I will forward this on to you'. Fen also described difficulties obtaining a source text in order to evaluate Edmonds's sample *Anna Karenin* translation (16 March 1950). Nabokov described the inadequacies of (Russian-English) dictionary entries while translating Pushkin's shrubs and trees (Nabokov in

Brower, 1959, p. 104); Vinay and Darbelnet voiced a desire for 'conceptual dictionaries with bilingual signifiers [...] But such dictionaries do not exist' (1995, p. 131). Jakobson's appeal is still more earnest:

> It is difficult to overestimate the urgent need for and the theoretical and practical significance of differential bilingual dictionaries with careful comparative definition of all the corresponding units in their intension and extension. Likewise differential bilingual grammars should define what unifies and what differentiates the two languages in their selection and delimitation of grammatical concepts. (1959, p. 140)

In light of such limitations, Edmonds's handling of the culture-specific lexis found in Tolstoi's *The Cossacks* [*Kazaki*] is particularly impressive; the source text includes Cossack- as well as Caucasian-specific references: чихир, абрек, кабардинец, карга, кошкильды, бешмет, кинжал, not all of which terms can be found even in more modern editions of the *Oxford Russian Dictionary* (1993/2000).[16] In the 1960s, if Edmonds experienced the same difficulties as Jakobson in obtaining a comprehensive bilingual dictionary, she would have had to consult a good, monolingual dictionary instead (or a well-informed native Russian-speaker) for a basic understanding of their meanings and then find a comparable term in English or otherwise resort to explicitation.

In spite of the exciting prospects of translation by mechanical means in the 1950s,[17] Savory remained unconvinced that human translators would soon be replaced by mechanical translation:

> [...] a computer has no background of knowledge and experience; it is no more than an efficient and, particularly, a rapidly working tool, which can work in the service of the human intellect to which it owes its existence. (1968, p. 171)

Savory argued in favour of the human artistry of translation (ibid., p. 41). He was not alone. The 1950s translator was portrayed by many as a craftsman, endowed with professional skills worthy of financial and reputational reward, not just a penny wordsmith guided by instinct and loosely-defined principles. Brower referred to the translator as a 'creator' (1959, p. 7), and Poggioli described the translator with more artistic imagery, as 'a Narcissus who in this case chooses to contemplate his own likeness not in the spring of nature but in the pool of art' (1959, p. 139). In 'Translation: The Augustan Mode' (1959), Douglas Knight ascribes four key attributes to the translator: the status of 'artist'; the status of scholar and linguist; to 'have the interests and insights of an educated but unspecialized reader'; finally, to be 'alive to the struggles and dilemmas of his culture' without which 'his work will lack the urgency which good translation needs' (p. 197). Similarly, according to Savory, 'rare qualities [...] are needed in a good translator, but linguistic knowledge and literary capacity will not, by themselves, ensure the best translation' (1968, p. 34). The translator must experience 'sympathy with the feelings of the author' (ibid.) or, as Venuti puts it, '*simpatico*' (1995, p. 273); familiarity with the subject of the work is essential (Savory, 1968, p. 34), as are 'insight, diligence and thoroughness' (ibid., p. 36). To meet all these necessary requirements, the 'good' translator is, therefore, something of a rare specimen:

> A translator who adequately fulfils the requirements outlined above and who is able to attain a faultless standard of translation is obviously not to be found easily. The art of translation ought, therefore, to be highly valued and the translator correspondingly well rewarded for his services. (Ibid., p. 35)

In reality, though, Savory's summary of the translator's work is less optimistic. He concludes that it is 'a hopeless, almost impossible task, in return for which he [the translator] will not receive a proportionate reward' (ibid.). As at other times in translation history, there is a clear disconnect in the 1950s between the translator's emboldened self-perception as artist, creator, scholar and linguist, and outside opinions about the profession. The 1950s–60s, though, form an era of artistic self-definition for the translator, through collective voices in Brower's anthology and *Delos*, collaborative organisations such as Penguin, and individual voices such as Savory and Nabokov. These strivings for professional recognition and status are significant, therefore, to our understanding of the development of Translation Studies for they predate the recognised start of the discipline by nearly twenty years.[18]

Soviet translation theory

From the 1920s onwards, Soviet translators and theorists (Kornei Chukovskii, Mikhail Lozinskii, Efim Etkind, Ivan Kashkin, Semën Lipkin, Nikolai Liubimov, Samuil Marshak, Nikolai Zabolotskii, among others) forged a parallel climate for translation and translation theory under the auspices of the Soviet school of translation – 'an esprit as well as an organisation' (Leighton, 1991, p. xvi) – sporting the (rather nebulous) strapline: 'translation is an art' (ibid., p. 6). The Soviet school initially emerged out of Maxim Gorkii's post-revolutionary (and pre-Penguin) World Literature [*Vsemirnaia literatura*] project, founded in 1918 alongside the World Literature Publishing House, to translate 'all the treasures of poetry and artistic prose created over a period of one and a half centuries of intense European spiritual creativity' (Gorkii, 1919). To this end, the translator, poet, journalist, and theorist Chukovskii was invited to produce a handbook benchmarking best translatorial practice. In terms which anticipate Lefevere's, he explains in *Vysokoe iskusstvo* (1965–67), translated by Leighton as *A High Art* in 1984, that:

In order to accomplish this, a theory of artistic translation was needed which would arm the translator with clear and simple principles [...]. Some of us had a vague sense of these principles but they had not yet been formulated. Gorky therefore proposed that several members of the editorial board [...] compile something like a manual for old and new masters of translation - we were to formulate the principles needed to help translators in their work. (p. 4)

Chukovskii's manual was a timely development, as can be seen from Mandelshtam's highly critical 1929 *Izvestiia* article '*Potoki khaltury*' ('Torrents of Hackwork'), which decries the flood of talentless, 'abominable' translations in the Soviet Union (Mandelshtam, 1929, pp. 81–83). Regarded as central to the Soviet school of translation, Chukovskii's much-refined observations on the art of translation, spanning from 1919 to 1968, 'raised the respect and prestige of the art of translation to a level that could not be comprehended in the West' (Leighton, 1984, p. xii). However, to regard translation purely as a creative art, rather than a calibrated science, risks a lack of prescriptive guidelines for practitioners. Consequently, Chukovskii's observations do not convince everyone. In *Translation and the Making of Modern Russia* (2016), Brian James Baer analyses the obstacles to quantifying the Soviet school of translation:

The tenets of the school were vaguely expressed, and typically in negative terms, that is, what the school was not. Moreover, what tenets were articulated changed over time in reaction to political and cultural shifts. As with socialist realist novels, the tenets of the Soviet School were not elaborated in theoretical theses so much as they were defined by exemplars, authoritative models. (p. 130)

Soviet translation theorists attempted to define their core tenets as the following: the rejection of literalism (*bukvalizm*) (Baer and Olshanskaya, 2013, p. xi) and "blandscript" (*gladkopis'*) (Leighton, 1991, p.13); the pursuit of precision, balance, and translatorial self-control; commitment to the source author; acceptance of translatability; and the principle of equivalent effect. The 'good' translator's qualities were also scrutinised, often defined by artistic analogies (the translator as actor, artist, portraitist). Zabolotskii (1954, pp. 109–110) captured the essence of the profession in a twenty-two-point taxonomy. Chukovskii referenced Russia's own history of translation in order to qualify his views. The poet, novelist, and playwright Aleksei Konstantinovich Tolstoi (1817–1875), for example, is praised for 'striving [...] to be as faithful to the original as possible, but only where *fidelity or precision do not harm the artistic impression*' (Chukovskii, 1965–67, p. 79, emphasis in original). In an essay published in volume iv of his *Sobranie sochinenii* (1963), Tolstoi expressed a principle of equivalent effect, which preceded Rieu's Western version by nearly a century. Chukovskii endorsed the effect, 'The reader of the translation must be carried into *the very same sphere* as the reader of the original, and the translation must act on the very same nerves' (1965–67, p. 80, emphasis in original). Like Jakobson and Quine, Chukovskii also explored the complexities of lexical equivalence when translating words such as *chelovek* (man, person) into English. On this occasion, he quotes Admiral A. Shishkov's book, *A Discourse on the Old and New Style of the Russian Language* (1803), which predates Jakobson by more than 150 years, and uses Venn diagrams most effectively to explain the extent of equivalence when translating Russian words into French (Chukovskii, 1965–67, pp. 55–58).

Consciously rejecting the formalistic methods of the 1920s–30s, the precursor of *bukvalizm*, Chukovskii noted that:

> [...] there are scores, even hundreds, of cases where such concern for precision led [...] to imprecision, and where concern for a strict correspondence in the number of lines drastically lowered their quality. [...] translators – even the best translators – made such huge sacrifices for this principle that they inflicted incalculable losses on Soviet readers. (Ibid., p. 179)

Chukovskii maintained that formalistic translation methods must give way to methods 'which are vital and creative' (ibid., p. 178), but even then, the 'good' Soviet translator must not get carried away. Liubimov, famous for his translations of Cervantes and Rabelais, highlighted two key dangers facing the translator, 'dreary, ponderous *bukvalizm* and wanton, foolhardy, slapdash ad libbing' (1982, p. 83, my translation). In order to avoid such dangers, Soviet scholars advocated that the Soviet translator step into the source author's mind and emotions, channel their creative energy into an accurate representation of the original. The translator should sacrifice their narcissistic self and any excesses of creativity for the sake of precision. The source text and the source author's intentions must be accurately conveyed, hence Liubimov's rejection of *otsebiatina*, 'ad libbing'. Chukovskii concurred:

> Art like this is accessible only to great masters of translation – the kind of translators who possess the priceless ability to overcome their own ego and transform themselves artistically into the author they translate. This demands not only talent, but a special versatility, a plasticity, a 'communality of intellect'. (1965–67, p. 40)

Chukovskii offers a recurring message that chance errors, 'slips of the vocabulary', may be forgiven; these are merely 'scratches and cuts which are easily treated' (ibid., p. 17).[19] By contrast, however, he believed that the distortion of an author's spirit – either by the 'total complex of concoctions which in their aggregate change the style' (ibid., p. 26) or by obliterating 'all the intonations, all the colour, all the characters' speech distinctiveness' (ibid.,

p. 16) – was tantamount to 'villainous murder', a 'criminal act' (ibid., p. 17). Using similar terms, Marshak, poet and translator of Robert Burns, wrote:

> Centuries of effort and experience have shown us that aspiring to literal accuracy can often lead to translational gobbledygook, to violence against one's own language, to the loss of the poetic value of that which is being translated. (1962, p. 93)

Soviet translators spurned, therefore, the 'sham precision for which the pedant-translators of the thirties strove' (Chukovskii, 1965–67, p. 79) and immersed themselves instead in the pursuit of artistic translation, committed to capturing the original author's spirit and style. Marshak consolidated the opinions of Chukovskii, Liubimov, and Lozinskii when he wrote in 1962 that:

> An actor may be liberated rather than constrained by his role, but only if he can pour himself into it, deeply, with his entire essence. The same goes for a translator. He should, so to speak, be reincarnated in the author, [...] fall in love with him, with his manner and language, in this way preserving faithfulness to his own language [...]. Impersonal translations are always colourless and lifeless. (p. 94)

For Liubimov, the translator, unlike the original author, has a dual responsibility: to the source author *and* the target reader. In order to serve author and reader successfully, the translator must become immersed in all life experiences, observe how people live, and have fully awakened senses. Marshak, like Liubimov and Chukovskii, also observed that 'Without a link to the real world, without profound observations on life, without a worldview, [...] without study of the language and of the various nuances of the spoken idiom, the creative work of the poet-translator is impossible' (1962, p. 92). The best way for the Soviet translator to honour the source text and source author, therefore, was by striving for the utmost equivalence and accuracy. Failure to do so, according to Liubimov, would be like 'putting a pane of distorted glass between the author and the reader' (1982, p. 8, my translation).

While Western translators were requesting better dictionaries and glossaries in the 1950s, Soviet translators were placing an emphasis on the *living* language, an ever-changing phenomenon outmanoeuvring the contemporaneity of dictionaries. According to Chukovskii:

> The nuances of human speech cannot be chased down in a dictionary. Therefore, the task of the translator, if he is an artist, consists of nothing less than finding as often as possible the equivalents for Russian and foreign words which cannot be located in a dictionary. (1965–67, p. 82)

Soviet translators should have a 'daily dose of synonyms' (ibid.); they should maintain a literary store-cupboard – *literaturnaia kladovaia* – of modern vocabulary and idioms (Liubimov, 1982, p. 53), and, above all else, should believe in the invincibility of the Russian language (ibid., p. 50). Translatability was regarded as one of the Soviet school's overarching principles. The Soviet theorist Rossels described translatability as the first principle of the Soviet school (Leighton, 1991, p. 13) and Lauren Leighton quotes the translator V. Koptilov as insisting that 'The virtuoso translator does not know the word "untranslatable"'(ibid., p. 207). For Soviet theorists, the translator should overcome all textual challenges. They should persevere until a practical solution is found to preserve the fabric and features of the text. As Baer puts it, the view that there were 'limits to translatability, [...] was anathema in Soviet culture of the time' (2016, p. 130).

Chukovskii, however, did not share Koptilov's complete conviction with regard to the translatability of colloquial speech. In his view, 'the Russian language has not the slightest lexical means' to cope with 'colorful dialects in translation' (Chukovskii, 1965–67, p. 128). Though unable to say exactly how colloquial speech should be rendered, Chukovskii's preference is for the translator to 'give us a sketch of a plot without even attempting to recreate foreign stylistics!' (ibid., p. 131). He firmly declared his dislike of: *muzhikification* (the inflicting of an improbable local dialect on characters); the localising of names; the literal rendering of idioms and making calques of foreign folk sayings. Highlighting his point, Chukovskii accused foreign translators of Russian writers of failings of this ilk and 'intolerable slovenliness' (ibid., p. 234). As Munir Sendich (1999) observes, 'There is hardly a single American, or British, translation of classical Russian literature that would satisfy the requirements Chukovsky's book prescribes for a good translation' (p. 55). Surveying attempts by Anglophone translators (and given the time of Chukovskii's writing, such attempts must have included those by Penguin translators), Chukovskii concluded despondently that 'because of these poor translations the reader across the ocean has not the slightest idea what Gogol, Chekhov, Leskov [...] is really like'. Any decent translations are exceptions, 'surprises, accidents' (Chukovskii, 1965–67, p. 236), and his faith in Soviet superiority is transparent when he laments, 'Can it be that we Soviet authors must silently and passively endure this insufferable lack of care for our labours?' (ibid.).

Magarshack's translation theory

Magarshack's notes and drafts include contemporary and historical references from both the West and the Union of Soviet Socialist Republics. His thirty-four-page lecture, 'General Principles of Translation from the Russian' (n.d.),[20] summarises milestones in the Western history of translation. Starting with Terence, he progresses to the (post-) Elizabethan English translators: George Chapman, John Denham, and John Dryden; to Dr Johnson's *Life of Dryden*; Alexander Fraser Tytler's *Essay on the Principles of Translation*; Johann Wolfgang von Goethe; and Matthew

Arnold's 'On Translating Homer'. Some of these references may be attributed to the first two issues of *Delos*, in which Magarshack underlined and annotated a number of features and extracts.[21] Not all aspects emanate from *Delos* though; Magarshack also drew on Sir Philip Sidney, Alexander Pope, Percy Bysshe Shelley, Constance Garnett, and Logan Pearsall Smith to support his translation observations. From the Soviet tradition, Magarshack's influences include Chukovskii's *Vysokoe iskusstvo*, which he quotes at length in his lecture, 'A Note on Translation of Chekhov' (n.d., pp. 2–3); Liubimov's *Perevod-iskusstvo*; Marshak's notes on translation; and finally, but more fleetingly, Semën Lipkin, Peretz Markish, and Wilhelm Levik, all contributors to *Masterstvo perevoda* ('The Craft of Translation'),[22] the Soviet equivalent to *Delos*.

Magarshack makes overt reference in his book synopsis to Nabokov's translation of *Evgenii Onegin*. Savory's influence can best be recognised in Magarshack's taxonomy for translation practice. Translatability and lexical equivalence feature too; where Jakobson built a discussion around the Russian words *syr* (cheese), *rabotnik/rabotnitsa* (worker), and Chukovskii discussed *chelovek* (person), Magarshack does the same, offering his own references, for example, to colours ('the Russian looks at the spectrum in quite a different way from the English speaking person' (Synopsis, n.d., p. 4)), and what he terms 'static' words ('such as the Russian word for <u>ruka</u> [sic], which includes the arm as well as the hand, leading to mistranslations which often destroy the effect of a whole scene' (ibid.)). Magarshack and Jakobson shared the same assessment of poetry translation: that 'poetry is untranslatable' (Synopsis, n.d., p. 2/1959, p. 143), and for Magarshack, it was specifically the inability to evoke the same response that made him so certain of poetry's untranslatability.

Like Savory and Brower, Magarshack also made an assessment in 'General Principles' of the modern state of translation in the United Kingdom and the United States, likening the Russian literary translator to 'the poet at the beginning of the Elizabethan age' (n.d., p. 1). Citing Sidney, for whom the translator is "Almost in as good a reputation as the mountibanks of Venice"(ibid.), Magarshack suggests that a new, energetic stage in the British literary canon was being forged through translation. In reality, it was Penguin and other commercial publishing institutions that were shaping Anglophone perceptions of the classic Russian literary canon by the titles they selected and sold, and, in Penguin's case, the translation style it supported. For Magarshack, though, this phase in Russian literary translation was novel and flourishing, albeit under-scrutinised and under-appreciated. Magarshack also noted the 'rather primitive stage' of Russian scholarship, as well as the noticeable absence from the literary field of 'many English critics of note who have enough Russian to be able to express an authoritative opinion on a translation of a Russian classic' (ibid.), a claim which sounds a familiar chord (see Virginia Woolf's evaluation of Russian literature in translation).

Magarshack turned to history in order to form his own definition of a 'good' literary translator's credentials. He articulates the Chukovskian belief, which underscores all of his, and Soviet, theorising, that the translator is an artist:

> In dealing with a work of art (and it is with this aspect of a translator's work that I am chiefly concerned) the translator performs a dual role: he is not only a craftsman, he must also be an artist, for unless he can breathe the spirit of art into his translation, the result is bound to be a travesty of the original. (n.d., p. 1)

In his 'General Principles' lecture, Magarshack manages to summarise his professional stance whilst positioning himself in an historical hall of fame. He identifies with the Elizabethan poets for their views opposing literal translation: with Chapman (1598), translator of Homer, for attacking 'the literal translation of an author as "A pedantical and absurd affectation"'(Magarshack, n.d., p. 2); and with Denham (1656), translator of Virgil, for branding the concept of the 'fidus interpres' as 'A vulgar error in translating poets' (ibid.). He lauds Dryden's (1680) condemnation of the 'verbatim translator and the imitator' (ibid.), and in praise of paraphrase – a principle of translation that Magarshack describes as being 'so lucid' (n.d., p. 3) – Magarshack devotes more than three pages of his lecture to Dryden, singling out Dryden's demand that the translator possess 'a perfect understanding of his author's tongue and an absolute command of his own' (Magarshack, n.d., p. 4). Magarshack asserts a key difference, though, between Dryden's translation and his own: Dryden was translating from a dead language. For Magarshack, there is more at stake when translating from Russian, a living language. Recalling Chukovskii and Liubimov, he notes that:

> [...] it is not enough for a translator to have learnt the language from books. The only way for a translator to master a language is by personal association with the people speaking that language in their own country. Scholarship by itself is not enough; for scholarship is only concerned with the dead bones of a language. What matters in a work of art, is its living soul, the living words, and not the words to be found in a dictionary; to apprehend the meaning of a living word, one must feel it rather than be aware of its sense intellectually. (Ibid., pp. 5–6)

Magarshack also found flaws in Tytler's rule regarding the treatment of idiomatic phrases. He describes Tytler as 'an erudite Scott' [sic] (ibid., p. 13), but cannot accept that the more challenging idiom should be dealt with by using 'plain and easy language', his fear being that 'it loses its salt' (ibid., p. 14). By introducing a discussion of idioms, Magarshack creates an opportunity to criticise his predecessor, Garnett. Critical of any translator unfamiliar with the living Russian language, he, like Chukovskii, accuses such a practitioner of leading the reader:

> [...] into the belief that it is the peculiar Russian national character that makes the Russians express themselves so strangely. Even where a translator is aware of the fact that he is dealing with an idiom, a clumsy, literal translation will very often destroy a dramatic scene. (Ibid.)

Magarshack supported his opinion with examples from Garnett's work. He singled out her literal translation of 'the Russian idiom *"pochemu nyet"*' as 'why not', as having been 'instrumental in producing in the minds of the English readers, a curious notion of the Russian as a queer person who responds to the most ordinary situation of social intercourse in a most peculiar way' (ibid., p. 14). Magarshack also criticised Garnett for her literal renderings in *Diadia Vania*:

> 'Nye pominayte likhom' as 'Don't remember evil against me.' [sic] ruins the whole scene, since no English speaking woman would say anything of the kind to a man she had confessed a minute ago that she was in love with [...]. Here we have the case of an everyday Russian idiom, [...] translated literally into an unidiomatic and curiously harsh phrase which does not give the actress playing Yelena the ghost of a chance of conveying the feelings of Chekhov's heroine, and must needs lead to a distortion of the scene on stage. (Ibid., pp. 14–15)

He dedicates another three pages (pp. 21–24) to the idiomatic errors he perceives Garnett to have made in her translation of Gogol's *Nevsky Prospekt*. Magarshack aligns his views with those of Chukovskii and Liubimov. Chukovskii wrote that the translator who lacks a working knowledge of the source language risks distorting the source message and even the source culture in their target text:

> Translators who do not know the phraseology of their foreign language are just such 'remarkable eccentrics.' Many of them know their foreign language only from the dictionary, and consequently do not know its most current idioms. They have never guessed that the English expression 'God bless my soul!' does not always signify literally what it says, but frequently just the opposite: 'Devil take me'. (1965–67, p. 93)

For Liubimov, the translator must have a natural, fully proficient knowledge of the source and target languages, people, and local culture:

> An organic connection with one's people, with one's life is the rule of art; it is its soil and its air. Without this connection art withers and degenerates. The call for a closer connection with real life is what is

most directly and immediately relevant to the writer-translator. Without a connection with the realities of life it is impossible to create a fully developed original work; likewise, without a connection to life a translation becomes anemic. (1963, p. 123)

Magarshack singles out the importance of a translator having 'Organic Contact with Life', a need for linguistic dexterity, both in the source and target languages, to ensure a credible transfer of a text's style, spirit, humour, idioms. Even though he never returned to Russia and never spoke Russian at home (Magarshack, 2015), Magarshack's emphasis on linguistic dexterity and contact with the 'living' language indicates that he saw himself as a prime example of a translator living and breathing both source and target languages. Developing this assertion further, he clearly believed his Russian birth, childhood, and youth to be sufficient for a person to 'feel' the deeper meaning of the Russian word. Magarshack appears to have believed that his life in Britain provided sufficient exposure to English for him to 'feel' the deeper meaning of the target language too and to render nuances accordingly in his Penguin translations. According to Magarshack, it is the translator's proficiency and creativity with both languages that will determine how effectively equivalence is achieved:

A creative writer selects his words for their evocative power; to translate him does not mean to substitute words in one language for words in another language: it means to evoke the same kind of emotions as the original author was successful in evoking. A translator who is insensitive to the reactions of his author's readers can produce only a travesty of his work. (n.d., p. 6)

Magarshack's approach applied the same principles of dynamic equivalence associated with Rieu (1955) and Nida (1964). Nida's essay does not feature in Magarshack's archive, nor is there a copy of Rieu's 'Translating the Gospels', however, given Magarshack's close working acquaintance with Rieu,[23] it seems likely that Rieu's approach served to reinforce views he already had. The prospect of repeat commissions at Penguin might have helped to consolidate Magarshack's like-minded views too, however. There is no way of discerning to what extent Magarshack's practice was already entirely formed, based on his pre-existing habitus, and coincided fortuitously with Penguin's strategy later; or to what extent his practice was formed purely to cater to Penguin's needs and out of a wholly conscious (and understandable) desire to secure ongoing employment. Although Bourdieu's concept of habitus can be useful, it can, at the same time, be too much of a blunt instrument for translation case studies, especially because habitus has come to be associated with translatorial subservience. Habitus feels like a poor fit for a man like Magarshack given his dispositions: pride in his Russian birth, a sense of entitlement about translating Russian literature, and a desire to be respected and recognised professionally in two nations.

Magarshack's theorising reveals a sense of entitlement and self-worth coupled with dissatisfaction at not being better respected in the field; being Russian-born but university-educated in the United Kingdom, he felt he should be respected, even admired, by both the Union of Soviet Socialist Republics and the United Kingdom for his contributions to Russian literary translation. Magarshack's dispositions fall less comfortably into Bourdieu's broad schema. A better term to suit Magarshack's dispositions, therefore, might be David Charlston's concept of translatorial *hexis*. Translatorial *hexis* 'embodies [...] a defiant, honour-seeking attitude in the philosopher-translator with regard to specific oppositions in the surrounding field' (ibid.). Charlston's adoption and exploration of the term *hexis*, which values (rather than overlooks) the 'subtle, conscious or unconscious textual interventions' (ibid., p. 54) found in the translated text, challenges Simeoni's 'component of "subservience" [...] detected in the translator's habitus' (ibid., p. 55). Charlston's application of *hexis* also goes beyond Sela-Sheffy's own challenge to Simeoni's model of subservience.

What can be concluded, if we revisit Rieu's mission statement for Penguin Classics, is that Rieu and Penguin would certainly have approved of Magarshack's apparent devotion to equivalence. In his compilation, *Penguin Portrait*, Hare observes Rieu's aspiration for equivalence:

> This was exactly the 'principle of equivalent effect' that Rieu strove to achieve in his translations, and those he commissioned: a certain quality in the translation capable of creating the impression on modern-day readers as the original had on its contemporaries. (1995, p. 188)

Comment on the effectiveness of Penguin's principle of equivalent effect rarely features in translation reviews at the time when Magarshack was active; instead, reviewers typically applaud the arrival of a fresh translation to suit the modern reader. In the case of Cyril Connolly's 1956 review of *The Idiot*, he goes further, praising Magarshack for managing 'to tidy up the verbiage of the leisurely nineteenth century classic' (*The Sunday Times*). Magarshack felt that it was important to bring the classic tale to the modern reader, but, according to his notes, not to modernise the classic tale in doing so.[24] Equivalence was not the only common ground between Rieu and Magarshack. Magarshack approved of Rieu's Dryden-style recommendation to paraphrase too (Rieu and Phillips, 1955, p. 157). Endorsing dynamic equivalence and paraphrase as pillars of his practice, Magarshack also felt it was imperative for the 'good' translator to know the source author's intentions, to 'possess the ability of crawling, as it were, into the mind of his author' (Synopsis, n.d., p. 4) and his author's characters. By implication, Magarshack is assuming that such authorial intentions can indeed be discerned. This approach also explains Magarshack's successful side line in biographies, an additional source of income, for which he became arguably more famous than for his translations:[25]

> Translator must have not only a perfect knowledge of the language of his author but also of his author's political and economic background: his biography, his contemporaries, his place in the literature of his country, the historic facts of his age mirrored, however faintly, in his works, etc. (Ibid., p. 3)

For Magarshack, a "successful" translation, therefore, results from a translator's ability to read the author's intentions and to locate the work in the source culture. The way in which a translator achieves this success, however, depends on the constituent parts of a translator's past: the combination of translation experience, creativity, and the translator's ability to use the target language, alongside an intimate knowledge of the source culture, history, and politics. This professional blend resonates with the general profile of a Soviet translator:

> [...] translators must have a scholar's knowledge of literature, geography, ethnography, history, social science, and philosophy. Soviet translators are in many cases [...] also authors of scholarly studies, literary histories, biographies, and standard historical-cultural works on the country of their foreign language. (Leighton, 1991, p. 14)

In these areas, Magarshack set himself apart from his nearest 'rival' Garnett, who preferred others (Stepniak and later her husband, Edward) to write the introductions to her translations (Garnett, 2009, p. 143). In his lecture, 'A Note on Translation of Chekhov', Magarshack makes no effort to disguise doubt in Garnett's Russian language and cultural skills. He argues that in order to achieve a 'proper' rendering of Chekhov, the translator 'must have a thorough knowledge of Russian, by which I do not mean a knowledge acquired by an academic study of the language, but one obtained from a long and close association with the Russian people' (ibid., p. 1).[26] He continues that:

> [...] it is a fact that some well-known translators of Chekhov's plays have only a hazy notion of Russian. This is certainly true of Constance Garnett who monopolised for such a long time the presentation of Chekhov's plays on the English stage and left a ghastly legacy of misconceptions and misrepresentations behind. (Ibid.)

Magarshack's evaluation of Garnett's efforts is harsh. By his disregard, even contempt, for Garnett's knowledge, Magarshack dismisses the notion that a non-native, self-taught Russian linguist could ever really grasp the meaning of all the words to be translated. On a deeper level, Magarshack is also doubting the extent to which a translator with such little contact with 'real' Russian life can truly feel and capture complex, anthropological concepts, such as the ubiquitous Russian soul, the 'style, the spirit, and the meaning' (Rieu, 1955, p. 154), concealed within an original Russian text. On this basis, Magarshack should also have applied the same criticism to Edmonds who, as has already been established, did not have a 'long and close association with the Russian people' either. There is no record, however, of Magarshack commenting on Edmonds's work and, in fact, contrary to Magarshack's opinion, Edmonds fared well in Henry Gifford's evaluation, as we have seen. (After Penguin, Edmonds 'became expert' at Old Church Slavonic and 'undertook the English translation of the Orthodox liturgy' (*The Telegraph*, 1998), requiring her to engage wholly with the Russian 'spirit'.) Instead, Magarshack was more critical of his fellow Russian-speaking Slav, Elisaveta Fen, whom he accused in her version of *Three Sisters* of propagating a 'Chekhovian sadness-cum-despair syndrome' and of becoming a 'victim of the general lunacy which is so characteristic a feature of the Chekhov cult' (1972, p. 16).

Magarshack made no allowance for Garnett's dedication, for the fact that she conducted her work in professional isolation, with few predecessors or resources to offer guidance or comparison. Nor would Magarshack acknowledge that, even in spite of the infrequent trips she made to Russia, Garnett had mastered enough of the language to translate seventy volumes of Russian literature (Heilbrun, 1959, p. 246) (considerably more than his own list of published, book-length works). Each generation of translators makes the best of their moment. If there is no legacy on which to build, then the translator can proceed only as best they can, using the available tools, knowledge, and experience.[27] Garnett may have produced 'Edwardian prose' (Remnick, 2005), she may have been 'totally lacking verbal talent' (Nabokov, 2011, p. 31) but even Nabokov credited her 'with a certain degree of care' (in her translation of *The Government Inspector*) (ibid.).

It is possible that Magarshack's discrediting of Garnett stemmed from rivalry, maybe even resentment, towards her for cornering three fundamental opportunities before him: namely, translating the Russian literary canon; being instrumental in constructing Russia's image abroad; and enjoying the reputation of a trailblazer. By displaying her abilities in a less positive light, Magarshack was encouraging his target audience to discard the old and take a (reasonably-priced, Penguin-published) chance on his own, 'living' translation instead. Commercial rivalry and struggle for ownership is recognised as being a default response among competing cultural producers (Bourdieu, 1993, p.41). Whereas modern Russian classic translators have numerous predecessors from whom they would wish to stand out as having achieved more, Magarshack had only the one major competitor in the United Kingdom. Magarshack's first Penguin publication arrived just five years after Garnett's death and represented the first significant challenge to her dominant English version of *Crime and Punishment*. Magarshack and Penguin would have been conscious that they were pitting themselves against Garnett's reputation, which they would somehow have to erode in order to claim it for themselves. Magarshack's criticism of Garnett became all the easier for the fact that, since she died in 1946, Garnett could hardly defend herself, and also because Magarshack was not her only critic.

For all his criticism, however, it seems only proper to draw attention to the fact that, by the same critical measure, Magarshack himself would not have had the native *English* fluency which Garnett boasted. As is frequently debated about bilingualism,[28] one might reasonably ask whether Magarshack's Russian had suffered for having left Russia at a relatively young age (twenty-one), and whether, in turn, his feel for the 'living' language of his source texts had diminished increasingly over time. With no Russian-interaction in the United Kingdom (Magarshack, 2015), Magarshack's mother tongue may well have become 'subtractive', a form of bilingualism where 'an individual may come to know and use English with greater fluency than their native language [...] and may actually involve the attrition of skills in the earlier language' (Altarriba, 2005). At the same time, though, one might also question the dominance of his English given that he apparently relied heavily on his wife, Elsie, to help with all his commissions (Magarshack, 2014, p. 2). Though professionally proficient, Magarshack's English, was still, nevertheless, that of an émigré.

One might wonder, therefore, the extent of Magarshack's own 'Organic Contact with Life' (Magarshack, n.d., p. 4), which he recommended all translators experience if they were to master their languages. Liubimov[29] remarked that, 'Study of living colloquial speech with its phraseology, specific expressions, and intonation can and should take place everywhere – in the street, on the train, at the store, at the office, at a meeting, and during a walk' (1963, p. 124). For him, it is the in-depth, native feel for a language that imbues an otherwise expressionless phrase with 'living, natural and clear colloquial intonation' (ibid.). An inside knowledge of the target language allows the translator the best possible chance of capturing idioms, inflections and nuances that occur in a local dialect, and of expressing the native mindset. Without such knowledge, the translator 'will not be able to expose the reader to the linguistic treasures of an original text, nor to follow its linguistic diversity' (ibid.). Yet, for most of his working life, Magarshack worked at his desk from home each day (*Chicago Tribune*, 1963) – a microcosmic setting, therefore – and did 'not have a very sociable life outside the family' (Magarshack, 2014, p. 3). Magarshack's daughter describes her parents as being 'both very isolated' (ibid., p. 2), which would make the advice he gave to others – 'Study of colloquial speech must be Conducted Everywhere' (see Appendix 2) – all the more difficult to carry out in his own case.

Magarshack's unusually emotional response to Garnett's work and her legacy of misconceptions signifies his enhanced sensitivity towards Russia's image abroad:

> If [...] a translation results in the creation of a spurious atmosphere, an atmosphere that is entirely alien to the particular work and could not

possibly be part of it, then the translation is not only wrong, but also harmful, it is liable to give rise [...] 'to much international depreciation, if not contempt'. (General Principles, n.d., p. 18)

Like the émigrés in Garnett's circle of friends, Magarshack, living in the West as a Russian émigré, seemingly shared that same desire to serve as a 'viaduct[s] for the flow of Russian literature' (Peaker, 2006, p. 2). He had an inside knowledge of the Russian cultural landscape – still regarded at that time as mystifying by most in the United Kingdom – and, as for Fen too, translation allowed him to continue to access this knowledge even in self-imposed exile. Magarshack also hoped to undo the harm done by his predecessors; as he suggests in his taxonomy, the Russian classics should be re-translated every twenty-five years, thus allowing for serious errors to be flushed out sooner than under Garnett's almost fifty-year reign. Regular re-translations would allow for the linguistic changes that occur as a language evolves.

Magarshack was preoccupied by the need for the West to recognise the greatness of Russian literature and its literary translator. In reality, achieving such recognition would have been an uphill struggle given the national memory of both the Crimean War and the Great Game a century before. Luckily for Magarshack, the convergence of opportunity and timing in the form of Penguin's Russian Classics was ideal, especially Penguin's focus on creating a library of Russia's cultural heritage that would transcend all eras. Magarshack (and, to a lesser extent, Fen) found their professional *raison d'être* in the West by providing a cross-cultural literary service – with a high degree of authenticity – which few in the United Kingdom were qualified at that time to offer. By constructing a persona around his ability to offer something that others generally could not (his potential rivals – Nabokov, Yarmolinksii, and latterly Gibian and Terras – settled in the suitably-distant United States), Magarshack was able to make a name for himself in the United Kingdom both as one of 'the keepers of an authentic Russian tradition and culture' (Bethea and Frank, 2011, p. 199) and as a '*cultural custodian* responsible for the shaping of local culture' (Sela-Sheffy, 2008, p. 611).

Nabokov is someone with whom Magarshack shared a cultural milieu, and whose opinions on translation Magarshack observed with interest. They both assumed gatekeeper positions, sharing the same contempt for the literary reviewer who 'neither has, nor would be able to have, without special study, any knowledge whatsoever of the original' (Nabokov, 1955, p. 115); to quote Magarshack, 'there are not many critics of note who have enough Russian to be able to express an authoritative opinion on a translation of a Russian classic' (n.d., p.1). They also agreed on the issue of underperforming translators: personified for Magarshack by Garnett and, for Nabokov, by any translator distinguished by 'sheer unacquaintance of Russian life' (Nabokov, 1955, p. 122). On the whole, however, Magarshack and Nabokov approached translation from very different angles and, for this reason, the task of recognising and evaluating Magarshack's theorising and Penguin practice becomes clearer when Nabokov is used as a foil.[30]

In 'Problems of Translation: *Onegin* in English' (1955), Nabokov lauds word-by-word faithfulness to the text:

> The term 'literal translation' is tautological since anything but that is not truly a translation but an imitation, an adaptation or parody. (p. 121)

Magarshack objected to Nabokov's devotion to literalism out of concern for the reader. He wrote that 'a translator who is insensitive to the reactions of <u>his</u> readers also produces merely a travesty of the original (example: Nabokov's translation of <u>Eugene Onegin</u>)' (Synopsis, n.d., p.1, Magarshack's underlinings). Magarshack continued in a public letter to *The New York Review of Books*:

> I warmly agree with Edmund Wilson's views of Nabokov's incompe-tence as a translator. In fact, his 'translation' of Eugene Onegin is a grotesque travesty of that great poem. It is yet one more sad example of how a man can be blind to his own shortcomings. (26 August 1965)

Magarshack's anti-*bukvalist* position strongly points to his support of the Soviet school of translation and, consequently, highlights Nabokov's dis-tance from it. In direct opposition to Nabokov's views that 'the term "free translation" smacks of knavery and tyranny' (1995, p. 114), Magarshack believed that 'purple passages [...] sound grotesque if translated literally into English' (n.d., p. 12). In more general terms, his view was that:

> We should pride ourselves less upon literality and more upon dexterity at paraphrase. It seems clear that, by such dexterity, a translation may be made to convey to a foreigner a more just conception of an original than the original itself. (Ibid., p. 17)

Magarshack believed that not just good work but 'excellence' could come from careful moments of textual deviation – 'Deviations from original sometimes harmful, sometimes acceptable, but sometimes excellent' (Appendix 2)[31] – a flexibility which, according to his later theorising, Nabokov's translation prac-tice could not have tolerated.

The two translators also differed over their use of footnotes, adopting entirely polarised positions. Where Nabokov stated about his *Onegin* trans-lation, 'I want translations with copious footnotes, footnotes reaching up like skyscrapers to the top of this or that page' (1955, p. 127),[32] Magarshack's view again echoes a more Soviet view of translatability:

> The thing to avoid in dealing with these [...] difficulties is the footnote; for a footnote is a translator's confession of failure. It immediately dis-tracts the attention of the reader from the text and, in a passage charged

with emotion, may destroy the whole effect the author has laboriously built up. Difficult words in the text have to be translated, not explained away. (General Principles, n.d., pp. 19–20)

The footnote debate is still being rehearsed in general terms (Landers, 2001, pp. 93–94; Ying, 2008; Lourie, 1992; and Newmark, 1988, pp. 91–93), with attempts to classify when footnotes are, or are not, acceptable or useful. Magarshack aimed to make the journey easy and accessible for all his target readers. In the spirit of Rieu's guidance for Penguin translations,[33] he avoided footnotes, often smoothed out syntax, and toned down Russianness (names are Anglicised – contrary to Chukovskii's advice – with additions of Mr and Mrs; patronymics are often omitted; and culture-specific references are paraphrased, Anglicised, or omitted). Magarshack satisfied the aspirations of the early Penguin Classics with these decisions, but he replicated this approach with other publishers too, suggesting a natural inclination towards domestication, but also a contemporary publishing trend to avoid unnecessary textual interruptions.

The final distinction that I would emphasise between these two translators concerns the size and identity of their intended target audiences. Savory (1968) identified four literary categories of translation attracting specific audience types operating on different levels of sophistication:

1 The translation of 'purely informative statements' (p. 20)
2 Almost characterless translations made 'for the general reader' (p. 21)
3 Works which, in the past, 'have so appealed both to translators and their critics' (p. 23)
4 The translation of all 'learned, scientific and technical matter' (p. 23)

Savory may have had Penguin Classics in mind when he identified the second audience. He wrote that 'Forty, even thirty years ago no publisher could for a moment have considered the production of large numbers of translated works in cheap paperback format: yet the miracle has happened' (1968, p. 47). Nevertheless, there is an implied sense of mild distaste about the 'characterless' universality of this category (and yet it was the general reader's vote of confidence for such literature that ensured Penguin's success – economically and symbolically – and that of its commissioned freelancers). Preferring the smooth, artistic rendering, Magarshack belongs to this second category. Magarshack defined a perfect translation as one that 'ceases to be a translation, when, that is, the English reader is not conscious of reading a work originally written in a foreign language' (General Principles, n.d., p. 30). Expanding this view further, he wrote:

The important point is that a translation can be enjoyed side by side with the original. A good translation of a work of art, in short, is not a substitute for the original, but a living copy of it […]. (Ibid.)

By contrast, Nabokov sits most comfortably within the third category of highly scholarly literary translation, aiming his rendering of *Eugene Onegin* at a more broadly intellectual audience. Nabokov '[...] certainly did not perceive translation, or any art, in terms of mass production or mass appeal' (Leighton, 1991, p.181). Nabokov's non-populist, *bukvalist* stance set him at odds with Magarshack's and Rieu's aspirations of readable translations for the general reader. For all Magarshack's criticism and comment about Nabokov's practice, though, Nabokov remained silent.[34] Yuri Leving describes Nabokov as a 'self-taught émigré maverick who virtually sensed the market with a gut instinct and learned to navigate it by trial and error' (2013, p. 103). In his multifarious literary roles, and with the film success of *Lolita*, Nabokov secured considerable economic and reputational capital and a key position in the United States as a representative of Russia abroad. He also went on to be published extensively by Penguin as a modern classic writer. In these various contexts, therefore, Nabokov became more famous than Magarshack, and presumably felt no need to compete with Magarshack over the finer points of translation.

A personal manifesto

Although Magarshack's private collection does not contain a copy of Savory's *The Art of Translation* (1968), Savory's memorable list of conflicting instructions for would-be translators is mirrored in Magarshack's own four-page checklist for translation, a taxonomy entitled 'General' (see Appendix 2 for the full transcript). Magarshack's checklist also contains contradictions and incompatibilities, but there is no way of discerning whether these are intentional. The list consists of unadorned maxims, which leave the reader occasionally having to infer his intended meaning. What is clear from these statements, though, is that he and his practice reflect a complicated amalgam of Western and Soviet norms influencing his various approaches to translation. Magarshack's taxonomy is an attempt to articulate the best of these Western and Soviet strategies and to evaluate the UK translation industry from a position of twenty years' experience; in doing so, it also embodies Magarshack's translatorial *hexis*. Magarshack's written allegiance to certain professional values (Charlston, 2013, pp. 56–57) provides insight into personal complexities. In a bid to classify Magarshack's rather haphazard manifesto, I have condensed the most common and striking statements to the following three categories, all of which 'reveal something about the complex, decision-making process' (ibid., p. 57) involved in Magarshack's translation practice. The three categories are: *Gatekeeping*; *Strategy and style*; *The "good" translator*. I shall now address each category in turn.

Gatekeeping

Magarshack includes a number of statements that are written from the position of someone straddling two identities. On the one hand, as a native

Russian, he has a justified claim on the source text, author, and culture, a sentiment which permeates his statements. There is a sense of national pride and ownership in Magarshack's statements. Yet, on the other, he expresses an unfulfilled self-worth, that of an aspiring but under-appreciated émigré:

> Translator must adopt the Very soul of the Author which must speak through his own Organs (p. 1)[35]
> True Character of Author's Style (Ibid.)
> Genius of Translator must be akin to that of Original Author (Ibid.)
> Translator must be Recognised as the Creator of a New Work (Ibid.)
> Translator must Serve Author more than Himself (p. 3)
> Must Keep Perfect Equilibrium between Literalness and Total Freedom: Can only be achieved by Translator who is a good Writer or Poet in his own right (Ibid.)
> Recognition of Translator's Art by Prizes (Ibid.)
> Defects of Standard Translations: Failure to Suggest Author nor merely Great Mind but Great Writer (p. 4)

These statements portray Magarshack as a translator who believed in fidelity to the source text and loyalty, bordering on subjugation, to the source author, as if the translator bears a special duty to guard and preserve the source culture on its journey into the target culture. Although he doesn't openly state as much, Magarshack constructed a case for regarding the translator, especially the loyal émigré translator, as a 'keeper' of the home culture (Bethea and Frank, 2011, p. 25), someone vested with the necessary skills, cultural background, and emotional sensibilities to interpret the source culture accurately and authentically. It is the gatekeeper's job to make the home culture available to an uninitiated target culture. (Elisaveta Fen expressed similar aspirations in her memoirs and unpublished diaries, which are stored at the Leeds Russian archive.) Without some cultural sign-posting, the target audience may 'find themselves in a foreign society and present [...] at a ritual to which they do not hold the key' (Bourdieu, 1993, p. 217). In *Gatekeepers: The Emergence of World Literature and the 1960s* (2016), William Marling explains further that without literary gatekeepers, a nation's literary canon may never be selected in the first place, or may never be properly integrated into the world literary canon. According to Marling, 'Translators are among the most important gatekeepers', they:

> [...] acquire, develop, and then exploit a double cultural competence, a mastery of two sets of cultural information, in the use of which they become aware of cross-cultural discrepancies. (Ibid., p.5)

Gatekeeper status was important to Magarshack. On the one hand, he wanted to take control of the way in which the source culture, his native literary canon, was being portrayed and Penguin, the publisher of the day, became his best vehicle for achieving that aim. On the other, he wanted status and identity for himself. He wanted to be regarded as one of only a very select few endowed with the necessary skills to redefine the 'real' Russia and classic Russian literature in the United Kingdom. He wanted to navigate a credible course for an enquiring target audience through the apparent 'otherworldliness' of Russian literature. By cultivating such a persona – that of a 'genius-creator' whose competence is portrayed as something 'of a unique, unexplained gift' (Sela-Sheffy, 2008, p. 615) – Magarshack was able to secure a 'privileged standing' (ibid.) in his field. In his letter to Glover on 18 June 1952, he projects the impression of a "genius at work" as a means of negotiating alternative payment terms between commissions; he wrote:

> I have now to sit down to do a translation of OBLOMOV, which is one of the greatest works of art in Russian literature and is written in a style that is not as slapdash as Dostoyevsky's. It will require a tremendous lot of concentration and careful adaptation of an appropriate English style.

He is also described in an interview for *The Stage* in 1956 as having established himself 'as a Chekhov propagandist' and is quoted as saying that his book on Chekhov has 'already influenced Chekhov production considerably' (Marriott, 1956, p. 8). Magarshack increased the value of his personal capital by emphasising his unique talents, which in turn increased his chances of obtaining ongoing work in the Russian literary translation market (a trend which Sela-Sheffy also identifies in her research into Hebrew translators (2008, p. 620)). Magarshack took care to emphasise that these select few are translators who possess 'genius' creativity, striking the right balance between respect for the original author and the reader's needs. Magarshack's view that the translator is the genius-creator of a brand new work was also shared by the Soviet school of translation. In *Vysokoe isskustvo*, Chukovskii defines the translator's burden of responsibility to match the original author's greatness:

> [...] a translator does not photograph an original text, he re-creates it through art. The text of the original serves him as material for a complex and often inspired creative work. The translator is first of all a man of talent. In order to translate Balzac, he must [...] impersonate Balzac by assimilating his temperament and emotional makeup, his poetic feeling for life. (1965–67, p. 6)

Magarshack defined translation in his own way, building on these creative metaphors and directly borrowing Marshak's (1956, p. 92) comparable analogy of translation as portraiture vs. photography:

> [...] a translation can be claimed to be perfect when it can be enjoyed side by side with the original. A good translation is a work of art,

in short, is not a substitute for the original, but a living copy of it, in the same way in which a portrait is a living copy of a person and photograph is not. (General Principles, Magarshack, n.d., pp. 30–31)

Lefevere also discusses translator genius. Unlike the Soviet school, which embraces the union of theory with highly artistic, 'genius' practice, for Lefevere, the labelling of a translator as 'genius' in the Western tradition comes at the price of such a union. He wrote:

[...] if a unique work of literature is well translated, the translator must, quite simply be a genius too, and like any genius he is liable to tread lonely clouds that soar high above all theory. (1981, p. 71)

In the Soviet tradition, all converging agents – publisher, editor, and translator – shared the same aim, of producing a cultural good of artistic merit. Translation assumed a level of prestige for the Soviets, discussed in terms of national talent, which has never been reached in the United Kingdom. In a world of ideological capital, however, the rewards were different for the Soviet translator; they received the prized, non–commercial status of artist. According to Chukovskii, 'a good translator deserves respect in our literary world because he is not a handyman, not a copyist, but an artist' (1965–67, p. 6). Echoing Chukovskii's view (but, it should be noted, not eschewing the gains of economic capital), Magarshack states in his taxonomy: 'Main thing in artistic translations is talent: knowledge of language is not enough' (General, p. 3). Magarshack's mantra for recognition indicates his perceived shortfall in capital; although he was constantly aspiring to even greater success, his achievements failed to satisfy. Even in his earliest stages of negotiation with Penguin over his contract for *Crime and Punishment*, Magarshack wrote to Glover stating that, 'I am no amateur, and my books have been published and are due to be published by well-known publishing houses, including Allen & Unwin, Faber & Faber, and John Lehmann' (3 March 1949). Sela-Sheffy observes from her own research that translators have been 'striving to establish translation as an autonomously gratifying art-trade in its own right, with its own distinctive aura', where the 'performers of literary translation [...] make claim to fame and maintain a public persona as "creative translators", sometimes to the point of gaining stardom as translators' (2008, p. 614). Magarshack does not at any point mention the translator's salary (or royalties) as a means of recognition, rather he appealed for prizes (General, p. 3) and labels such as 'Genius' and 'Creator' (ibid., p. 1). What Magarshack was looking for on top of economic capital, therefore, was public and professional acclaim, reputational capital, a form of worth that symbolised national, even international, acceptance and deference expressed towards him, as an émigré.

Strategy and style

The next grouping of statements informs us of Magarshack's remit as a commissioned freelancer to ensure a style that would satisfy both Rieu's and Chukovskii's notions of equivalent effect:

> Translator must figure to himself in What Manner the Original Author would have expressed himself if he had Written in the language of the translation (p. 1)
> Style and Manner of Writing Same as the Original (Ibid.)
> Translation must have all the Ease of the Original Composition (Ibid.)
> Ease must not degenerate into licentiousness (Ibid.)[36]
> Prose works more Difficult to Render than Verse because of idiosyncratic style (Ibid.)
> Faithfulness to Tone, Mood and Content of Original while thinking: How would original author have said this if he had been writing in English? (p. 2)
> Deviations from original sometimes harmful, sometimes acceptable but sometimes Excellent (Ibid.)
> Translator must be able to imagine clearly and distinctly the inner portraits of the characters of original (p. 3)

When taken together, the above statements reiterate Magarshack's sense of fidelity to the source author and original text, but they also show that he is now turning his thoughts to the target reader too. Thus Magarshack's practical role becomes one of intermediary between text and reader. Magarshack's observations echo Rieu's edict that 'If you're going to apply the principle of equivalent effect, you've got to examine very carefully the style, the spirit and the meaning of the original' (1955, p. 154). Magarshack, however, refracted the principle into individual commands: produce equivalent responses in the target reader, honour the author's style and spirit, recreate the ease of the original. Magarshack's statement on textual deviation also chimes with Rieu's views. In his interview, Rieu gives one of his own examples, from Luke 22:15, where deviation is, in his opinion, preferable to a literal translation:

> [...] the words, 'with desire I have desired' are not English and never have been. The idiom is not even Greek. It is one of Luke's bits of Semitic Greek, going straight back to the Hebrew. And here we're all justified in abandoning the phrase, however hallowed it may seem. (Ibid.)

It follows from Rieu's justification for deviation, therefore, that a key question in his practice, and similarly for Magarshack, was audience: for whom did the original author write, and for whom must the translator recreate? Rieu explains:

> [the Gospels] were written, not for the man on the street, but for the man in the congregation, and [...] we must not write down to him [...]. There is good reason for thinking that the original audience of the Gospels found them just as difficult as we do; and therefore, if we paraphrase or lower our standard of English to make things crystal clear [...], we're going beyond our jobs as translators. (Ibid.)

Magarshack also valued audience, observing:

> If a certain phrase or word used in a certain context raises a smile from the Russian reader, then it is the business of the translator to make sure that the same kind of smile is raised in an English reader, or else that passage might as well be left untranslated.
>
> A writer does not work in a vacuum: he writes for an audience. Eliminate the audience and you eliminate art. (General Principles, n.d., p. 6)

Magarshack ascribed success in achieving an appropriate transfer of the original's flavour into the target text to the power of visualisation. More than once, he discusses the need for the translator to capture a visual image of the source author's intentions and to 'feel' through creativity how best to render an image through words. Magarshack's advice is couched in artistic, sensory terminology, where authorship and translation are acts of creative skill to be performed before an audience. On handling the Russian verb, for example, he combined visualisation with Soviet discipline:

> To a remarkable visual artist like Gogol, [...] the Russian verb offers countless opportunities for painting a whole picture in two or three words. It is hardly ever possible to obtain the same effect in English, and what the translator has to do first of all is to visualise the picture clearly and then reproduce it with the utmost economy and precision of which he is capable. (General Principle, n.d., p. 24)

Furthermore, according to Magarshack, the translator's work, compared to the author's job, is considerably more demanding (Sela-Sheffy, 2008, p. 617). As we have seen, Magarshack was keen to point out this view to Penguin on receiving Glover's letter (26 May 1954) regarding excessive corrections to the *Oblomov* page proofs. In Glover's letter, he reminds Magarshack of the contractual clause, which 'provides that any author's corrections in excess of an amount equal to 10% of the composition charge for the book should fall on the author'. Appalled by the notion of not being 'likely to get any royalties for a year or more' if he has to foot 10% of the composition charge, Magarshack makes the distinction in his reply to Glover between the nature of an author's and a translator's corrections. He wrote, 'I disagree with your point about the difference between an original work and a translation. It is just a translation that requires a great deal more changing' (27 May 1954).

The "good" translator

Having established the strength of Magarshack's belief in the principle of equivalent effect, this section groups those statements that Magarshack issued as an experienced language specialist, adding his own views to the questions of the day, namely, which skill-sets and background a "good" translator must possess, and which influences hamper a translator's progress:

> Perfect Knowledge of Language of Original (p. 1)
> Complete Acquaintance with the Subject (Ibid.)
> Only Realism founded on Solid and Firm Foundation of Life and not Book Knowledge results in fruitful and Active Method of Artistic Translation (Ibid.)[37]
> Impossible criticise translation from a language the Critic is only vaguely familiar with (p.3)
> Importance of thorough knowledge of background (Ibid.)
> Parochialism of assigning review books to Professors of the language in question (Ibid.)
> Translator's Organic Contact with Life (p. 4)
> Translator must Live in Country whose language is that of the Translation (Ibid.)

Many of these statements are standard views, shown by Munday (2008, pp. 23–27) to be long held by practising translators (Luther, Tyndale, Dolet, etc.). (Of the five most important principles of translation set out by Dolet, for example, the top two match Magarshack's own statements.) It makes best practical sense for the translator to have complete acquaintance with the subject, the language of the original and target cultures, and a thorough knowledge of the background to a text. Perhaps predictably, Magarshack's observations reveal more about the UK translation industry. He argued that the Russian-English literary translation scene was being misinterpreted and misrepresented by ill-informed critics with minimal knowledge of Russian. At the same time, however, he expressed disgruntlement that only Professors of Russian were being assigned books to review. Magarshack's views are steeped in frustration: at critics who might destroy a translator with ill-informed verdicts, and at monopolising academics, paid and recognised for their critiques while, on both counts, proven practitioners like him remained repeatedly overlooked. I maintain that Magarshack articulated a sense of the devaluation of professional translators' knowledge, which continues to prevail today (translation scholar Mona Baker discusses this professional malaise in *In Other Words* (1992, p. 2)); but in spite of this, Magarshack in the 1960s was better established and better respected than his average modern counterpart. Throughout his career, Magarshack had a very clear sense of and belief in his status and worth, and held firm aspirations to change the (self-) perception of the translator.

Recommendations for teaching translation

Magarshack concluded his theorising with a comment on the present and a vision for the future. He urged British universities to disseminate their knowledge of Russian language and literature, lamenting that even by the 1970s, chairs of Russian language and literature at British universities were still thin on the ground:

> [...] the academic mind in this country is still apt to regard Russia as a 'terra incognita' and the study of Russian literature as so exotic an occupation that only a few cognoscenti are fit for it [...] it is as important now as a chair of French or German language and literiture [sic], or even a chair of Latin and Greek. (n.d., p. 33)

By establishing full academic recognition of Russian letters in multiple UK universities, Magarshack hoped to create a 'nucleus of informed opinion' (ibid.) and a new generation of better-informed translators and critics. After twenty years of mistrust and criticism for academics and critics, Magarshack finally acknowledged that fair academic evaluation might be a useful tool: let academia work constructively within the field, rather than without.

In terms of training future translators, he envisaged (with some degree of foresight) British universities stationing students with creative writing ability at Russian universities, thereby enabling them to become immersed in the study of Russian language and literature. The combination of natural literary talent and exposure to Russian life, he hoped, would go on to produce the ideal cadre of future translators. His acknowledgment that translation should be taught in British universities and his views on how this might be achieved were perhaps inspired by the long-held Soviet commitment to sponsoring literary translators to train at the Gorkii Literary Institute and in higher education institutions (Komissarov in Baker and Saldanha, 2009, p. 522). Whether aspiring Soviet translators gained sufficient, or indeed any, practical language experience in the West is questionable.

Conclusion

This chapter combines historical and sociological approaches in order to analyse the intellectual manifestations of Magarshack's personal and

professional experiences, which present themselves in his previously unexplored private papers and theorising. The events and dispositions that
constitute his habitus and which have been discussed in relation to his
theory-writing include: his post-emigration relationship with Russia; his
desire to be remembered in the Union of Soviet Socialist Republics and
respected intellectually in the United Kingdom; his concern about the distorted image of Russia created by non-Russians in English translation; his
criticism and envy of Garnett (as a non-native Russian) for monopolising
the field of Russian literature in translation; his convergence with Rieu's
(Penguin's) translation strategy and conscious divergence from Nabokov's;
his self-image as a specially privileged gatekeeper; and his craving for professional recognition as a literary genius-creator. The interpretation of this
complex amalgam of experiences and associated responses – Magarshack's
'slow process of inculcation' (Simeoni, 1998, p. 5) – has enabled us better
to understand the values, motivations, and occasional contradictions in
Magarshack's own translation theorising, and it will enable us in the next
chapter to evaluate his translated text with new insight.

As an émigré straddling two cultures, Magarshack's combined knowledge of Soviet as well as European translation traditions enabled him to
circumvent binary restrictions in practice, to adopt a liberating notion
of translatorial latitude. This approach may yet mark him out as something of a theoretical pioneer in Russian-English translation in the West.
Western translation approaches have often crystallised into an irresist-
ible duality which has preoccupied theorists as far back as St. Jerome
and Schleiermacher. Such thinking has led the Western school to seek an
all-encompassing and universal theory, 'a consensus on how translations
should be approached and studied' (Arrojo, 2013, p. 123), which hints at a
more predictable and formulaic approach to translation. For Magarshack,
theory existed as a response to a practical problem, a view shared by the
Georgian poet-translator Elizbar Ananiashvili:

> When Soviet translators began their campaign to educate critics, they
> could point out that theory had been developed in practice [...] the
> greatest value of Soviet translation theory is that 'it does not prescribe
> norms and point to rules,' but rather generalizes experience with the
> intent of helping practice. (Leighton, 1991, pp. 70–71)

Magarshack's affinity with the Soviet school of translation, however, lacked
criticism, suggesting a potential bias or naivety on his part. Willing blind-
ness (as it would be termed in the twenty-first century) regarding aspects of
the Soviet regime was not entirely uncommon among Russian exiles:

> Curiously, a number of Soviet émigrés – many of whom left the USSR
> owing to dissatisfaction with the regime – seemed to share the official
> view of Soviet cultural accomplishments. True, they lacked reliable

information; but their somewhat idealized picture of Soviet literary translation may also have had a psychological foundation in a need to believe that their country of origin did have some redeeming qualities. (Friedberg, 1997, p. 6)

If there is naivety on Magarshack's part, it can perhaps be attributed to his ongoing sense of marginalisation, to the fact that after such a long career in English words working for a number of respected British publishing houses, he could still be regarded as a foreigner. As we have seen in the preceding chapter, though, Magarshack would have struggled with Soviet editorial control. The relative autonomy he enjoyed as a Western translator contrasts greatly with the micro-managed world of the Soviet translator, for whom, according to Baer, 'the term "free", which is often used to describe the Soviet School approach, is something of a misnomer insofar as the practice of translation was in fact highly constrained' (2016, p. 130).

Throughout his career, Magarshack saved his most assertive letters and acerbic criticism for editors, academics, and literary critics, in fact for any-one who challenged his work. See, for example, his letter of 12 March 1964 to Penguin Classics editor Mr Plaat, in which he writes concerning changes to his Chekhov stories, 'I should like to protest at the way alterations were made in my text without my knowledge or consent. I am appalled at the way two stories had their titles altered'. He adopted an even more defen-sive tone when challenged by Robin Milner-Gulland over his translation of Pasternak's biography; Magarshack regarded 'his frenzied attempt to cast a slur on my reputation as a personal attack by some disgruntled academic' (29 April 1971). Magarshack's correspondence reveals huge respect for Rieu, and yet other letters to Penguin editors reveal a frequently frustrated or resistant Magarshack, sometimes a caustic one. It was his dogged asser-tiveness combined with queries over his translations that resulted in him ultimately falling 'out of favour' (Cochrane, 24 January 1964). For these rea-sons, therefore, it is unlikely that Magarshack would have flourished under the rigour of the more controlling system of editorship that prevailed in Soviet Russia.

But it is clear that Magarshack – even having made his living and rep-utation working for Penguin, the most recognisable publisher of the day – sought Soviet-style affirmation in the West, calling in his taxonomy ('General') for professional prizes to raise the status of the UK trans-lator. Rather than attempt to battle for this development in his early years as an emerging translator, with little power, position, or influence over the field, Magarshack raised the idea late in his career once he had safely distinguished himself (Bourdieu, 1993, p. 184) as a reputable name in the literary field. This assertion challenges Bourdieu's generalised estimation of the translator (2008, p. 148) as a figure seemingly at the margins of the field and without prospects for professional satisfaction or progression. Magarshack cuts a very different figure compared to his Penguin successor Ronald Wilks, whose personal and professional difficulties, as we will see in Chapter Four, correspond more closely to Bourdieu's estimation of the translator as dissatisfied and reactive. Magarshack's career demonstrates a developing social identity, an ability to maximise opportunities and to construct a secure position in the field as an essential bridge between cultures and also as a creative artist (Sela-Sheffy, 2008, p. 620). Magarshack used the symbolic capital he had acquired at Penguin to best effect as a lever with which to challenge his industry's norms – urging the industry to place greater value on the translator's role – and also to further his own reputation. Magarshack received words of praise for his achievements at Penguin – W.J. Igoe wrote in the *Chicago Tribune* that 'Magarshack has done more than any other writer [or, indeed, group of writers] to make Russian literature available in worthy form to the English-speaking reading public. The list of authors he has brought us is awe-inspiring' (1963, p. 3). Magarshack would no doubt have rejoiced in the emergence since of numerous prestigious literary translation awards (various PEN translation awards, the EBRD Literature Prize, the International Booker Prize, and previously the Rossica Prize and Rossica Young Translators Prizes) and, with them, the long-overdue recognition that the literary translator is a creative agent (or even artist), entitled to a small share in the fame of the original text – and thus, in Venuti's terms, fully culturally visible.

Notes

1. Based on personal and shared experiences as an undergraduate; and reminiscences of the Cambridge Russian Programme (Briggs email to C McAteer, 18 August 2014).
2. For a full list of the BBC's airings of Magarshack's translations, see: <http://genome.ch.bbc.co.uk/search/0/20?q=David+Magarshack#search> [Accessed 15 June 2017].
3. It is worth noting that Magarshack translated more than Fen and Edmonds and the contrast in numbers, therefore, may not necessarily represent quality.
4. Magarshack was no doubt aware that translators could receive the Stalin Prize for translation in the USSR; Mikhail Lozinskii, for example, was awarded the Stalin Prize in 1946 for his translation into Russian of Danté's *Divine Comedy* (Baer and Olshanskaya, 2013, p. x).
5. As Claire Warden notes in '"A Glimpse of Another Russia": Elisaveta Fen's Chekhov Translations' (2018), Fen makes clear her feelings about Bolshevism in a book proposed (but never realised) in 1939, under the title *Russia – My Country*. Fen wrote 'Propaganda, as a means of persuasion, can be overdone, and produce counter-suggestibility. Communism can provide a substitute for religion only up to a point. Bolshevism has some hold on the Russian mind, but is it a permanent hold? Is all Russia behind Bolshevism? The answer to these questions must be emphatically: No!' (MS 1394 253).
6. Other translators of the time put more faith in back translation.
7. Also demonstrated in articles: 'Gogol: A Great Russian Humorist', *Radio Times*, 1952; and 'The Translator's Art', *Times Educational Supplement*, 1969.

8. Gollancz was the founder member of the Left Book Club and a board member of the Anglo-Soviet Public Relations Committee throughout 1941–42. He exchanged correspondence with the Communist party between 1939–42 (Gollancz archive online).

9. This view is supported by the fact that Gollancz commissioned only this one book on the principles of literary translation. Kevin Crossley-Holland, editor at the time of Magarshack's terminated commission, can recall no further Gollancz publications of this ilk (e-mail to C McAteer, 14 April 2016).

10. Letter from Cooper to Cochrane, 1 November 1970.

11. 'Notes on the Translation of Chekhov' was aired in an abridged, twenty-minute broadcast, 'The Mystery of the Red Coffin', on 13 December 1981. According to the Features' Editor, the lecture was well received. 'It's fairly rare, sadly, to get reaction to programmes on Radio 3, and I think it shows that David's words struck a powerful chord. [...] I would have thought it would be very worthwhile publishing it' (Plowright, 1982). Staff at the BBC Genome Project have been unable to locate any copy of the transcript.

12. See Crossley-Holland's letter to Magarshack's literary agent, Peter Grose at Curtis Brown Ltd: 'I am really so sorry that David Magarshack feels he must cancel the contract for THE PRINCIPLES OF TRANSLATION, [...] when a book is overdue in this way it becomes more and more of a millstone. He is very much the best man (in my opinion) to write this book' (16 May 1973).

13. See Andrew Chesterman and Emma Wagner (2002, pp. 1–12), Jean Boase-Beier (2006, pp. 47–56), and Christopher Whyte (2015, p. 285).

14. See James S. Holmes's view in the 1970s regarding Russian translation theory that 'there is a great deal going on that is inaccessible to us' (1994, p. 93), and more recently, Anthony Pym and Nune Ayvazyan who asked, 'Could we really have ignored the Russians so completely?' (2014, p. 1). (Sergei Tyulenev emphatically refuted this rhetorical question (2015, pp. 342–346).)

15. Nabokov cited as incompatibilities: the greater number of rhymes in Russian; the limitation of one stress per word in Russian; higher frequency of polysyllabic words and full articulation of syllables in Russian; a rarity of inversion in Russian verse; frequency of modulated lines in iambic tetrameter (1955, p. 118).

16. Чихир (chikhir) is a Caucasian wine; абрек (abrek) is a Caucasian partisan-warrior (historical); кабардинец (kabardinets) is a native of the North Caucasian region of Kabardino-Balkaria; карга (karga) is a (carrion) crow; кошкильды (koshkil'di) is a Chechen settlement; бешмет (beshmet) is a Cossack/Caucasian outer-coat; кинжал (kinzhal) is a (Caucasian) tribal dagger.

17. Anthony Oettinger dedicated an essay to automatic translation (1959, pp. 240–267); Vinay and Darbelnet also explored the latest technological developments. However, not until several decades later with statistical machine translation did machine translation seem feasible.

18. The discipline is generally considered to have begun with James S. Holmes's 1972 paper, 'The Name and Nature of Translation Studies' (Munday, 2008, p. 9).

19. This is a far more lenient view than that held by Ginzburg, whom Chukovskii quoted as stating that 'not only the fate of a translation, but the professional fate of the translator hangs on a single word' (Chukovskii, 1965–67, p. 11), and the formalistic Nabokov, who famously wrote that, 'The clumsiest literal translation is a thousand times more useful than the prettiest paraphrase' (1955, p. 115).

20. Referred to hereafter as 'General Principles'.

21. The most annotated articles are by Goethe and Arnold in *Delos* Book 1; and by Dryden in *Delos* Book 2.

22. All three translators feature in the 1963 edition, <http://padaread.com/?-book=22183&pg=515> [Accessed 12 March 2019].
23. Magarshack's correspondence with Plaat, Managing Editor, Penguin, 12 March 1964, reveals his respect for Rieu: 'He saw seven of my Penguin books through the press and I shall never forget his marvellous tact and consideration'.
24. He states in his taxonomy that the translator 'Must not attempt to translate slang or colloquialism into current slang or colloquialism of England or America' (General, p. 1).
25. Magarshack's obituary in the *Times*, 29 October 1977, only cited Magarshack's role as a biography writer. No mention is made of Penguin or the many translations he had published throughout his career.
26. Magarshack repeatedly emphasises the need for the translator to know the source culture. Although socialising in Russian exile circles in London, Garnett only visited Russia twice in her lifetime (Garnett, 1991, p. 115 and p. 208) and made little secret about her reliance on dictionaries (ibid., p. 76).
27. When asked at the Litquake Translation Panel 'whether a bad translation was better than no translation at all', translator Katherine Silver replied, 'Garnett was a trailblazer working under adverse conditions, a translator who made it possible for the Pevears of the world to now perform what is [sic] perhaps more faithful renditions of the great Russian novels' (Ciabattari, Book Critics, 2009).
28. See Baker, 'When the second language and culture [...] replace or demote the first language, a subtractive form of bilingualism may occur. This may relate to a less positive self-concept, loss of cultural or ethnic identity, with possible alienation or marginalization' (2011, p. 72).
29. Magarshack described Liubimov as 'one of the finest Russian translators, [who] insists that translation is an art. A man who dedicates himself to artistic translations' (n.d., Box 13).
30. In a similar fashion, Nabokov has also been compared to Jakobson in Baer's essay, 'Translation Theory and Cold War Politics, Roman Jakobson and Vladimir Nabokov in 1950s America' (2011, pp. 171–186).
31. Magarshack does not cite specific examples of his work as excellent deviations, but his departures from Russian-naming norms could arguably be considered excellent at a time when the UK's mass lay-readership, only just accessing the previously elitist world of Russian literature, was attempting to grapple with consonant-rich Russian names.
32. Nicholas Warner argues that Nabokov's fixation with footnotes reflects more his own narcissistic attempts to divert attention away from the source author and back to himself (1986, p. 168).
33. See Rieu's letter to Kitto, 21 October 1944.
34. Magarshack's letter to *The New York Review of Books* criticising Nabokov's translation of *Onegin* was published in the same issue (26 August 1965) as Nabokov's own response to Wilson's review. There is every likelihood that Nabokov would have been aware of Magarshack's views.
35. Magarshack's capitalisation.
36. Magarshack is referring to the risk that an excessively 'free' translator might gravitate towards grammatical or stylistic liberties.
37. Magarshack's underlining.

References

Anon., 1998. Obituary, Rosemary Edmonds, 21 August [online] Available at: *The Telegraph Historical Archive*, [Accessed 16 March 2018].

Anon., 2018. Genome Radio Times 1923–2009, *BBC*, [online] Available at: <http://genome.ch.bbc.co.uk> [Accessed 17 May 2019].

Altarriba, J., 2005. Bilingualism. In: P. Strasny, ed. *Routledge Encyclopedia of Linguistics*. London: Routledge.

Arrojo, R., 2013. The Relevance of Theory in Translation Studies. In: C. Millán, and F. Bartrina, eds. *The Routledge Handbook of Translation Studies*. Abingdon and New York: Routledge, pp. 117128.

Baer, B.J., 2016. *Translation and the Making of Modern Russian Literature*. New York and London: Bloomsbury Academic.

- ed., 2011. *Contexts, Subtexts and Pretexts. Literary Translation in Eastern Europe and Russia*. Amsterdam/Philadelphia: John Benjamins.
- and Olshanskaya, N. eds., 2013. *Russian Writers on Translation: An Anthology*. Manchester: St. Jerome, pp. iii–xiv.

Baker, C., 2011. *Foundations of Bilingual Education and Bilingualism*. 5th ed. Bristol, Buffalo, Toronto: Multilingual Matters.

Bethea, D., and Frank, S.., 2011. Exile and Russian Literature. In: *The Cambridge Companion to Twentieth-Century Russian Literature*. Cambridge: Cambridge University Press.

Boase-Beier, J., 2006. Loosening the Grip of the Text: Theory as an Aid to Creativity. In: M. Perteghella, and E. Loffredo, eds. *Translation and Creativity, Perspectives on Creative Writing and Translation Studies*. London and New York: Continuum, pp. 47–56.

Bourdieu, P., 1993. *The Field of Cultural Production*. Cambridge: Polity Press.

- 2008. A Conservative Revolution in Publishing. Translated from French by R. Fraser. *Translation Studies*, 1(2), London: Routledge, pp. 123–153. http://dx.doi.org/10.1080/14781700802113465.

Briggs, A.D.P., 2014. Private email to C. McAteer, 18 August.

Brower, R.A., ed.1959. *On Translation*. New York: Oxford University Press.

Charlston, D., 2013. Textual Embodiments of Bourdieusian Hexis, *The Translator*, 19(1), pp. 51–80, DOI: 10.1080/13556509.2013.10799519.

Chekhov, A., *Plays*, Translated from Russian by E. Fen., 1954. Harmondsworth: Penguin

Chesterman, A., and Wagner, E., 2002. *Can Theory Help Translators? A Dialogue Between the Ivory Tower and the Wordface*. Manchester: St. Jerome.

Chukovskii, K., 1965–67. *Vysokoe iskusstvo*. Translated from Russian by L. Leighton. In: L. Leighton, ed. 1984. *The Art of Translation. Kornei Chukovsky's 'A High Art'*. Knoxville, TN: The University of Tennessee Press.

- 1968. *Vysokoe iskusstvo*. Moscow: Sovetskii pisatel'. [pdf] Available at: <http://samlib.ru/w/wagapow_a_s/chuk-tr.shtml> [Accessed 24 November 2015].

Ciabattari, J., 2009. Guest Post by Scott Esposito: Report on the NBCC

Reads/Litquake/City Lights Translation Panel, [blog] 19 October, Available at: <http://bookcritics.org/blog/archive/nbcc_reads_litquake_city_lights> [Accessed 22 April 2016].

Crossley-Holland, K., 2016. Private email to C. McAteer, 14 April.

Fen Archive, MS1394. Leeds: Leeds University Special Collections, Russian Archive.

- Fen Memoirs, *Russia – My Country*. MS 1394/253.
- Letter Fen to Rieu, 16 March 1950, MS 1394/6581.

Friedberg, M., 1997. *Literary Translation in Russia*. University Park, PA: Pennsylvania State University Press.

Garnett, R., 2009. *Constance Garnett – A Heroic Life*. London: Faber and Faber.

Gollancz Archive, n.d., A Catalogue of the Papers of Victor Gollancz, [online] Available at University of Warwick: <https://mrc-catalogue.warwick.ac.uk/records/GLL> [Accessed 29 February 2020].

Gorkii, M., 1919. World Literature. Translated from Russian by J. McGavran. In: B.J. Baer, and N. Olshanskaya, eds. 2013. *Russian Writers on Translation: An Anthology*. Manchester: St. Jerome, pp. 6566.

Hare, S., 1995. *Penguin Portrait: Allen Lane and the Penguin Editors, 1935–1970*. London and New York: Penguin.

Heilbrun, C., 1959. *The Garnett Family, The History of a Literary Family*, [online] Ann Arbor: ProQuest Dissertations Publishing. [Accessed 22 May 2017].

Holmes, J.S., 1994. *Translated! Papers on Literary Translation and Translation Studies*. Amsterdam: Rodopi B.V.

Hunnewell, S., 2015. Richard Pevear and Larissa Volokhonsky, The Art of Translation [interview] *The Paris Review*, 4(213).

Jakobson, R., 1959. On Linguistic Aspects of Translation. In: L. Venuti, ed. 2004. *The Translation Studies Reader*. Abingdon and New York: Routledge, pp. 138143.

Knight, D., 1959. Translation: The Augustan Mode. In: R. Brower, ed. *On Translation*. New York: Oxford University Press, pp. 196–204.

Komissarov, V., 1998. Russian Tradition. In: M. Baker and G. Saldanha, eds. 2009. *Routledge Encyclopedia of Translation Studies*, 2nd edition. Abingdon and New York: Routledge, pp. 517–524.

Landers, C.E., 2001. *Literary Translation: A Practical Guide*. Clevedon: Multilingual Matters.

Lefevere, A., 1981. Translated Literature: Towards an Integrated Theory, *The Bulletin of the Midwest Modern Language Association*, 14(1), pp. 68–78.

Leighton, L., 1991. *Two Worlds, One Art*. DeKalb, IL: Northern Illinois University Press.

Leving, Y., and White, F., 2013. *Marketing Literature and Posthumous Legacies: The Symbolic Capital of Leonid Andreev and Vladimir Nabokov*. New York: Lexington Books.

Liubimov, N., 1982. *Perevod-Iskusstvo*. Moscow: Sovetskaia Rossia. [pdf] Available at: <http://imwerden.de/pdf/ljubimov_perevod-iskusstvo_1982_text.pdf> [Accessed 15 July 2016].

Lourie, R., 1992. Raskolnikov Says the Darndest Things, *The New York Times*, 26 April [online] Available at: <http://www.nytimes.com/1992/04/26/books/raskolnikov-says-the-darndest-things.html?pagewanted=all&_r=0> [Accessed 02 February 2016].

Magarshack, D., 1972. *The Real Chekhov*. London: George Allen & Unwin Ltd.

Magarshack Archive, MS1397. Leeds: Leeds University Special Collections, Russian Archive.

- Anon., 1951. Review *Crime and Punishment. Yorkshire Observer* (Bradford), 13 December.
- Anon., 1954. Goncharov in English, *The Scotsman*, 14 October, Box 17.
- Anon., 1958. Review *Brothers Karamazov. The Listener*, 20 March.
- Anon., 1965. Chekhov and Gogol Transfers. *The Times Literary Supplement*, 8 April, Box 11.
- Article, 1969. The Translator's Art, *Times Educational Supplement*, 16 May, Box 13.

- Connolly, C., 1956. True Genius. [review] *Sunday Times*, 15 January, Box 17.
- Crossley-Holland K., 1973. Letter to Peter Grose Esq., 16 May, Box 1.
- *DELOS* 1–6, Austin, Texas: National Translation Center, Box 20
- Igoe, W.J., 1963. 'The Gift of Tongues'. [article] *The Chicago Tribune*, 20 October, Box 11.
- Plowright, P., 1982. Letter to Elsie, BBC London, 8 February, Box 1.
- Powell, A., 1992. Letter to Elsie, 15 March, Box 1.

Magarshack, D., n.d., A Note on Translation of Chekhov, Box 13.

- n.d., The Art of Translation, Synopsis, Box 13.
- n.d., A Note on Translation of Chekhov, Box 13.
- n.d., General. [taxonomy] Box 13.
- n.d., General Principles of Translation from the Russian. [unpublished paper] Box 13.
- 1952. Gogol: A Great Russian Humorist', *Radio Times*, 15 February, Box 25.
- 1964. Letter to F. Plaat, 12 March, Box 1.
- 1965. Letter to Editors. [online] *The New York Review of Books*, 26 August. Available at: <http://www.nybooks.com/articles/archives/1965/aug/26/other-comment-2/> [Accessed 24 July 2015].
- 1965. Other Comment (In response to: The Strange Case of Pushkin and Nabokov). *The New York Review of Books*, 26 August. [online] Available at: <http://www.nybooks.com/articles/1965/08/26/other-comment-2/> [Accessed 21 April 2016].
- 1971. Letter to Mr Rosenthal, 29 April, Box 1.
- Nikolai Lyubimov [Magarshack's notes], Box 13.

Magarshack, S., 2014. Letter to C McAteer, 19 December 2014.

- 2015. Interview with C McAteer, Camden, London, 20 February 2015.

Mandelshtam, O., 1929. Torrents of Hackwork. Translated from Russian by N. Olshanskaya. In: B. J. Baer & N. Olshanskaya, eds. 2013. *Russian Writers on Translation: An Anthology*. Manchester: St. Jerome, pp. 81–83.

- *Potoki khaltury*. [online] Available at: <http://rvb.ru/mandelstam/01text/vol_2/03prose/2_249.htm> [Accessed 15 July 2016].

Marling, W., 2016. *Gatekeepers: The Emergence of World Literature and the 1960s*. New York: Oxford University Press.

Marriott, R.B., 1956. Mr Magarshack Bangs Chekhov's Cymbals and Drums, *The Stage*. 16 August.

Marshak, S., 1956. The Art of the Poetic Portrait. Translated from Russian by B.J. Baer. In: B.J. Baer, and N. Olshanskaya, eds. 2013. *Russian Writers on Translation: An Anthology*. Manchester: St. Jerome, pp. 9092.

- 1962. The Poetry of Translation. Translated from Russian by J. Cieply. In: B. J. Baer & N. Olshanskaya, eds. 2013. *Russian Writers on Translation: An Anthology*. Manchester: St. Jerome, pp. 93–95.

May, R., 2000. Russian Literary Translation into English. In: O. Classe, ed. *Encyclopedia of Literary Translation into English, Vol. 2, M-Z*. London and Chicago: Fitzroy Dearborn, pp. 1204–1209.

Meylaerts, R., 2006. Conceptualizing the Translator as a Historical Subject in Multilingual Environments, A Challenge for Descriptive Translation Studies? In: P. Bandia, and G.L. Bastia, eds. *Charting the Future of Translation History*. Ottawa: University of Ottawa Press, pp. 5979.

Morson, G.S., 2010. Potemkin Translators, The Pevearsion of Russian Literature, *Commentary*, 130(1), (Jul/Aug), pp. 92–98.

Munday, J., 2008. *Introducing Translation Studies, Theories and Applications*. 2nd ed. London and New York: Routledge.

Nabokov, V., 1955. Problems of Translation: *Onegin* in English. In: L. Venuti, ed. 2004. *The Translation Studies Reader*. Abingdon and New York: Routledge, pp. 115–127.

- 1959. The Servile Path. In: R. Brower, ed. *On Translation*. New York: Oxford University Press, pp. 97–110.
- 2011. *Nikolai Gogol*. London: Penguin Classics.

Newmark, P., 1988. *A Textbook on Translation*. Hemel Hempstead: Prentice Hall International.

Nida, E., 1964. Principles of Correspondence. In: L. Venuti, ed. 2004. *The Translation Studies Reader*. Abingdon and New York: Routledge, pp. 153167.

O'Brien, J., 1959. From French to English. In: R. Brower, ed. *On Translation*. New York: Oxford University Press, pp. 78–92.

Oettinger, A., 1959, Automatic (Transference, Translation, Remittance, Shunting). In: R. Brower, ed. *On Translation*. New York: Oxford University Press, pp. 240–267.

Peaker, C., 2006. *Reading Revolution: Russian Émigrés and the Reception of Russian Literature in England, c. 1890–1905*. Ph.D. University of Oxford. Available at: <http://ora.ox.ac.uk/objects/uuid:c21af242-f696-4a7c-8f8e-5f9df9ea111c> [Accessed 26 January 2016].

Penguin Archive, Bristol: Bristol University Arts Library, Special Collections.

- Letter Rieu to Kitto, 21 October 1944, DM1938.
- Letter Glover to Seeley, 13 March 1947, DM1107/L23.
  - Letter Magarshack to Glover, 3 March 1949.
- Letter Magarshack to Glover, 18 June 1952, DM1107/L35.
- Letter Glover to Magarshack, 26 May 1954, DM1107/L40.
  - Letter Magarshack to Glover, 27 May 1954.
- Letter Cochrane to Duguid, 24 January 1964, DM1107/L143.
- Letter Joshua Cooper to Cochrane, 1 November 1970, DM1952/329/044/L258.

Poggioli, R., 1959. The Added Artificer. In: R. Brower, ed. *On Translation*. New York: Oxford University Press, pp. 137–147.

Postgate, J.P., 1922. *Translation and Translations, Theory and Practice*. London: G. Bell and Sons, Ltd.

Powell, A., 1958. Review. *Punch*, 234 (6137), 2 April, p. 459, [online] Available at: *Punch Historical Archive* <http://gdc.galegroup.com> [Accessed 30 July 2018].

Proffer, C.R., 1964. Dead Souls in Translation. In: *The Slavic and East European Journal*, 8(4), (Winter), pp. 420–433, [online] Available at: <http://www.jstor.org/stable/304423> [Accessed 13 June 2016].

Pym, A., and Ayvazyan, N., 2015. The Case of the Missing Russian Translation Theories. *Translation Studies*, 8(3), pp. 321–341. http://dx.doi.org/10.1080/14781700.2014.964300.

Quine, W., 1959. Meaning and Translation. In: R. Brower, ed. *On Translation*. New York: Oxford University Press, pp. 148–172.

Remnick, D., 2005. The Translation Wars, *The New Yorker* (7 November) <http://www.newyorker.com/archive/2005/11/07/051107fa_fact_remnick> [Accessed 30 September 2016].

Rieu, E.V., and Phillips, J.B., 1953. Translating the Gospels. *The Bible Translator*, 6(4) (October 1955), pp. 150–159.

Savory, T., 1968. *The Art of Translation*. London: Jonathan Cape.

Sela-Sheffy, R., 2008. The Translators' Personae: Marketing Translatorial Images as Pursuit of Capital, *Meta: Translators' Journal*, 53(3), pp. 609–622. Available at: <http://id.erudit.org/iderudit/019242ar> [Accessed 26 April 2017].

Selver, P., 1966. *The Art of Translating Poetry*. London: John Baker.

Sendich, M., 1999. *English Counter Russian. Essays on Criticism of Literary Translation in America*. New York: Peter Lang.

Simeoni, D., 1998. The Pivotal Status of the Translators' Habitus, *Target*, 10(1), pp. 1.39.

Steiner, G., 1975. *After Babel: Aspects of Language and Translation*. London: Oxford University Press.

Tolstoi, A., 1963. *Sobranie sochinenii* (5 vols.; Moscow), vol. iv, p. 214.

Tyulenev, S., 2015. A Response to 'The Case of the Missing Russian Translation Theories'. *Translation Studies,* 8(3), pp. 342–346. http://dx.doi.org/10.1080/147817 00.2014.996247.

Venuti, L., 1995. *The Translator's Invisibility*. London and New York: Routledge.

• 2004. *The Translation Studies Reader*. 2nd ed. Abingdon and New York: Routledge.

Vinay, J., and Darbelnet, J., 1958. Stylistique comparée du français et de l'anglais. Translated from French by J. Sager and M.-J. Hamel, 1995. In: L. Venuti, ed. 2004. *The Translation Studies Reader*. 2nd ed. Abingdon and New York: Routledge, pp. 128–137.

Walkowitz, R.L., 2007. Unimaginable Largeness: Kazuo Ishiguro, Translation, and the New World Literature. *Novel*, 40(3), p. 221. [pdf] Available at: <http://rci.rutgers.edu/~walkowit/pubs/UnimaginableLargenessNOVEL.pdf> [Accessed 21 October 2016].

Warden, C., 2019. "A Glimpse of 'Another Russia'": Elisaveta Fen's Chekhov Translations. *Theatre Survey*, 60 (3), pp.414–433.

Warner, N.O., 1986. The Footnote as Literary Genre: Nabokov's Commentaries to Lermontov and Puškin. *American Association of Teachers of Slavic and East European Languages,* 30(2), pp. 167–182, [online] Available at: <http://www.jstor.org/stable/307594> [Accessed 20 June 2016].

Whyte, C., 2015. Brodsky Translating Brodsky: Poetry in Self-Translation. By Alexandra Berlina, with a foreword by Robert Chandler, *Translation and Literature*, 24(2), pp. 283–286.

Ying, H., 2008. Footnotes like Skyscrapers, *Olympic Voices from China*, [online] Available at: <http://www.wordswithoutborders.org/article/footnotes-like-skyscrapers> [Accessed 25 April 2016].

Zabolotskii, N., 1954. Translator's Notes. Translated from Russian by N. Olshanskaya. In: B.J. Baer, and N. Olshanskaya, eds. 2013. *Russian Writers on Translation: An Anthology*. Manchester: St. Jerome, pp. 109–110.

3 Putting translation theory into practice

Introduction

The existence of Magarshack's theoretical reflections lends an extra dimension of analysis which can be applied to his works. It is rare for a translator to leave this much reflective material, but Magarshack's papers make it possible to explore the rationale behind some of the practical decisions he was consciously making in his translation process. We can also interpret this data in order to ascertain the extent to which his practice was influenced, even constrained, by his personal set of dispositions (his translatorial *hexis*) and the dispositions of the field, such as his good, but non-native English; his commitment to creating an image of Russia alternative to that generated by Garnett; his use of his position as a cultural gatekeeper to determine which culture-specific terms should be paraphrased or simply omitted. Given that Magarshack's livelihood was dependent on his (primarily Penguin) translations, and that his reputation and financial success were founded on his translation practice, textual analysis of his translations is essential for this case study. I shall, therefore, combine Magarshack's primary concerns and principles as outlined in his notes, lectures, interviews, and articles on translation theory with an analysis of his Penguin practice and professional idiosyncrasies as seen in his first Penguin commission, his 1951 translation of Dostoevskii's *Crime and Punishment*.

This chapter will ascertain whether Magarshack's image of Russia from an émigré perspective can be considered any more realistic than Garnett's. On a broader scale, I will gauge how representative Penguin's Russian Classics were of their original texts. I will analyse whether there were occasions when the essence of a source text might have been compromised for the sake of Rieu's aspirations to mass accessibility or for a translator's personal preferences, and, indeed, how significant these compromises were, provided that the translations met the immediate needs of their large and relatively uninitiated target readership. Finally, I shall examine observations on Magarshack's work by his reviewer contemporaries, and others made by reviewers since.

Although I will necessarily refer to other translations by Magarshack, the Penguin publication of *Crime and Punishment* is my primary interest for two particular reasons. First, there is considerable archival material for this translation because it was Magarshack's first Penguin commission and thus heralded a significant point in his career. This commission signified his move away from journalism and crime-writing and launched him instead into translation and biography-writing. Secondly, *Crime and Punishment* exemplifies a wide range of the textual complexities one would expect any translator of a Dostoevskii novel to face. In his own inimitable way, Nabokov summarised these complexities as 'the repetition of words and phrases, the intonation of obsession, the hundred-percent banality of every word, the vulgar soapbox eloquence' (Bowers, 1981, p. 78). Magarshack's *Crime and Punishment* is a good standard, therefore, for how he typically approached his translations of Dostoevskii (works by Dostoevskii accounted for four of Magarshack's seven Penguin translations), and also for evaluating later translators of Dostoevskii.

Magarshack in theory: aims of literary translation

The methods which Magarshack explained in his private papers and strove to implement in practice single him out from his Russian-English literary predecessors. However, they align him with later translation theorists and their preoccupations, as I will show below. When reading Magarshack's methodology in his notes on translation, it soon becomes possible to recognise which passages express the reality of his practice and which do not. At times, there is a disconnect between the two. There are plausible explanations for these disparities. Magarshack composed his views while looking back upon his career and on events in his personal life (emigration to the UK, his need to make a living, and his desire for self-validation and recognition). In this instance, the disparity may simply arise from the fact that his mental image of his experiences and achievements may have differed from reality, becoming distorted with the passage of time. The other consideration (drawing yet another historical parallel with Dostoevskii) is that Magarshack's professional practice was pressured. Translation was Magarshack's way of earning a living, and he worked with more than one publishing firm. This would have meant that in reality he spent less time on his projects than would have been the case if money and time were no object. Certainly, in his correspondence with Glover, Rieu referred to possible haste on Magarshack's part when assessing his draft manuscript for *Crime and Punishment*, 'I think he has made the thing very readable. But the TS [typescript] shows signs of hasty work, as I thought it would' (8 October 1949).

Both in his general notes on translation and in his book synopsis, Magarshack summarises the core values, as he perceived them, of the translator's job:

> Chief aim of translation: what matters in a work of art is living soul of the language which translator has to feel rather than apprehend

intellectually; a translation ought to produce same effect as the original work. (Synopsis, Magarshack, n.d.)

The principle of equivalence emerges as Magarshack's primary criterion by which to judge a "successful" translation, echoing Rieu's position and views from translation theory at the time (see Chapter Two). This is the same benchmark I shall also use to evaluate Magarshack's practice. In order to reach a combined overall effect of equivalence, Magarshack broke down the translator's key practical concerns and considerations into six main areas of work for the literary translator:

- Idioms
- Spurious Atmosphere
- Background
- Period Style
- Meaning of words
- Parts of speech

Failure to achieve equivalence in these areas was of great concern to Magarshack. Whereas Chukovskii saved his most cutting opinions for Fell's non-equivalence in translating Chekhov (1965–67, pp. 13–17), Magarshack saved the greatest share of his condemnation for Garnett. In 'Translation and the Individual Talent' (2006), Timothy D. Sergay draws attention to the tendency translators have exhibited down the decades of erasing the literary efforts and progress made by their translator predecessors (p. 38). Magarshack does not just erase Garnett's efforts at equivalence, he point- edly deconstructs them. One of his chief criticisms concerns the way in which Garnett's literal renderings fostered what he called a 'spurious atmos- phere' of incorrect information about the Russian people, culture, and way of life. Magarshack defined this phenomenon as when 'an English reader finds the work of a Russian author quaint, bizarre, and, as the phrase goes, "so Russian", then a new element has crept into the work of the Russian author which does not exist in the original' (General Principles, n.d., p. 16). He used Garnett's translation of Chekhov's *Diadia Vania* as an example; specifically, her rendering of Elena's parting words to Astrov. He wrote:

> "Nye pominayte likhom" as "Don't remember evil against me" ruins the whole scene, since no English speaking woman would say anything of the kind to a man she had confessed a minute ago that she was in love with, if indeed any English speaking woman would say anything of the kind to anyone. (Ibid, p. 14)

Rather than rely on a plain and easy, or literal, rendering of a nation's phraseology, and risk distorting the way in which the nation is regarded by the rest of the world, Magarshack believed that a truly competent

translator should capture the sense through accurate and careful paraphrase. In Magarshack's opinion, the translator's creation of a spurious
atmosphere perpetuates false impressions and national stereotypes, which
become accepted by the target culture and ultimately become extremely difficult to reverse. He wrote, for example, that:

> The phrase – the harsh realism of the great Russian classics – is one of
> the stock phrases one meets over and over again in serious English peri-
> odicals. That it is utterly false, that, for instance, Dostoevsky's great
> novels are full of laughter as well as tragedy, has yet to be proved to the
> English reader. (n.d., p. 18)

It is clear from his notes how keenly Magarshack felt that power, influence,
and responsibility are vested in the translator to convey a faithful likeness
of the original text, but not a literal copy. He argues that Garnett's literal renderings created a distorted image of the Russian as 'incompetent,
gloom-sodden, bizarre, and even grotesque' which has 'become so generally
accepted that it even colours the views of serious authors on Russian affairs'
(ibid., pp. 17–18), although he does not give examples of such authors or
affairs.

In his second edition of *Tolstoy or Dostoevsky* (1967), George Steiner wrote
that Magarshack's Dostoevskii translations 'supersede those that have
gone before'. Rachel May made more detailed assessment of Magarshack's
achievements:

> Most notable among the new popularizers of Russian literature
> was Magarshack, whose translations, most notably for Penguin
> Books, became almost as ubiquitous as those of Constance Garnett.
> Magarshack's approach, which still shows some tendency toward clari-
> fication and simplification of style, is more sympathetic than Garnett's
> to psychological complexities in the various characters. He allows their
> syntax to remain confused, breaks up their sentences with exclamations
> and repetitions, and otherwise avoids smoothing out their language.
> (1994, pp.43–45)

In his review of Magarshack's translation of *The Idiot* in *The Slavic and
East European Journal* (1958), George Gibian compared Magarshack
with Garnett too, remarking that 'again and again […] in descriptions,
narrative, and particularly dialogue, Magarshack is idiomatic and fluent,
whereas Constance Garnett puts an undesirable, even if only thin, cur-
tain of awkwardness and unnaturalness between the reader and the novel'
(p. 153). Magarshack advised translators – if they aspired to deal with idioms in a thoughtful and creative way – to immerse themselves fully in the
living language. The careful selection of a comparable target equivalent
might be one way of dealing with the idiom, where one source idiom is

exchanged for a comparable target idiom. Alternatively, if appropriate, a Russian literary reference can be matched with an equivalent English one, a strategy of translation by cultural substitution (Baker, 1992, p. 31). On this point, Magarshack cited the example of Gogol's intertextual reference to Griboedov's *The Misfortune of Being Too Clever* ('Zephyrs and amours') and suggested exchanging Griboedov for Shakespeare, using the Hamlet quote 'Primrose path of dalliance' instead (General Principles, n.d., p. 19). In the absence of an idiomatic target equivalent, or even out of a desire to draw the reader's attention to a specific expression from the source text and thus hopefully retain some of the original flavour, Magarshack advised the translator to turn to Pearsall Smith, Sterne, and Dr. Johnson, all of whom advocated 'new-minting' an expression in the target language if necessary (ibid., p. 15). However, it is worth remembering that Magarshack's Russian was used only in a translation capacity and his literary English was very much a desk-bound phenomenon (Magarshack, 2015). This means that his languages would not, perhaps, have been as fresh as he himself advocated. Let us now draw on a textual approach, therefore, and analyse translational aspects from selected passages in Magarshack's Penguin translation of *Crime and Punishment*. A traditional text-based analysis will enable us to assess whether May's and Gibian's views of Magarshack's skill compared to Garnett's are well-founded, or whether Donald Rayfield's appraisal in the *TLS* might prove more accurate (that 'Dostoevsky does not suffer too much from David Magarshack's version, standard since the 1950s, its blandness notwithstanding' (2018)). Text-based analysis will also allow us to evaluate the extent to which Magarshack's practice concurred with his own translation theory.

Penguin's re-voicing of Dostoevskii's *Crime and Punishment*

Dostoevskii incorporated a range of stylistic devices in order to create a polyphony of character idiolects. Nicolas Pasternak Slater, translator of Oxford University Press's 2017 version of *Crime and Punishment*, described Dostoevskii's dialogue as 'the most difficult part of the novel to translate, but at the same time one of the most rewarding' (cited in *The Bloggers Karamazov*, 2018). Among the literary devices which Dostoevskii utilised to construct character voices are idiomatic and colloquial expressions – used by Marmeladov, Porphirii, and more peripheral characters (Razumikhin, Lebeziatnikov, Nastas'ia, and Koch, etc.); humorous accents or manners; and minor characters with exaggerated foreign accents such as Mrs. Lippewechsel, Louisa Ivanovna, and "Achilles", the policeman who witnesses Svidrigailov's suicide. When rendering idiomatic expressions, Magarshack attempted, in most cases, to match the sense of a source text idiom with a comparable phrase, but without necessarily employing a matching idiom. For example, in Part One, Chapter Three,

Magarshack embellishes Dostoevskii's description of Nastas'ia – '[она] смеялась неслышно, колыхаясь и трясясь всем телом' (1973, p. 26) – with an Anglicised idiom, 'she laughed silently, rocking to and fro and shaking like a jelly' in order to embolden the imagery. A neutral translation of the original would be: '[she] laughed silently, rocking and shaking her whole body'; Magarshack introduced an idiomatic simile for heightened effect. He enhanced idiomatic imagery elsewhere, always to heighten suspense or melodrama:

> 'Гм, это правда', - продолжал он, следуя за вихрем мыслей, крутившимся в его голове (Part One, Chapter Four, 1973, p. 36)
> 'Hmm, it's true – he continued, following a whirlwind of thoughts, which swirled in his head' (literal translation)
> 'Well, I suppose that's true enough,' he continued, following the train of his thoughts, which went whirling through his brain like a blizzard' (1951, p. 59)

Here the 'whirlwind' ['вихрь'] is original, but Magarshack has incorporated 'like a blizzard' for additional emphasis, and has also changed the original order to introduce the English expression 'train of thought'. These two examples illustrate Magarshack's theory that:

> Each idiom had therefore better be considered within its context. The translator must not only grasp the full dramatic implications of the Russian idiomatic phrase, but be able to re-live the emotions for each particular situation. (General Principles, n.d., p. 15)

Where the idiom in the source text presented some difficulty, Magarshack either compensated for the absence of an immediate idiomatic match by augmenting the remainder of the sentence – a strategy which Sendich recognises in *The Idiot* as one of Magarshack's 'most obvious' (1999, p. 141) – or he subdued the diction in order to concentrate on conveying the essence of the source message. In the case of the latter technique, rather than attempt to replicate all source text subtleties (via emphatic markers and verbal colloquialisms) in English, Magarshack constructed a more conservative mood through his lexical choices. Take, for example, the following passage in Part Six, Chapter Four, when Svidrigailov is discussing with Raskolnikov his intentions to marry the sixteen-year-old Resslich daughter:

> 'А что ж? Непременно. Всяк об себе сам промышляет и всех веселей тот и живёт кто всех лучше себя сумеет надуть. Ха-ха! *Да что вы в добродетель-то так всем дышлом въехали?* Пощадите, батюшка, я человек грешный. Хе-хе-хе!' (1973, p. 370) (My italics here, and below, highlight the idiomatic pitch of the passage)

The passage translates literally as:

> 'Well, and so what? Absolutely. Each looks after himself and the one
> who lives happiest is the one who can hoodwink himself the best. Ha-ha!
> *And what's making you go headlong at virtue, battering ram and all?* Give
> me a break, father, I am a sinful person. Ha-ha-ha!'

Ready's translation captures the idiomatic flavour of the original, and also
remains true to the sense:

> 'Why on earth not? Most definitely. Every man must look after him-
> self and no one has more fun than the man who deceives himself best.
> Ha-ha! *What are you doing charging at virtue with a battering ram?* Be
> merciful, father. I'm just a sinner. Heh-heh-heh!' (2015, p. 577)

Contrast Magarshack's version:

> 'Why not? I shall most certainly marry her. Everyone thinks of himself,
> and he who deceives himself best, lives merriest. Ha, ha! *And what have
> you suddenly become so virtuous for?* Spare me, my dear fellow, I am a
> miserable sinner. Ha, ha, ha!' (1951, p. 493)

Magarshack's rendering 'And what have you suddenly become so virtuous
for?' conveys the meaning, yet by choosing to omit '*vsem dyshlom*' from
the original (Ready's 'battering ram'), he fails to evoke the same expressive effect. Magarshack's omission leads to a tempering of Svidrigailov's
idiolect and also, therefore, of his characterisation. In another example,
from Part One, Chapter Six, Magarshack chose the expression 'making
speeches' (1951, p. 85) to render 'ораторствуешь' (1973, p. 55). Magarshack's
safe lexical choice lacks the vibrancy of the source verb, which could be
rendered by more colloquially evocative verbs like 'spout off', 'mouth off',
or, even the rather fitting and vernacular 'speechify' (Ready, 2015, p. 81),
a lexical decision which augments characterisation. In a similar instance,
Ready again matches Dostoevskii's idiomatic reference to the character
Zametov in Part Two, Chapter Four, 'руки греет' (1973, p. 104), which translates literally as '[he] warms his hands'. Ready uses a comparably idiomatic
colloquialism 'With a greasy palm' (2015, p. 161), whereas Magarshack's
'[t]akes bribes, though' (1951, p. 151) lacks the force of the original.
Dostoevskii actively emphasises this idiom, repeating it three times in quick
succession; Magarshack's smooth rendering diminishes the colloquial richness of the source text. Some of Magarshack's lexical choices, therefore,
lead to textbook use of language, rather than the 'living language' which he
repeatedly prescribed in his notes.

In Part One, Chapter One of *Crime and Punishment*, Dostoevskii uses
a simile where Raskolnikov is pondering the merits of getting back to his

room without alerting his landlady to his presence. The phrase he uses is 'лучше проскользнуть [...] кошкой' (1973, p. 6), translated literally as 'better to steal by like a cat'. Dostoevskii repeats this feline metaphor in Part One, Chapter Six when Raskolnikov is setting off on his journey to the pawnbroker: 'осторожно, неслышно, как кошка' (ibid., p. 57), which translates literally as 'carefully, soundlessly, like a cat'. In each case, Magarshack adopts more typically Anglophone collocations, choosing to shift his focus from cat to mouse: 'as quietly as a mouse' (1951, p. 19) and 'taking the utmost care to be as quiet as a mouse' (ibid., p. 88). On the surface, Magarshack's renderings may appear to convey the silence of Raskolnikov's movements and, therefore, be technically correct, but they lack the source text's cat-like stealth, the very quality most suited to Raskolnikov the murderer. By playing cat-and-mouse with Dostoevskii's lexical intentions, no matter how subtle, Magarshack has unwittingly diminished Dostoevskii's message. He subscribes to a degree of 'qualitative impoverishment' described by Antoine Berman as 'the replacement of terms, expressions and figures in the original with terms, expressions and figures that lack their sonorous richness or, correspondingly, their signifying or "iconic" richness' (1985, p. 283). In the same way that he accused Garnett of doing with her '*pochemu nyet*' (see Chapter Two), Magarshack created his own spurious atmosphere regarding Russians and their emotional responses. In sociological terms, it could be said that Magarshack's lexical choices compromise the classic Russian literary mood, the *illusio*. The translation scholar Jean-Marc Gouanvic notes the following with regard to French translators of US science-fiction novels:

> The translator's task is to deliver the novel's rhetoric, and to do so with a similar plausibility to that of the original [...]. If the translator does not perform his or her task, the translated text will not contain the same *illusio* potential as the original. This would lead the work to be 'unsuccessful' [...]. (2010, p. 127)

It is possible that Magarshack was attempting to Anglicise his lexis to suit Penguin's stylistic norms. As a former crime-writer, he would have been aware of Penguin's penchant for Agatha Christie's novels, for example, and he was equally aware of her commercial success (Yates, 2006, p. 33). But by modulating Dostoevskii's style in this way, Magarshack compromised some of the Russianness of the source text. Sendich remarks that '[i]n his efforts to convey the most minute tonalities of the original, Magarshack has occasionally ruined the style' (1999, p. 141). He has 'Englished' (Fitzpatrick, 2007) the text in his own way, which cannot go unnoticed. Penguin's reply to the US reader Richard D. Mical, who was 'uncomfortable' about Magarshack's British-English rendering of *Crime and Punishment*, makes quite clear that Penguin felt no concern about Magarshack's Anglicisms or about the ethno-centric position of the Penguin publishing house. Penguin editor James Cochrane replied, 'David Magarshack's translation was certainly intended for a British audience and I wonder what you had in mind when you expressed doubts about that' (13 January 1966). It is not just the reading public who noticed the Englishness of Magarshack's translations, though; critical reviewers commented on his 'Englished' style too. On 8 April 1965, the *TLS* reviewed his Faber and Faber translation of Chekhov's *Platonov*. After fleetingly thanking Magarshack for providing the first ever full version of the play, the anonymous reviewer proceeds to criticise him. First, Magarshack is attacked for being 'less than charitable towards Mr. D. Makaroff's version of 1961', recalling Sergay's observation that each translator, looking back on their predecessors' efforts, should do so with respect or else expect to suffer criticism themselves at some point (2006, p. 39). The reviewer's main accusation, however, is that Magarshack's translation is:

> [...] perfectly readable but scarcely speakable; it has been translated into a bastard idiom that is not colloquial English and never was. Much of Mr. Magarshack's version seems to aim at an Edwardian or Victorian diction such as might have been spoken in Chekhov's lifetime. This is an obvious and legitimate approach, but requires far more careful treatment than one might expect: only a master of pastiche could nowadays manage it successfully. In Platonov the cumbrous Victorianisms tend towards bathos [...].

Magarshack would have disliked this accusation. In 'General Principles', Magarshack specifically points out the need to *avoid* period English when translating classic Russian literature, which suggests that, in practice, he himself was aspiring to create a very different effect:

> Why, if Shakespeare is translated into modern Russian, should Gogol be translated into early nineteenth century English? The advocates of this procedure fail to perceive two things; first that the translator is as much a child of his age as the original author was a child of his. Consequently, if he is to transmute a Russian work of art into an English one, he can only do so in the language of his time. Secondly, a translator is writing for the people of his own day and [...] to obtain the utmost response from his public, he has to write in the language they speak and not in the language their fathers or forefathers spoke. (n.d., p. 20)

Criticism of translating Russian into 'period' English has tended on the whole to be directed at Garnett. Brodskii observed caustically that '[t]he reason English-speaking readers can barely tell the difference between Tolstoy and Dostoevsky is that they aren't reading the prose of either one. They're reading Constance Garnett' (Rodensky, 2013, p. 224). More than merely confirming Magarshack's view of Garnett, Brodskii's remark also confirms Magarshack's own earlier concerns about the Anglophone world's skewed vision and reception of Russian literature. The criticism levelled at

Magarshack in his *Platonov* review tars him with the same brush as Garnett. However, in Magarshack's Dostoevskii translations, one senses that he was consciously trying to create an equivalent literary style, one which would convey an impression to the modern reader that was simultaneously true to Dostoevskii and relatively domesticated. Magarshack achieved this style more consistently than did Garnett. Peter France, in 'Dostoevskii Rough and Smooth' (1996), endorses this view:

> Garnett's prose was seen as somewhat too formal and Edwardian. So the versions of several novels produced by David Magarshack, and subsequently published by Penguin Books, tend to bring Dostoevskii's voices into line with modern English usage; the result is readable, but even more domesticated than Garnett's. (p. 76)

The *TLS* reviewer's notion that Magarshack was trying to capture a Victorian or Edwardian diction may have arisen from Magarshack's treatment of idiomatic expressions which, as we have seen in the above examples, were not entirely successful in reflecting the emotional range or energy of the source text. As the critics' opinions show, not everyone liked Magarshack's style or deemed it successful, but May at least acknowledges Magarshack's attempts to capture different conversational styles and voices in the text:

> David Magarshack's translations of Russian classics are more attentive to the stylistic idiosyncracies [sic] of the various authors and to the voices within the texts. [...] Garnett's version stays closer to the meaning of the words but strays much further from their effect. [...] Magarshack's is more impetuous in his speech, less grammatical – (possibly too much like a London barfly) – and far more believable. (1994, p. 44)

Taking into account France's and May's references to Dostoevskii's voices, and the anonymous reviewer's accusation of a bathetic 'bastard idiom', we can deduce that Magarshack was at least striving to achieve a new form of characterisation through the vehicle of language. He did not apply 'period' English as such, but regional, modern English, recognisable to the Penguin general reader. Magarshack perceived his style of English as one that made the text more easily accessible and alive to the target reader. He made his desire for domesticated translations known when he was interviewed by W.J. Igoe for the *Chicago Tribune*, remarking that he wanted his work to be 'Englished as a work of imagination' (1963, p. 3). Magarshack domesticated dialogue in a way which Garnett never attempted. In order to convey the polyphony present in Dostoevskii's original novel in such a way as to be accessible to the modern reader, Magarshack combined the old with the new. He did this by imparting idiomatic Englishness to Dostoevskii's characters, for example to Marmeladov with his comic bombast; to the servant

Nastas'ia with her deliberate Victorian-style vernacular ('I'll fetch you the bread in a jiffy, sir; but wouldn't you rather have some cabbage soup instead of sausage? I've some lovely cabbage soup left over from yesterday. Kept it specially for you, I did', p. 46); and to Razumikhin with his educated student voice ('you see, Roddy, I admit that you're a clever fellow, only you're a damn fool all the same!' p. 187, and 'What rot!' p. 269). Magarshack wrote that the translator must avoid 'current slang or colloquialism of England or America' (General Principles, n.d., p. 1), and yet he experimented with British vernacular when voicing peripheral characters. Consequential characters in *Crime and Punishment* adopt hybrid forms of diction. Some – like the madam Mrs. Lippewechsel and Louisa Ivanovna – speak in character with Anglicised, at times almost comedic, German ('"Oh *mein Gott!*" she threw up her arms in dismay. "Your husband vos drunk and by horses vos run over! To ze *Spital* viz him! I'm ze landlady here!"' (1951, p. 200)). Others – the tavern landlord, for example, who jeers Marmeladov in Part One, Chapter One, and the onlookers at the horse flogging in Raskolnikov's dream in Part One, Chapter Five – switch between the correct register of classic literature and the inflections associated with May's 'London barfly' (1994, p. 44). The barfly intonations are comparatively few and tentative in *Crime and Punishment*, but the landlord's quips and the anonymous crowd's accusations of Mikolka in Raskolnikov's dream represent the genesis of a voice which will become recognisably associated with the lower classes in Magarshack's future Dostoevskii translations:

> 'What a comic!' the landlord said in a loud voice. 'And why ain't you working? Why ain't you got a job, seeing as how you're a civil servant?' (1951, p. 30)
> 'Aye, you ain't got the fear of God in you after all' (Ibid., p. 77)

By the time Magarshack translated *The Idiot* (1955) for Penguin, he was ready to equip a key character, Rogozhin, with a more sustained 'barfly' voice. He achieved this voice by introducing double negatives and the occasional use of "ain't", a speech pattern often associated either with the regional, colloquial dialect of someone from the South East of England (Pearce, 2007, pp. 173–4), or with anyone who is unaware of the grammatical norms of 'correct' English. The result is that Magarshack's Rogozhin, and other occasional background characters, end up speaking a pseudo-Bill Sikes dialect ('You won't do nothing of the kind' (Dickens, 2007, p. 369), 'there ain't a stauncher-hearted gal going' (p. 376–7)). In this respect, Magarshack's approach resembles that of Edmonds in *The Cossacks* (1960). Edmonds also infused her text with regional dialect in order 'to represent the peasants' speech, which is very different from normal Russian' (Rieu, 8 August 1959). According to Rieu's internal memorandum of 23 July 1959, her attempts are 'a sort of mixture of Devon and Cockney' with which he was not entirely happy. He advised Edmonds of the need for some revision.

In his final note on the subject to 'DLD' [Duguid], Rieu wrote that 'her revision is a considerable improvement, though I have pointed out one or two minor inconsistencies. I have also suggested the addition of a note on this dialect and the manner in which she has attempted to present it in translation' (11 August 1959). The Penguin archive does not contain Edmonds's first typescript showing her attempts to render dialogue before Rieu's suggestions and her published version does not contain either of Rieu's suggested notes in the front of her book. What is interesting, however, in light of Rieu's comments to Edmonds, is that Henry Gifford specifically singled out Edmonds's efforts at rendering dialogue as being particularly effective. It is also curious that no such critical comments appear about hybrid dialogue in Penguin's correspondence with Magarshack.

Magarshack's and Edmonds's strategy for rendering dialogue is akin to a method of translation which Chukovskii criticised as 'vulgarized translation' (*'vulgarizatorskikh perevodcheskikh metodov'* (1968, Chapter Five)). Chukovskii, representing the Soviet tradition, was not alone in criticising this method. From the Western Translation Studies tradition, Berman expresses similar concerns about attempts to transfer a vernacular:

> The effacement of vernaculars is thus a very serious injury to the textuality of prose works. [...] Unfortunately, a vernacular clings tightly to its soil and completely resists any direct translating into another vernacular. [...] An exoticization that turns the foreign from abroad into the foreign at home winds up merely ridiculing the original. (1985, p. 286)

Had the strategy been applied consistently, Magarshack's efforts might have resulted in masterful characterisations of Dostoevskii's characters. There are, however, incongruous moments in Magarshack's vernacular creations, which sound too cultured and refined for their actors and prevent Magarshack's creativity from succeeding. (The roguish and characteristically coarse-mouthed Rogozhin refers to Myshkin repeatedly as 'old man' and asks 'Hark, do you hear?' (1955, p. 655) for example.) Incongruities aside, it is commendable of Magarshack (and Edmonds in *The Cossacks* too) to attempt to transfer idiolect into another language in anything like a comparable and convincing way, not least of all because Magarshack, as an émigré, could only base such insider knowledge of language on observation, not on 'cradle' colloquialisms. Even his wife, Elsie – North Yorkshire-born and Cambridge-educated – would no doubt have struggled to write convincingly in (or even advise her husband on) localised South-East diction. What is perhaps important at this time was the attempt to stretch translation norms, and the fact that Magarshack – as his notes on translation theory also indicate – was consciously striving to break Garnett's rigid, formulaic mould (correct English, one Edwardian voice serves all); France endorses this view in his acknowledgement that Magarshack was trying to 'bring Dostoevskii's voices into line with modern English usage' (1996, p. 76).

The difficulty in bringing Dostoevskii's voices into the modern day continues. Connor Doak's review of Ready's Penguin re-translation of *Crime and Punishment* describes the rendering of Dostoevskii's dialogue as 'perhaps Ready's greatest achievement [in this translation]' (2015, p. 299), conveying the 'energy and the colloquialism of the original Russian' (ibid.). Ready's renderings capture more colour than his predecessors' efforts, but the problem of hybrid diction persists. Like Magarshack, Ready has applied a vernacular effect to the diction of Dostoevskii's lesser characters but, rather than conforming to village diction as the source text indicates in Part One, Chapter Six, the maidservant Nastas'ia adopts a South-East, Dickensian intonation, for example, 'You says you used to teach children – so why ain't you doing nothing now' (p. 36), 'Are you sick or ain't you?' and 'Are you or ain't you eating?' (p. 83). The occasional use of Anglicisms in dialogue from various characters (and in the narrative) – 'Load of cobblers!' (p. 30), 'A fine pickle!' (p. 60), 'Mummy' (p. 69), 'poppycock' (p. 240), 'A smashing lad! A smashing lad!' (p. 533), 'ragamuffin' (p. 603) – not only 'raises the unwelcome spectre of Constance Garnett' (Bird, 2014, p. 5), but also jolts the reader from an otherwise convincingly Dostoevskian narrative. In Part Two, Chapter Six, Ready makes a bystander wail over a suicidal woman in a mixture of Yorkshire, Scottish, and, again, South-East inflections in the space of two sentences:

> Only t'other day she tried to do herself in, and we had to take the noose off her. I was only going to the shop just now, left my wee girl to keep an eye on 'er – and look! (p. 205)

Contrast Magarshack's stylistically neutral, and internally consistent, version:

> Tried to hang herself the other day, she did. Just cut her down in time. I ran out to a shop, left my little girl to look after her – but she's gone and done it again! (p. 189)

For a contemporary counterpart to Ready's version, I cite Pasternak Slater's rendering of the same passage. Like Magarshack, he produces a concise and conversational effect, still in keeping with the *illusio* of nineteenth-century literature but without relying on the unstable, if courageous, device of dialect:

> The other day she tried to hang herself, we cut her down. I'd just gone out to the shop, and left my little girl to look after her – and now look what she's done! (2017, p. 153)

The issue of how far, or whether, dialogue should be domesticated is one which separates Magarshack, Edmonds, and Ready from the Soviet translation tradition. Here they deviate from Chukovskii's translation theory, which Magarshack otherwise quoted with full approval. In *Vysokoe iskusstvo*, Chukovskii wrote of the absurdity and incompatibility of having English mouths speak 'ineffably' Russian words – 'напрасно влагает в уста англичанам русские простонародные слова' (Part One, Chapter Five) – such as '*tiaten'ka, mol, uzho, inda* [...] and it is strange to read how British ladies and gentlemen tell each other *batiushka* and *tiu-tiu!*' (1965–67, p. 99). The same notion also works in reverse: Russian characters should not adopt local, British diction or Anglicised names. Chukovskii ridicules such practices thus:

> The result is as if Dickens's Mr. Squeers, and Lord Mulberry Hawk and Lord Verisopht were so many Ivan Trofimoviches living in Kolomna and passing themselves off as Englishmen when they are really straight out of Saltykov-Shchedrin or Ostrovsky. (Ibid.)

At the same time, it is possible that Magarshack, Edmonds, and Ready might have earned some Soviet recognition for attempting to avoid *gladkopis*, or 'blandscript' (Leighton, 1991, p. 91) in their dialogue by injecting colloquial colour. Magarshack was certainly aware of the translator's difficulty of capturing idiolect; he wrote in his taxonomy (see Chapter Two):

> Problem of Creation of Literary Types: Characteristic Speech of Any Character in Original has to be carefully re-created: translator therefore must possess flexible and versatile command of words: he has no right to impoverish author's language. (n.d., p. 4)

Aside from dialect and domesticated dialogue, Magarshack's translation of *Crime and Punishment* demonstrates a number of other domesticating techniques, which also appear in his other Dostoevskii translations. He employed recognisably British-flavoured references throughout the novel such as, for example: 'comic fellow' (p. 30), 'a veritable Bedlam' (p. 34), 'in a jiffy' and 'Oh, blast' (p. 46), 'dirty ruffian' (p.65), 'a few *yards* from the last *kitchen-garden* in the town stood a *pub*' (p. 73, my italics); 'rotter' (p. 142), 'a crafty rascal' (p. 194), 'you're a nice chap, but [...] you're a bit of a rake, and a dirty rake at that' (p. 225). Such stylised lexis only appears within dialogue; rarely, if ever, does it form part of the narrative. Thus, over the course of the entire novel, there is a combined overall impression of English domestication. Gibian (1958, p. 153) noted this same tendency in his review of Magarshack's translation *The Idiot*, drawing parallels between Garnett's and Magarshack's Britishisms ('Cricket terms (Garnett: bowled over, Magarshack: stumped),[1] and English words (pavement for sidewalk) abound').

References to everyday Russian *realia* are also frequently shorn of their foreignness, as if the setting of the book should largely conform to

British-style living. The pawnbroker Alyona Ivanovna is described in the opening chapter as wearing a rather complicated-sounding 'old, tattered fur-lined jacket, yellow with age' (1951, p. 23) rather than the neat 'истрепанная и пожелтелая меховая кацавейка' (1973, p. 8) from the original (literally 'a frayed, yellowed, fur-lined *katsaveika*'); and in Part One, Chapter Five, Magarshack explains the culture-specific funeral dish *kutya* (p. 73) by paraphrase. These are both examples where Magarshack's decision to paraphrase, rather than provide a footnote, results in a clumsy or verbose translation. Magarshack domesticates the Russian preference for eating horseradish (хрен) on its own – which Marmeladov refers to in Part One, Chapter Two – into a more recognisably British condiment: 'horseradish sauce' (p. 37); the Russian soup *shchi* (щи) becomes 'cabbage soup' (p. 46); and Pulkheria Raskolnikov's reference in the original to the holy Feast of the Assumption (госпожинок) becomes a secular calendar date 'August 15th' (p. 56), shorn of all religiosity. Like Gibian, Leighton recognised the regularity of Britishisms in Magarshack's work from as early as his translation of *Crime and Punishment*:

> [...] a translation characterized by overly obvious British words and expressions sounds artificial to an American, while a strongly Americanized translation becomes an irritant to British readers. In either case, the reader begins to question the language of the original text [...]. [...] Magarshack's Britishisms are too obvious. 'Oh rot!' 'I daresay,' 'what a funny crowd you all are' – these choices are too inimitably British to sound natural in a novel by Dostoyevsky. (1991, p. 137)

Magarshack, keen to convey himself as bilingual gatekeeper, made Russian literature easy for his readers. As can be discerned from his notes on translation, the proliferation of 'overly obvious British words and expressions' should be interpreted as surface manifestations of Magarshack's background. By demonstrating an impressive, native command of his adopted language, dextrously used as a way of recoding Russian culture to suit his British reader (and satisfying Magarshack's British commissioning publisher), Magarshack was also communicating to his host country a willingness to integrate and a deservedness to be accepted and regarded as a literary success in the UK.

Where terms pose a problem of equivalence, Magarshack provided a polished and paraphrased, but often neutralised, version. In these instances, the culture-specific subtleties of the original are often lost, replaced by a more pedestrian paraphrase. Magarshack's preference for paraphrase over explanatory notes for his readers aligns him with Rieu's personal position on footnotes and with Penguin's informed view that 'there are a large number of readers who feel offended by what they regard as an insult to their general culture'.[2] Edmonds, on the other hand, struck a less dogmatic approach, making very occasional use of footnotes where she deemed necessary.

Only one note is used in *Anna Karenin*, for example, but for *The Cossacks*, she used several concise notes in order to explain culture-specific Caucasian or Cossack lexis.

Magarshack's avoidance of footnotes points to his support for the Soviet belief in translatability. As Leighton explains:

> Soviet translators excel at solving problems of translation. This is one reason for their high standards. They cannot and do not claim to have solved all problems satisfactorily, but it can be said that Soviet translators put many problems in their place. [...] By putting problems behind them in this way, Soviet translators have freed themselves to address problems that have not yet been approached or that have been avoided in other worlds. (1991, p. 120)

As shown already in Chapter Two, Nabokov's translation of Pushkin's *Eugene Onegin*, with its copious use of the footnote, is popularly regarded as a model of literalism, *bukvalizm*, the polar opposite of the Soviet translation tradition (ibid., p. 180). On this basis, therefore, Magarshack's translations can be more closely aligned to the techniques of Soviet translators. For Magarshack, the footnote was out of bounds, it was a 'translator's confession of failure' (General Principles, n.d., pp. 19–20):

> To obtrude a Russian word in the English text and then add a long footnote to 'explain' it, seems a curiously topsy-turvy sort of proceeding, since there is no reason why the explanation should not be embodied in the text. (Ibid.)

However, the question of tackling untranslatability through intratextual expansion appears, in some cases, to have resulted in a strategy of translation by omission instead for Magarshack, no doubt in an attempt to smoothe syntax and provide an easier read. See, for example, the scene in Part One, Chapter Two when Marmeladov's confession monologue to Raskolnikov is interrupted:

> [И] раздались у входа звуки нанятой шарманки и детский, надтреснутий семилетний голосок, певший 'Хуторок'. (1973, p. 18)
> [And] from the entrance, the sounds carried of a rented barrel-organ accompanied by a small, cracked, seven-year-old voice which sang 'Khutorok'. (literal translation)

Magarshack omitted the finer details to produce a smoother syntax and an easier read:

> [...] and from the entrance to the pub came the shrill voice of a seven-year-old boy singing a popular song. (1951, pp. 36–37)

By contrast, Ready's version provides the original's message in entirety and even includes a footnote about the song which is being performed:

> [...] and the sounds of a rented barrel organ and a cracked, seven-year-old voice singing 'Little Farm' carried over from the entrance. (p. 25)

As Baker observes, the strategy of omission is not harmful *per se* (1992, p. 40); in the above example, the risk is mainly that of descriptive loss, or erosion. Descriptive loss can become harmful, however, when the omitted information is crucial to the novel's dénouement. In 1978, Penguin Australia received a letter of enquiry from Grant Wallace, a lecturer at Heywood High School, Victoria, who wrote:

> Recently, I was discussing <u>Crime and Punishment</u> with my form 6 literature class when I came upon two lines which were not in the copies that the students had.
>
> I particularly noted the difference because this early reference to Lazarus (mentioned in the two lines) is taken up again a few chapters later when Raskolnikov pleads with Sonia to read out the passage about Lazarus from the Bible. The inclusion of the two lines is essential to the understanding that the police inspector has caused Raskolnikov to think seriously about redemption. I am curious to know why the two lines are present in the 1969 reprint and not in the 1977 reprint. (04 August 1978)

The two lines from Part Three, Chapter Five to which Wallace refers appear in the source text (in my italics) in the following section:

– И-и-и в бога веруете? Извините, что так любопытствую.
– Верую, - повторил Раскольников поднимая глаза на Порфирия.
– И-и-и в воскресение Лазаря веруете?
– Ве-верую. Зачем вам все это?
– Буквально веруете?
– Буквально. (1973, p. 201)
– A-a-a-and, do you believe in God? Excuse my curiosity.
– I believe, - repeated Raskolnikov, lifting his eyes towards Porfirii.
– *A-a-a-and in the raising of Lazarus, do you believe?*
– *I-I-I believe. What's all this to you?*
– Do you believe in it literally?
– Literally.
     (literal translation, my italics)

Ready (2015, p. 313) renders this passage in full (with my italics) as:

> 'And... you believe in God? Please forgive my curiosity'.
> 'I do', repeated Raskolnikov, lifting his eyes towards Porfiry.

'And... you believe in the raising of Lazarus?'
'I... do. But why are you asking?'
'You believe in it literally?'
'Literally'.

Magarshack's rendering, however – appearing in the first edition in 1951 up to 1969, and then again after 1977 – offered the following redacted exchange between Porfirii and Raskolnikov, where no mention of Lazarus is made:

'And – do you believe in God? I'm sorry to be so curious'.
'I do', replied Raskolnikov, raising his eyes to Porfiry.
'Literally?'
'Literally'. (1951, p. 278)

Wallace's observation is, therefore, correct. According to Penguin Classics editor Will Sulkin's reply, the omission was not an error but was, in fact, a conscious decision on Magarshack's part:

I'm afraid I can only go some way in answering your query. That is to say our files suggest that it was quite a deliberate step on the part of the translator, David Magarshack to remove the two lines in question – that he asked for this 'correction' to be made. What we don't have on file is an account of his motives. Nor, of course, can I refer this to Mr. Magarshack who died some time ago! (18 August 1978)

It is perhaps on account of such a significant omission that David McDuff, Penguin's next Dostoevskii translator (see Chapter Four), committed himself to restoring Dostoevskii's 'sound, tone and timbre' and attempting 'to echo in English the syntax and word order of the Russian' (France, 2000, p. 596). He achieved this aim with varying success, however. According to France, 'the resulting English sometimes seems distinctly odd – deliberately so, of course'. Regarding McDuff's replacement Dostoevskii translations for Penguin, France notes that 'At times, the convoluted style might make the reader unfamiliar with Dostoevsky's Russian question the translator's command of English. More seriously, this literalism means that the dialogue is sometimes impossibly odd – and as a result rather dead' (ibid.). From McDuff's version of *Crime and Punishment*, France might include the following examples of laboured dialogue between characters such as the tavern landlord and Marmeladov ('"Hey funny man! [...] Why don't you do any work, why don't you do any serving, if you're a civil servant?"' (McDuff, 1991, p. 44)); between Raskolnikov and Nastas'ia ('"One can't go and give lessons to children if one doesn't have any boots. Oh, in any case, I don't give a spit."' (ibid., p. 62), and between Mikolka and the crowd in the horse dream ('"Flog her to death!" cried Mikolka. "It's come to that. I'll do it myself!"' (ibid., p. 92)).

Above all other translation strategies, the domestication of Russian names is perhaps the most discussed of Magarshack's techniques among reviewers. Reviews of the time appear uncertain about whether Magarshack should have strayed so far from translation tradition with his British adaptation of Russian names, which involved increasing the usage of Mr., Mrs., and Miss and significantly reducing the frequency with which source text patronymics were faithfully transferred. In de Mauny's *TLS* review for Magarshack's translation of *The Devils* (1953), he distinguished Magarshack's work from Garnett's on the strength of this practice, and makes his ambivalence known:

> There is one point, however, on which Mr. Magarshack's tact as a translator may be questioned; for he has largely abandoned the use of patronymics ('*Mr.* Verkhovensky had declined *Mrs.* Stavrogin's proposal... '). His aim was no doubt the laudable one of sparing his readers confusion, for who has not sometimes lost his way in those tangled thickets of proper names? Yet, it might also be argued that, ultimately, we get to know these characters all the better for our initial struggle to grasp who is speaking to whom. (30 April 1954)

According to Magarshack, the translator's ultimate aim is to avoid causing the target reader uncertainty or confusion. In reality, however, switching between Russian names, patronymics, and diminutives in a text has all too frequently caused the English target reader discomfort. (The sense of foreignisation caused by the presence of Russian names in translations continues to affect Anglophone readers, suggesting it is perhaps one of the most untameable of culture-specific concepts in Russian-English literary translation. It is this very concern that a perplexed Oliver Bullough addressed, for example, in his online blog for *The Guardian* as recently as 2007, 'Why Must Russian Characters Have Quite So Many Names?'.) For Magarshack, there are two aspirations concerning the transfer of names which the translator must achieve: clarity and equivalent status. As he explained:

> The principles that should be applied in translations to Russian proper names must first of all aim at avoiding confusion in the mind if [sic] the English reader, and, secondly, at reproducing the different attitudes towards the person addressed. Since the difference between the use of the surname and the name and patronymic is rather slight, the English way of address – Mr. Ivanov – is to be preferred to the use of the name and patronymic, which, I suggest, should be used sparingly and only where their use could not possibly lead to any confusion in the mind of the English reader. (General Principles, n.d., p. 26)

In one respect, it is fortunate that English has the forms of address Mr., Mrs., Miss, which can, at least, come close to replacing the same level of formality of the Russian name and patronymic in the source text. This approach, taken with reduced references to patronymics, may well result in less confusion among readers. Edmonds included paratextual notes at the front of her *Anna Karenin* and *War and Peace* translations in order to explain the Russian concept of patronymics and to justify her reasons for omitting them where possible, in favour of the character's surname. She also explained her grammatical preference for uniformly rendering feminine Russian surnames as their masculine versions, starting with Anna Karenin, but including Countess Tolstoy, Madame Blavatsky, etc.

Magarshack's use of the English 'Mr, Mrs and Miss' equivalents, on the other hand, glosses over the key social signifiers which are present in the source text. Magarshack refashioned names almost to the point of ethnocentrisms (Berman, 1985, p. 287). The difficulty posed to the translator by Russian names reaches a new, yet more complex level when diminutives, which convey a mood or a person's attitude, have to be transferred. Natalia Strelkova, in her handbook on translation practice, offers the following summary of the difficulties facing a translator when handling Russian diminutives:

> [...] there is the wide (and some would say 'wild') variety of diminutives in use in various situations, e.g., for Мария: Маша, Машка, Машенька, Машкин, Машутка, Мариванна [...], then there is: Маруся, Маруська, Муся, Мусенька[3] (that's nearly a dozen already.) [sic] [...] Short of disregarding these [...], you either resort to footnotes, or compile a general introduction listing all the variants contained in the original. Then again, like many translators, give up trying and just transliterate, or keep repeating the same 'generic' ID name so as not to further confound the reader. (2012, p. 82)

She concludes insightfully:

> Despite all their good work, the earliest translators of the Russian classics [...] never adequately coped with diminutives. These cannot always be just 'translated'. They sometimes need compensation, or a different approach to the context. More often than not, a diminutive is not meant as a unit in and of itself. It can influence an entire text or part of it by setting the stage for the attitude of the author or his characters. Nuances that vary from favourable (friendly, familiar) to unfavorable (hostile, mocking), in addition to the neutral (objective) function, [...] all can be reflected in a diminutive suffix, hardly noticeable on the page, but by implication, important in putting across the attitude of the author. (Ibid., p. 83)

We must acknowledge, therefore, that great care is required here and the translator faces an almost impossible task in conveying the multifarious emotional subtleties encapsulated by a name. The translator must find an adequate solution which does not result either in absolute ethnocentrisms, or absolute foreignisms. Names in *Crime and Punishment*, as with all Dostoevskii's novels, take the source reader through the whole spectrum of moods and feelings felt towards a character. During the course of the source text, for example, the full name Rodion Romanovich Raskolnikov is referred to as Rodion Romanovich (formal, including patronymic), Rodion Romanich (spoken form of patronymic suggesting affection and familiarity), Rodya (familiar), and Rodka (light-hearted, affectionate in this case),[4] all of which emotional shades of meaning should be conveyed as convincingly as possible wherever necessary. Magarshack upheld this same view and attached importance to the translator as a cultural custodian to get the transfer of such sophisticated information right:

> [...] the Christian name, Ivan, can have a number of diminutives, such as Vanya, Vanyushka, or Van'ka. Now, all these different modes of address obviously express a different attitude of the person using them towards the person being addressed. To disregard this difference of attitude is both to distort the author's meaning and to confess to the inadequacy of the English language to express such shades of meaning. (General Principles, n.d., p. 25)

To exemplify his rationale further, he explains how the name 'Ivan' transfers to a sliding scale of English equivalents:

> Thus the English equivalent of Vanya would be Johnnie, and of Vanyushka – dear Johnnie, darling Johnnie, and so on. But Van'ka is what the dictionaries would call vulgar, expressing as it does, contempt and derision. (Ibid., p. 26)

Luckily for Magarshack, Dostoevskii did not stray too frequently beyond the use of surnames for many characters in *Crime and Punishment*.[5] Where characters keep their patronymics, however, Magarshack almost invariably omits them. On the occasions where Dostoevskii constructed a shift in textual mood by adopting the diminutives Rodya or Rodka, Magarshack relied on his solitary Anglicised version 'Roddy'. Magarshack's degree of success in this area of his practice is evaluated by Leon Burnett (2000):

> The new translator had certain 'blind spots' when it came to the matter of style. The attempt at assimilation went a stroke too far. His decision, for example to call Raskolnikov 'Roddy', in an attempt to solve the tricky problem of how to render Russian diminutives in English, was too much for one exasperated critic. (p. 370)

Where 'Rodya' and other characters' expressive forms like 'Sonechka', 'Dunechka', 'Nasten'ka' (and the ultimate 'Nastas'iushka' (Part Two,

Chapter Two), and 'Afrosin'iushka' (Part Two, Chapter Six,)) are used in the source text to denote affection, Magarshack clarified the emotional range with the sole addition of qualifying terms as described above, 'my dear Roddy' (1951, p. 48), 'dear Dunya' (ibid., p. 55), and 'darling Roddy' (p. 55) for 'бесценный мой Родя' ('my treasured Rodya', Part One, Chapter Three). However, there are key occasions where Magarshack simply glossed over the distinction altogether, offering no suggestion of added feeling. The letter, for example, that Pulkheria Raskolnikova sends to her son in Part One, Chapter Three uses the diminutive Dunechka twenty-one times in the original. The same form does not feature once in Magarshack's version (or McDuff's), where she appears (albeit consistently) only as Dunya. Magarshack was not alone in his decision to overlook diminutive refractions; Garnett (1914) also made no target language reference to Dunechka. In more modern versions, however, the translators Pevear and Volokhonskaia (2007), generally noted for their restoration of Dostoevskii's idiosyncrasies (Hunnewell, 2015), include eighteen of Pulkheria Raskolnikova's references to Dunechka; Ready (2015) includes sixteen; and Pasternak Slater (2017) includes them all. Similarly, in Magarshack's and Garnett's translations, the characters Sonia, Nastas'ia, and Afrosin'ia only ever appear in neutral forms, never the expressly affectionate diminutive variations (Sonechka; Nasten'ka, Nastas'iushka; Afrosin'iushka) which feature in the original. The omission of such fine detail means that emotional shifts are unclear; they possibly even go unnoticed by the target reader, thereby leading at best to a dampening, and at worst to a potential distortion, of the novel's atmosphere. Pevear and Volokhonskaia, Ready, and Pasternak Slater, however, restore these characters to their familiar forms, thereby ensuring that the subtleties derived from these naming decisions are made visible to the target reader (even though such detail may lead to confusion in a reader unfamiliar with Russian naming conventions).

Garnett, Magarshack, and more recently, McDuff, do not include a list of names to accompany their *Crime and Punishment* translations, although Rieu originally suggested this idea to Magarshack. In his letter to Glover of October 1949, on receipt of Magarshack's manuscript, Rieu wrote 'I am suggesting to him [Magarshack] that it would be helpful to have a list of characters at the beginning'. There is no further progression of this idea in later correspondence, however, and the book was published without a list of names; nor are there any character lists in Magarshack's subsequent Penguin translations. The target reader is left dependent on the translator's rendering of names in the text itself. By contrast, Pevear's and Volokhonskaia's, Ready's and Pasternak Slater's more recent versions of *Crime and Punishment* not only include paratextual character lists, but also go so far as to explain the meanings behind the names chosen by Dostoevskii (the 'speaking names' (Ready, 2015, p. xlvi)), which would otherwise be lost on the target reader. They provide guidance on patronymics, how to pronounce names, including where to place stresses.

McDuff's 1991 re-translation of *Crime and Punishment* signifies Penguin's move towards offering a more comprehensive paratextual package. His and subsequent versions seek to maximise the target reader's literary comprehension. McDuff provides a brief note on the source text, a note about denominations of Russian money in 1865, a twenty-one page introduction, and fifteen pages of end-notes. Ready and Pasternak Slater have since gone further, providing, in addition to their introductions, a chronology of main events in Dostoevskii's life, a bibliography for further reading, and Pasternak Slater even includes a note on the Russia-specific Table of Ranks and a map indicating key locations in the story. Compared to Magarshack's relatively meagre paratextual contribution (only the introduction, although this was standard for Penguin translators of his generation), the assistance editors and translators now offer to readers is greatly enhanced and is, presumably, appreciated by many, especially undergraduate students; but, where paratextual information occasionally extends to more than eighty pages (Ready's Penguin version, for example), there is scope too for the uninitiated, general reader to feel more daunted than they might previously have done with an early Penguin Classic.

Magarshack's attempt at assimilation – in rendering dialogue, naming practices, culture-specific paraphrasing, and use of Anglicisms – singles him out from his predecessors. As Burnett suggests above, Magarshack's dedication to assimilation not only reveals an attempt to stretch translation norms (albeit under the auspices of the broader Penguin mission), but it also reflects the extent of Magarshack's own attempts to convince his audience of his near-native language skills and to be assimilated in British cultural circles (Magarshack, 2015). There is, therefore, a deeper context to Magarshack's practice, which has emerged only through close analysis of his notes on translation and his translation practice. There is, at times, a disconnect between Magarshack's theorising and practice (supporting Gouanvic's and Pym's views that Bourdieu's model has limitations when action is theorised), but scrutiny of both agent (archival material) and agency (textual analysis) has revealed the complexities of Magarshack's dispositions: a man caught between two cultures and seeking mastery and acceptance in one, if not both, of them. Bourdieu's simplistic view that 'Sociology treats as identical all biological individuals who, being the products of the same objective conditions, have the same habitus' (1990, p. 59) serves only to highlight the limitations of the habitus model when it is applied to a microhistorical case study.

Magarshack: reviewed within and without

In March 1955, four years after Penguin published Magarshack's *Crime and Punishment* translation, George Macy, founder of the Limited Editions Club, New York (Majure, 2012), enquired about letting his Club use a Magarshack translation (in this case, *The Idiot*). Macy's enquiry resulted in the first note of doubt in Magarshack's translation competence, largely unquestioned up until this point by Penguin. Glover updated Macy on the latest publications in the Penguin Classics series, praising in particular Magarshack's translations of *The Devils, Crime and Punishment*, and *Oblomov*:

> I think it has generally been agreed in the case of all these translations that they are considerably superior to the previous translations of Dostoyevsky and Goncharov's work that have appeared in England. (9 March 1955)

Glover informed Macy that Penguin had just received Magarshack's manuscript for a new translation of *The Idiot* and Macy's reply (15 March 1955) reveals that the Limited Editions Club had also been making preparations for a publication of *The Idiot*, with new illustrations and a revised version of Garnett's translation courtesy of Ukrainian-born scholar, biographer, and translator Dr Avrahm Yarmolinskii (Liptzin, 2007). Macy, however, expressed an interest in seeing the first chapter of Magarshack's typescript with a view, potentially, to:

> [...] taking out a copyright in America upon this translation, which could then be assigned to Penguin. I could pay two hundred and fifty pounds for the permission which I require, a sum which I hope our friends at Penguin will consider generous. (15 March 1955)

Macy's response to Magarshack's sample translation was not as effusive, however, as Penguin (and Magarshack) might have desired:

> [...] I have persuaded a man who is something of an expert in Dostoievsky, and in translations from the Russian, to read this typescript and to compare it with the existing translation by Constance Garnett. I send you now a copy of his report, which will, I am sure, be at least interesting to you and your colleagues.
>
> As a result of having this report, I have decided that I might as well proceed with the use of the Garnett translation, having it 'corrected' by an expert. (16 May 1955)

The report is not included in the Penguin archive. In its absence, we can only surmise from Macy's letter that his expert (who remains unidentified) could not find sufficient change or novelty in Magarshack's version to warrant the Limited Editions Club paying for a stake in Penguin's work. Glover sent a copy of the reader's report to Magarshack, 'not with the least idea of forwarding the particular view, for for all I know you may have a very good answer to every point, but I thought at any rate it might interest you' (20 May 1955). Considering his opinion of Garnett's work, Magarshack's pride must have been dented to learn that 'they have decided not to use your version but prefer instead to use the Garnett translation revised and amended' (ibid.). In her contribution 'Translation and the Editor', which featured in the first issue of *Delos: A Journal On and Of Translation* (1968), Helen Wolff makes the observation, that:

> Translators are for the most part very sensitive people, just as sensitive, I have found, as first-rate photographers and probably for the same reason. Translation and photography leave a doubt as to the 'uniqueness' of the performance. Someone else may try the same and do the 'copying' just as well if not better. Translators by and large are defensive, and understandably so. (p. 165)

This is a passage underlined by Magarshack in his own copy of *Delos*. Wolff's evaluation of the translator's sensitive disposition is not far off the mark, it seems. Magarshack sent an apparently defensive counter report to Glover (again, there is no copy in either the Magarshack or the Penguin archives), only to find out later that his response had been sent on to Macy (and his evaluator). On finding out that his views had been passed on to the US expert, Magarshack wrote to Glover:

> Thank you for your note of May 24th. I did not know you were going to transmit a copy of my letter to the source from which the criticisms came and I am wondering if I shouldn't have used more moderate language. Quod licet Iovi non licet bovi, as the Latin tag has it. Still, they may as well have it. (25 May 1955)

In the absence of Magarshack's counter report, the above passage at least provides some insight into Magarshack's emotional response to the reader and reveals more about the dispositions he embodied: he is simultaneously sensitive, defensive, self-assured, and proud. By contrast, Macy's subsequent reply, with its jocular admission of baiting, reveals his (and Glover's) position of editorial advantage:

> In Latin America, people pay admission fees in order to watch two cocks battling, so it seems unfair that you and I should be getting, gratis, a ringside view of two 'experts in Russian' battling with each other. It seems unfair, also, that my cock should be resting behind anonymity. So I am sending him a copy of the note from Magarshack which you have sent me [...], and I am asking him, in all fairness, to release me from the pledge of anonymity by writing directly to you or directly to Magarshack in explanation of his own criticisms. There is no doubt that he is an expert, or that he is well-known to Magarshack. I am almost inclined to add that there is no doubt they are both right in their own way. (10 June 1955)

This exchange represents the first significant question mark over Magarshack's practice. It would have been relatively easy for Magarshack to explain away isolated instances of lay readers writing to Penguin with comments and criticisms of his first three contributions to Penguin's Russian Classics. Textual flaws spotted by a peer, however, would have required considerably more explanation. Expert peer review comes with questions of its own, for example: 'What characterizes good or bad reviewers, good or bad reviews, not only from technical or scientific points of view, but also considering its linguistic, form and content, features?' (Ausloos, M., Nedic, O., and Fronczak, P., 2015, p. 348). Without specific details of this unknown reviewer's parameters for evaluation, it is impossible to validate the findings, and given the creative nature of translation, as Macy himself pointed out, there is reasonable scope for both language specialists to be right, each in their own way.

One potential outcome for Magarshack could have been that Penguin might have opted for the same route as Macy, to dust off Garnett's version of *The Idiot* and produce all subsequent translations in the same way: at a reduced cost, offering a revised edition, and effectively de-commissioning Magarshack's services.[6] However, a decision to edit and revise would probably not have been deemed in keeping with the Penguin Classics ethos, as conceived by Rieu, of producing 'readable and attractive versions of the great writers' books in modern English' (1946, p. 48).[7] One need only look at the end-pages of *The Idiot* (1955) to find Penguin's advertisements for other newly translated texts, including *Crime and Punishment* where, in this case, rather than divulge any meaningful details of the storyline or of Dostoevskii's exalted position in the Russian literary canon, Penguin describes (in glowing terms) the new translation by Magarshack in three separate instances. Having gained their readership's confidence with the initial success, Penguin consolidated this by advertising all of Magarshack's other translations. In their advertisement for Goncharov's *Oblomov*, the concluding line of an already brief résumé reminds the target audience of the winning partnership between translator and publisher:

> This translation is by David Magarshack, the translator of Dostoyevsky's *Crime and Punishment* and *The Devils* in the Penguin Classics. (End-pages, *The Idiot*, 1955)

By repeatedly mentioning Magarshack and by identifying him as one of the key names in Penguin Classics, Penguin played to a target audience which would be attracted to newly updated versions of classic literature, rather than settling for Garnett redux, because they knew they could trust the product they would receive. One may reasonably conclude, therefore, that Penguin consciously fostered the perception that translations require generational updates. This acceptance paved the way for plenty of future sales and also justified the cost of regularly commissioning new translation work.

At the very least, Macy's reader's report would have prompted Penguin to keep a watchful eye on Magarshack's work rather than to continue to accept at face value the quality of his translations. The worst outcome from this could have been Magarshack's replacement by a different translator. Rather inauspiciously for Magarshack, Glover's penultimate letter in this exchange thanks Macy for the reader report and states:

> I was very interested to have your reader's report and it was good of you to send it. It is certainly one that our Editorial Board will be glad to have in relation to possible future work by Magarshack. (20 May 1955)

Famed as Penguin's prime translator of Dostoevskii, having translated *Crime and Punishment, The Devils, The Idiot,* and with *The Brothers Karamazov* set to follow, Penguin built Magarshack up to be a recognisable part of the Penguin brand. Though, admittedly, on a small scale, Magarshack was now ineluctably entwined with the success of Penguin's Russian Classics. The readers who were now accepting of and enthusiastic for Magarshack's work, as their letters show, would no doubt have been disappointed (even mistrustful) had he been replaced. In this scenario, Penguin, might have suffered decreased sales as a result. Which publisher would risk jettisoning a popular and recognised translator, one proven to be beneficial, perhaps crucial, to the success of the Russian Classics endeavour? Moreover, if the formula has worked thus far, why risk change for its own sake? With Magarshack's name so clearly associated by now with Penguin's Dostoevskii translations, this acknowledgement is perhaps another reason why Penguin Classics (UK) chose to differ from the critical opinion sent over from America.

For American readers, correspondence in the Penguin archive confirms an unease with the 'Britishness' of Penguin's translations (as evidenced by Richard D. Mical from Massachusetts who wrote of *Crime and Punishment* that, 'I feel a little uncomfortable reading David Magarshack's translation. I wonder if it were intended for an English (i.e. British) audience' (19 November 1965)). Although Magarshack's Penguin translations were stocked and successfully sold in the United States, Macy was probably right in 1955 to consider his US readership's preferences and to pursue his initial idea of an American-English revision of Garnett's work. Coming from a tradition of 'neither great surges of russophobic curiosity nor the periods of indifference, but rather a steady increase of interest' from the 1870s onwards (May, 1994, p. 17), the US reader would no doubt have had a far clearer idea in the mid-twentieth century about the sort of translation they preferred than their average, newly initiated, ordinary reader counterpart in the United Kingdom.

Not all contemporary reviewers voiced praise, therefore, for Magarshack's work. Magarshack's biography *Dostoyevsky* (1962) is also criticised in the *Slavic Review* for being 'pedestrian, careless, unprincipled, and naggingly uncharitable to the "genius" which it acknowledges but never shows in its subject' (Fanger, 1964). Such criticism would have been keenly felt by Magarshack, who impressed in his notes the utmost importance of researching, understanding, and 'crawling, as it were, into the mind of his author and his characters' (Synopsis, n.d., p. 4). As already shown in Chapter Two, Magarshack believed that without an in-depth knowledge of the source author – effectively, the author's habitus and social trajectory – then the translator could not hope to transfer the essence of the source text. If Fanger felt that Magarshack had failed to understand and relate to Dostoevskii, then, by Magarshack's own definition, it is possible that Magarshack might indeed have failed in transferring the essence of Dostoevskii to his translations. This is exactly how some reviewers have assessed his work.

In more recent years, Magarshack's translation technique has been described as bland, as if Dostoevskii's vibrant 'edginess' had been all but ironed out:

> At a time when the creative role of translation was coming to the fore, there was a flat-footedness about the Penguin Dostoevskii. The sense of excitement that some of Garnett's early readers had apparently felt upon encountering an uncouth guest in the library had been replaced by a bourgeois feeling of familiarity in the presence of an interesting, but domesticated, foreigner in the drawing room. (Belatedly, the bland cohesion of Magarshack's English has been tacitly acknowledged in the decision by Penguin to commission a new series of translations from Dostoevskii mainly by David McDuff, an out-and-out literalist, whose versions are to be commended for their uncompromising determination to convey every stylistic peculiarity and lexical repetition found in the Russian.) (Burnett, 2000, p. 370)

Larissa Volokhonskaia, the female and Russian half of the ubiquitous 'Pevear and Volokhonsky' translation team, is still more direct and critical in her evaluation of Magarshack's efforts, especially his translation of *The Brothers Karamazov* (1958), to which she and her husband attribute their debut foray into translation. In an interview for *the Paris Review*, Volokhonskaia said:

> I had my Russian edition of Dostoevsky, and I decided to read along. Dostoevsky had always really gripped me. Usually if you read in your native tongue, […] you just read. You follow the plot, the characters, you hope maybe this time this one won't murder that one! But now I started actually looking at the language. I said, How is Magarshack going to translate this? And lo and behold, he didn't. It wasn't there. The jokes, or the unusualness, just disappeared. (Hunnewell, 2015)

What Volokhonskaia found in Magarshack's style instead was: 'Something very bland. Something tame, not right. The meaning is there, but the style, the tone, the humor are gone' (ibid.).

Magarshack's treatment by modern translators calls to mind Sergay's argument that translators disrespect their predecessors. Magarshack found this out for himself; he was criticised for *his* translations after criticising Garnett for all her translations and Makaroff for his *Platonov*.

> When revoicing foreign texts which others have already lovingly revoiced into the language we share with them, surely an attitude of simple respect for those others should have some place in our 'rejoicing'. After all, far sooner than we'd like, and particularly if we attempt retranslations of classics, we ourselves will be 'others' for someone else. (Sergay, 2006, p. 39)

In terms of the British readership, the paying customers, it seems that Magarshack's efforts at revoicing Dostoevskii were largely well received. This reception can partly be ascribed to the fact that Garnett's translations, the only standard for Dostoevskii in English translation for the preceding forty years, had grown linguistically stale over time. In his review of Magarshack's *The Idiot*, Cyril Connolly suggested as much:

> Great books require re-translating at least every fifty years, for our written language must grow more rapid and easy on the eye as it adapts itself to the pace of contemporary living. That is why Mr. David Magarshack has made such a good job of 'The Idiot'. He has an ear for the modern cadence, for the moving expression, and he manages to tidy up the verbiage of the leisurely nineteenth-century classic. (*Sunday Times*, 15 January 1956)

Conclusion

After decades of waiting for Garnett's replacement, it is significant that Magarshack was the man finally chosen and commissioned by Penguin to replace Garnett's Dostoevskii, with all the benefits of a big patron and publishing infrastructure to back him up. By sharing Rieu's vision of domesticated, accessible translations, and harnessing Penguin's mould-breaking success, Magarshack was in an ideal position to justify some experimental methods in bringing the text closer to the reader (his approach to Russian names, dialogue, realia, paraphrase, for example), methods which Garnett herself had not tried.

From the close textual analysis of his translations and reference to Magarshack's archived notes, it has become clear that there are contradictions between some of Magarshack's theorising and his practice. There are also mixed views about the success of his practice. Whereas Edmonds was praised specifically for her rendering of dialogue, Magarshack's dialogue had a mixed reception. As regards his handling of culture-specific references, Magarshack's tendency to omit or neutralise awkward references suggest he interpreted the gatekeeper's remit differently to Edmonds, who provided her readers with notes where necessary. It has become clear from this synthesised analysis of textual and archival material that Magarshack wanted to enable his readers to engage emotionally with Russian literature (and thus persuade them to keep buying his translations). He wanted them to relate to the characters in the novel without an excessive number of obstructive foreignisms and footnote interruptions, and to enjoy a version of Dostoevskii that had been previously inaccessible. However, I have also ascertained some of the reasons behind Magarshack's translatorial contradictions and aspirations, which emerge from his personal set of dispositions, his *hexis*: his need to earn a living; his wish, as an émigré, to be recognised by his host nation as an artist; his wish to replace Garnett as the new biggest name in Russian literary translation; and his commitment to creating a more realistic image of Russia than the one created by Garnett.

Magarshack's methods might seem naive, his renderings incongruous and quaint at times from our twenty-first-century vantage point, where the 'modern cadence' has moved on yet again and there are now easily accessible and plentiful re-translations from which to choose. However, Magarshack's translations are not without impact or legacy and should be duly recognised as representing a decisive moment in the field of Russian literature in translation. Penguin's next Dostoevskii translations by McDuff, for example, have been described as tending 'toward verbose, stilted phrasings and overuse of annotations, so that his versions do not seem worthy replacements for Magarshack's earlier Penguin Classics' (May, 2000, p. 1208). From the perspective of Translation Studies, it is of great interest that Magarshack – drawing on his émigré background – turned to both Western and Soviet traditions in order to guide his translation practice through fundamental decisions. Of even greater value is the realisation that when he felt the need to satisfy a new level of domestication, which he deemed most appropriate for Penguin's Russian Classics, he was prepared to move beyond the norms of both West and East and introduce his own, personal methods of domestication to bring the reader closer still to the text. What is also clear from his theoretical musings is that, ahead of his time, Magarshack anticipated many of the ideas and themes which have since occupied (and continue to occupy) translators of Dostoevskii and translation scholars.

In the same way that Garnett's Edwardian style of translation prompted Magarshack to strive for a vernacular opposite, Magarshack similarly helped to galvanise a new aspiration for Russian literary translation. He placed a renewed focus on capturing Dostoevskii's stylistic peculiarities and idiosyncrasies (as emulated, with mixed success, in subsequent translations by McDuff, Ready, and Pevear and Volokhonskaia). Magarshack's part in revoicing Russian literature in translation should qualify him (even posthumously) to receive the respect and recognition of which Sergay writes. It is undoubtedly significant that the 2017 Nobel Prize in Literature laureate

Kazuo Ishiguro singled out Magarshack and his translation style, specifically for their influence on his writing:

'I often think I've been greatly influenced by the translator, David Magarshack, who was the favourite translator of Russian writers in the 1970s. And often, when people ask me who my big influences are, I feel I should say David Magarshack, because I think the rhythm of my own prose is very much like those Russian translations I read'.

Ishiguro values not just any Dostoevsky, but Magarshack's Dostoevsky, and one begins to suspect that he rather likes the idea that his own novels are imitating translations. (Walkowitz, 2007, p. 221)

Notes

1. For the sake of clarification, I maintain that Gibian was wrong to equate both these terms to cricket; whilst cricket uses the term, 'to bowl an over' this is not the same thing. The *Oxford Dictionary of English* makes no connection between 'to be bowled over' and cricket (2010); the term is more likely to relate to its earlier origins of skittles (*OED*, 2016). Similarly, 'to be stumped' is an obsolete ploughing term originating in the US, used to describe 'the obstruction caused by stumps in ploughing imperfectly cleared land' (ibid.).
2. Letter from Cochrane to Miss Atkins, 13 January 1966, regarding footnotes which offer a translation of the French used in the Russian original.
3. Strelkova's list of names translates as: 'Mariia: Masha, Mashka, Mashen'ka, Mashkin, Mashutka, Marivanna [...] then there is: Marusia, Marus'ka, Musia, Musen'ka'.
4. Dostoevskii's use of the 'ka' suffix for, for example, Gan'ka – Gavril Ardalionovich – in *The Idiot* assumes more habitually negative and contemptuous overtones.
5. Ready divides his list of characters into those whose surnames are predominantly used throughout the book, and those whose names appear in multiple forms.
6. Magarshack's pride would, no doubt, have prevented him from considering any role other than primary translator. Magarshack would almost certainly have shared Chukovskii's scorn 'of any translator who would practice the outmoded method of "correcting" an original masterpiece to accommodate the tastes of a current reading public' (Leighton, 1984, p. xiii).
7. Macy himself observed that Penguin displayed 'an almost-reckless desire to have new translations made' (15 March 1955) and, judging by the number of new Penguin Russian translations, this mission formed an important part of Penguin's sales pitch.

References

Ausloos, M., Nedic, O., and Fronczak, P., 2015. Quantifying the Quality of Peer Reviewers Through Zipf's Law. *Scientometrics* (2016), [pdf]106(1), pp. 347–368. DOI: 10.1007/s11192-015-1704-5.

Baker, M., 1992. *In Other Words: A Coursebook on Translation*. Abingdon and New York: Routledge.

Berman, A., 1985. Translation and the Trials of the Foreign. In: L. Venuti, ed., 2004. *The Translation Studies Reader*, 2nd Edn. New York and London: Routledge, pp. 276–289.

Bird, R., 2014. Forever Young, *The Times Literary Supplement*, 19 September, pp. 4–5 [online] Available at: The Times Literary Supplement Historical Archive.

Bourdieu, P., 1990. *The Logic of Practice*. Translated from French by R. Nice. Stanford, California: Stanford University Press.

Bowers, F. ed., 1981. Vladimir Nabokov: Lectures on Russian Literature, [online] Available at: <https://archive.org/stream/VladimirNabokovLecturesOnRussianLiterature/ Vladimir_Nabokov_Lectures_on_Russian_LiteratureBookFi.org_djvu.txt> [Accessed 09 November 2015].

Bullough, O., 2007. Why Must Russian Characters Have Quite So Many Names? *theguardian.com* Books blog, [blog] 21 March. Available at: <http://www.theguardian. com/books/booksblog/2007/mar/21/whymustrussiancharactersha> [Accessed 23 November 2015].

Burnett, L., 2000. Fedor Dostoevskii 1821–1881, Russian Novelist, Short-Story Writer and Journalist. In: O. Classe, ed., *Encyclopedia of Literary Translation into English A-L*, Vol. 1. Chicago and London: Fitzroy Dearborn Publishers.

Chukovskii, K., 1965–67. *Vysokoe iskusstvo*. Translated from Russian by L. Leighton. In: L. Leighton, ed. 1984. *The Art of Translation. Kornei Chukovsky's 'A High Art'*. Knoxville, TN: The University of Tennessee Press.

• 1968. *Vysokoe iskusstvo*. Moscow: Sovetskii pisatel'. [pdf] Available at: <http:// samlib.ru/w/wagapow_a_s/chuk-tr.shtml> [Accessed 24 November 2015].

de Mauny, E., 1954. New Translation (Review Magarshack's translation, *The Devils*), *The Times Literary Supplement* Digital Archive [Accessed 03 October 2016].

Dickens, C., 1837–8. *Oliver Twist*. Reprinted by Penguin Group, 2007. London: Penguin Red Classics.

Doak, C., 2015. Reviewed Work: Crime and Punishment: A New Translation by Fyodor Dostoevsky, Oliver Ready, *The Slavic and East European Journal*, 59(2), pp. 298–300.

Dostoevskii, F., 1866. *Prestuplenie i nakazanie*. In: *Polnoe sobranie sochinenii v tridtsati tomakh*, Moscow, 1973 (Vol VI).

• *Crime and Punishment*, Translated from Russian by C. Garnett., 1914. London: Heinemann.
• *Crime and Punishment*, Translated from Russian by D. Magarshack., 1951. Harmondsworth: Penguin.
• *Crime and Punishment*, Translated from Russian by D. McDuff., 1991. London: Penguin Books Ltd.
• *Crime and Punishment*, Translated from Russian by O. Ready., 2015. London: Penguin Books Ltd.
• *Crime and Punishment*, Translated from Russian by N. Pasternak Slater., 2017. Oxford: Oxford University Press.
• *The Idiot*. Translated from Russian by D. Magarshack., 1955. Harmondsworth: Penguin.

Fanger, D., 1964. Review: *Dostoevsky*, by David Magarshack, *Slavic Review*, 23(2), pp. 386.388.

Fitzpatrick, J., 2007. (thesis) *Russia Englished: Theorizing Translation in the 20th Century* [microfilm] Ann Arbor: ProQuest LLC.

France, P. ed., 1996. Dostoevskii Rough and Smooth, *Forum for Modern Language Studies*, XXXIII(1), 1997, pp. 72–80. [pdf] Available at: <http://fmls.oxfordjournals. org/content/XXXIII/1/72.full.pdf+html> [Accessed 30 November 2016].

- 2000. *The Oxford Guide to Literature in English Translation*. Oxford and New York: Oxford University Press.

Gibian, G., 1958. Review: The Idiot by Fyodor Dostoyevsky, David Magarshack. *The Slavic and East European Journal,* 2(2), (Summer).

Gouanvic, J., 2010. Outline of a Sociology of Translation Informed by the Ideas of Pierre Bourdieu. *MonTI* 2, pp. 119–129.

Hunnewell, S., 2015. Richard Pevear and Larissa Volokhonsky, The Art of Translation [interview] *The Paris Review*, 4(213).

Leighton, L., 1984. *The Art of Translation, Kornei Chukovsky's 'A High Art'*. Knoxville, TN: The University of Tennessee Press.

- 1991. *Two Worlds*, *One Art*. DeKalb, IL: Northern Illinois University Press.

Liptzin, S., 2007. Avrahm Yarmolinsky. In: M. Berenbaum and F. Skolnik, eds. *Encyclopaedia Judaica*. 2nd ed. Detroit, MI: Macmillan Reference USA.

Magarshack Archive, MS1397. Leeds: Leeds University Special Collections, Russian Archive.

- Anon., 1965. Chekhov and Gogol Transfers. *The Times Literary Supplement*, 8 April, Box 11.
- Connolly, C., 1956. True Genius. [review] *Sunday Times*, 15 January, Box 17.
- Igoe, W.J., 1963. 'The Gift of Tongues'. [article] *The Chicago Tribune*, 20 October, Box 11.
- Magarshack, D., n.d., The Art of Translation, Synopsis, Box 13.
  - n.d., Garnett and prudery. [Magarshack's notes] Box 27.
  - n.d., General. [taxonomy] Box 13.
  - n.d., General Principles of Translation from the Russian. [unpublished paper] Box 13.

Magarshack, S., 2014. Letter to C McAteer, 19 December 2014.

- 2015. Interview with C McAteer, Camden, London, 20 February 2015.

Majure, B., 2012. A Brief History of the Limited Editions Club, [online] Available at: <http://www.majure.net/lechistory.htm> [Accessed 29 November 2015].

May, R., 1994. *The Translator in the Text: On Reading Russian Literature in English*. Evanston, IL: Northwestern University Press.

- 2000. Russian Literary Translation into English. In: O. Classe, ed. *Encyclopedia of Literary Translation into English, Vol. 2, M-Z*. London and Chicago: Fitzroy Dearborn, pp. 1204-1209.

Oxford English Dictionary, 2020. *Oxford English Dictionary Online*, [online] Oxford: Oxford University Press. Available at: <http://www.oed.com> [Accessed 2 March 2020].

Pasternak Slater, N., 2018. Translating Crime and Punishment: A Conversation with Michael Katz and Nicolas Pasternak Slater, *The Bloggers Karamazov* [blog] 14 March. Available at: <https://bloggerskaramazov.com/2018/03/14/katz-paster-nakslater-1/> [Accessed 19 June 2019].

Pearce, M., 2007. *The Routledge Dictionary of English Language Studies*. London and New York: Routledge.

Penguin Archive, Bristol: Bristol University Arts Library, Special Collections.

- Letter Rieu to Glover, 8 October 1949, DM1107/L23.
- Letter Richard D. Mical to Gentleman, 19 November 1965.
- Letter Cochrane to Mr Mical, 13 January 1966.
- Letter Mr Grant Wallace, Heywood High School, Victoria, 4 August 1978.
- Letter Sulkin to Wallace, 18 August 1978.
- Letter Cochrane to Miss Atkins, 13 January 1966, DM1107/L35.
- Letter Glover to Macy, 9 March 1955, DM1107/L54.
- Letter Macy to Glover, 15 March 1955.
- Letter Macy to Glover, 16 May 1955.
- Letter Glover to Magarshack, 20 May 1955.
- Letter Magarshack to Glover, 25 May 1955.
- Letter Macy to Glover, 10 June 1955.
- Internal memo Rieu to DLD [Duguid], 23 July 1959, DM1107/L139.

  - Internal memo Rieu, 8 August 1959.
  - Internal memo Rieu to DLD [Duguid], 11 August 1959.

Rayfield, D., 2018. Who-knows-he-dunit? Donald Rayfield on the Difficulties of Translating Dostoevsky, *The TLS* (16 January) <https://www.the-tls.co.uk/articles/public/crime-and-punishment-translation/> [Accessed 24 April 2019].

Rieu, E.V., 1946. The Penguin Classics, *Penguins Progress*. 1 (July).

Rodensky, L. ed., 2013. *The Oxford Handbook of the Victorian Novel.* Oxford: Oxford University Press.

Sendich, M., 1999. *English Counter Russian. Essays on Criticism of Literary Translation in America.* New York: Peter Lang.

Sergay, T., 2006. Translators and the Individual Talent: The Splendid Isolation of Our Retranslators of Russian Classics, *Translation Review*, 71(1), pp. 3740.

Steiner, G., 1975. *After Babel: Aspects of Language and Translation.* London: Oxford University Press.

Strelkova, N., 2012. *Introduction to Russian-English Translation, Tactics and Techniques for the Translator.* New York: Hippocrene Books, Inc.

Walkowitz, R.L., 2007. Unimaginable Largeness: Kazuo Ishiguro, Translation, and the New World Literature, *Novel*, 40(3), p. 221.

Wolff, H., 1968. Translation and the Editor, *Delos: A Journal On and Of Translation*, 1, Austin, TX: National Translation Center.

Yates, M. ed., 2006. *The Penguin Companion.* Chippenham: Octoprint.

4   Penguin Russian Classics after 1964

Introduction

E.V. Rieu retired at the age of seventy-seven, having facilitated 200 newly translated titles into print. At his retirement party on 22 January 1964, surrounded by 'eminent names from the world of publishing and some 50 translators' (Platt, 2008, p. 14), Rieu expressed, with typical wit, his gratitude for the guidance given by his freelancers: 'I initially was uncertain whether Goncharov had written *Oblomov* or vice versa. Now, of course, I know that Oblomov was the author' (Rieu in Eliot, 2018, p. 380). Rieu's successors at the helm of the series were Dr Robert Baldick (1927–1972), fellow of Pembroke College, Oxford, scholar and translator of French literature with whom Rieu had discussed Penguin's Russian Classics from early on; and the Oxford University-educated classical scholar and translator, Betty Radice (1912–1985) who had worked as Rieu's assistant between 1959 and 1964. Baldick features for only a short period in the Russian section of the Penguin Classics archive as he died unexpectedly of a cerebral tumour on 24 April 1972 at the age of forty-five (Tilby, 2010). He served, however, as an intermediary between Penguin Classics editors and the Oxford scholars who could identify titles from the Russian literary canon for Penguin to translate. Baldick's opinion was also sought on the quality of translations; it was his blessing, for example, that guaranteed Foote's 1966 translation of Lermontov's *A Hero of Our Time*,[1] and his negative evaluations of Magarshack's 1964 Chekhov translation, *Lady with Lapdog and Other Stories*[2] and of Edmonds's 1966 translation of Tolstoi's *The Kreutzer Sonata* that hurried their careers at Penguin to a close. In addition to scholarly rigour, Baldick is also remembered for bringing a professional awareness of the translator's worth to Penguin Books. His obituary in the *Times* described him as making sure 'that translators were paid a proper fee for what is a specialist job' (25 April 1972).

Radice, by contrast, enjoyed a long career as the Penguin Classics editor, a role which she found herself performing on her own after Baldick's death and that of his successor, C. A. Jones, in 1974 (Radice and Reynolds, 1987, p. 12). Radice's editorship lasted twenty-one years, from 1964 until her own death from a heart attack in 1985. It is remarked several times in commentaries about this period of Penguin Classics history, that her tenure was more challenging in many respects than Rieu's, especially given the company's shift towards commissioning increasingly scholarly introductions and translations. Her son, William, wrote at some length in his introduction to *The Translator's Art* about the difficult position she found herself in, under scrutiny from all sides:

> These were demanding aims: to produce books that were authoritative works of scholarship and of high literary merit, as well as readable and appealing in the manner of the early Penguin Classics. They made Betty Radice's task far more strenuous than Rieu's, and far more open to attack, from scholars and academics on the one hand, from poets and aesthetes on the other. (Ibid., p. 22)

Radice's editorship involved her making choices between academic rigour and readability. Her son refers to the article she wrote for *The Times Higher Education Supplement* in which she states revealingly that 'I can't please everyone, and sometimes wonder if I may end by pleasing nobody but myself' (1984). Rieu had pursued an autonomous mission of his own for readable, affordable, quality translations, then a novelty in the field of publishing which would suit and attract a nation of dedicated, knowledge-thirsty followers.[3] By contrast, Radice's term as editor converged with a trend for a more scholarly *skopos*,[4] which influenced the nature of the textual rendering and the tone and content of paratextual inclusions. This change in *skopos* reflected the evolving characteristics and aspirations of Penguin's readership. In the introduction to her translation of Pliny's *Letters*, Radice strove to create a more instructive summary of the text. Her conscious departure from Rieu's view that 'the Penguin Classics must be free of the dead weight of scholarly apparatus' arose primarily from the demands of the end user, namely, the growing use of translations in 'schools and university teaching [...] and the way in which readers with sophisticated literary sensitivity were expecting to find in English translations the poetic and aesthetic qualities of the original' (Radice and Reynolds, 1987, p. 22). Whereas Rieu's job had been to innovate while attracting the cautious but curious target reader, Radice's mission was to develop, instruct, consolidate, and deepen their knowledge.

As Rieu's protégée, Radice, according to her son, excelled at human interaction. Radice is described as being, like Rieu, 'meticulously courteous to all her translators and correspondents, never failing to answer letters promptly, at surprising length, and often in long hand' (ibid., p. 18). Based on the correspondence found in the Penguin Russian Classics folders, Rieu's and Radice's code of conduct was highly principled and robustly upheld; their example also suffused the practices of those working alongside them. Even when faced with difficult letters to write, the Penguin tone remained impeccably polite; when the answer was no, the message was clearly but courteously conveyed; when faced with a disgruntled translator (as shown in Chapter One with the challenging tone frequently adopted by Rosemary Edmonds, for example), there was a concerted effort to pacify.[5] The overriding impression is that editors generally tried to help their translators with deadline flexibility, payment, and even procurement of source texts. Finally, if a translator's standard of work slipped and a message of termination became inevitable, this task was also performed respectfully. Some exceptions, as we will see during the course of this chapter, include the case of Babette Deutsch.

A new cohort of Russian translators

With the departure of the earliest cohort of translators – either voluntarily, as appears to have been the case with Gardiner, or through forced ejection (Fen, Edmonds, and Magarshack) – Penguin commissioned a new set of freelancers. Their job was to take Penguin Russian Classics into the Black Cover series and beyond into Penguin Modern Classics, Penguin Twentieth Century Classics, and Penguin International Writers. Those translators who, like Foote (Lermontov's *A Hero of Our Time* (1966)), Freeborn (Turgenev's *Sketches from a Hunter's Album* (1967), *The Home of the Gentry* (1970), *Rudin* (1975)), and Pushkin co-translators Deutsch and Yarmolinskii (*Eugene Onegin* (1964)), witnessed the period of transition immediately following Rieu's departure, formed the cast of the next cohort of translators.

These "Black Cover" Russian titles which were commissioned during the post-Rieu era demonstrate a shift in Penguin's focus. Lesser-known works by Chekhov, Gogol, Dostoevskii, Pushkin, and Tolstoi were translated by new names, for example: Jessie Coulson (probably a student of J.R.R. Tolkien at Leeds University, and the first female lexicographer to have her name included in the Oxford dictionary (OED, 2018)), Jane Kentish (a Sussex University graduate of the Russian language, who negotiated her translation of Dostoevskii's *Netochka Nezvanova* with Penguin from the remove of Colombo, Sri Lanka) and Ronald Wilks. Of the Black Cover cohort, Wilks (1933–2016) was especially long-serving. His first Penguin commission was published in 1966 and his last in 2009. He translated a wide range of Russian authors for Penguin: Gorkii's autobiographical trilogy (*My Childhood* (1966), *My Apprenticeship* (1974), *My Universities* (1979)), Gogol's *Diary of a Madman and Other Stories* (1972), seven compilations of Chekhov's short stories (including *The Kiss and Other Stories*, *The Duel*, *The Steppe*, *The Shooting Party*, and *Ward No. 6*), Saltykov-Shchedrin's *The Golovlyov Family* (1988), Tolstoi's *How Much Land Does a Man Need?* (1993), Sologub's *The Little Demon* (1994), Pushkin's *Tales of Belkin and Other Prose Writings* (1998), and Dostoevskii's *Notes from Underground* and *The Double* (2009).

Wilks is described in his short (unpublished) obituary as having 'gained a scholarship to Trinity College Cambridge from Wanstead Grammar School

[...]. Ronald studied Russian, Spanish and Philosophy at Trinity between 1954–1957 after training as a Naval Interpreter for National Service' (Trinity College, 2016). There is no account in archived correspondence of how Wilks became a translator for Penguin but, for the first years of his Penguin tenure, Wilks's letters indicate that he worked by day for the family business, Wiltoys (N. Wilks & Sons Limited),[6] a manufacturer of wooden jigsaws and educational games. Wilks invited Penguin to contact him there should they have any queries about proofs because 'I'm at the above number most of the day' (21 September 1971), suggesting either that he was not wholly reliant on translation to earn his living, or that he was not sufficiently established as a translator to be able to rely solely on his freelance earnings.[7] It is clear that he enjoyed cordial relations with his Penguin editor James [Jim] Cochrane. In 1972, several years into his Penguin tenure, Wilks revealed that he had submitted his thesis ('I hope to have the result in about 6 weeks' time. Until then I shall be vegetating – and worrying myself stiff!' (26 October 1972)), and he concluded with an invitation for Cochrane:

I hope that you may be able to come for my celebratory party, should I become Dr. Wilks. It seems that I have a very good chance, but nothing is certain. The thesis comes out at 360 pages – and very large ones! (Ibid.)[8]

The openness with which he treated his editors during their many years of collaboration provides the researcher with an ideal opportunity to chart the highs and lows of the modern, freelancing literary translator's life (at least until the late 1980s, after which letter exchanges are replaced by telephone calls and, eventually, emails, and archived material at Penguin generally becomes scarce). Magarshack had shared financial concerns most frequently with his editors (usually out of the necessity to hasten advance payments), and he proudly affirmed the rights and prestige of the translator. Wilks, by contrast, shared considerably more detail about his personal life and the everyday, practical preoccupations facing a freelance Penguin translator during the 1970s. He expressed hope (for his PhD) and, later, joy at his impending fatherhood; he admitted to "translator's-block" and acknowledged the toll that solitude can take on the translator. In response, Penguin treated Wilks with understanding; the editors helped wherever possible with his practical appeals and offered (professional) sympathy over more personal troubles.

In 1971, Wilks wrote with apparent good humour regarding the proofs for *Diary of a Madman*; he explained to Miss Gill Woodeson at Penguin's Editorial Department that 'Gogol' is the despair of most translators – the long sentence on p. 10 of The Overcoat is a very famous one and just one example of the difficulties!' (post-card, 16 September 1971). His next letter to Miss Woodeson, just one week later, clarifies further, 'As I mentioned, Gogol is generally thought to be the most difficult of all Russian writers: it is with great relief that I now turn to Gorky' (21 September 1971). The relief, however, proved only short-lived. Cochrane's internal memorandum a few months later to Penguin Classics editor Fred Plaat includes an appeal:

> Ronald Wilks, the translator of Gorky: <u>My Childhood</u> and <u>My Apprenticeship</u>, is rather bored with his solitary life as a Russian translator and research student and has offered his services for proofreading or any editorial work. (8 May 1972)

In *Becoming a Translator* (2008), Douglas Robinson observes that 'translating [...] involves a good deal of repetitive drudgery that will simply never go away. [... I]f you can't learn to enjoy even the drudgery, you won't last long in the profession' (p. 34). In Wilks's case, the lot of the solitary translator incurred considerable boredom, culminating in the delayed completion of his translation of Gorkii's *My Universities* by several years. According to an internal memorandum to Penguin Classics editor Will Sulkin on 15 July 1975, Wilks 'had a skin disease, various relatives of his died, and these misfortunes meant that he could not continue with work on MY UNIVERSITIES [sic] at the time'. Sulkin resumed contact with Wilks, who replied on 21 April 1976. Wilks described himself as 'almost too ashamed to write' and confirmed that 'a succession of domestic traumas over the past three years has been offputting [sic], to say the least'. His letter concludes on a note of obvious concern about his ongoing career prospects at Penguin, 'I am sure that I have injured my reputation with Penguin irreparably and quite justifiably. I am very, very sorry about it all'. However, contrary to Bourdieu's statement that publishers as 'holders of economic and political power [...] are dominant over all' (Speller, 2011, p. 14), Penguin was both sympathetic and ready to show clemency, as Rieu would have expected. In 'A Classic Education' (1984), Radice claims to have taken her lead from Rieu in clarifying the duty of care Penguin editors should show towards their translators:

> He [Rieu] knew [...] from his own experience that translating is a demanding and solitary discipline, so that whereas some forge ahead with confidence, others need periodic reassurance and an editor must be prepared to give help when asked, however time-consuming it may prove. (p. 17)

Sulkin's response to Wilks balances concern with the appropriate measure of reassurance:

> Please don't feel guilty about the delayed delivery. I appreciate that times have been extremely difficult for you. Further, almost all books have suffered delays in publication over the past two years or so: even if you had managed to stick to the delivery deadline the typescript would probably be languishing still on the shelf in my office. (4 May 1976)

When Wilks eventually submitted the final Gorkii proofs, his accompanying letter indicated a more optimistic outlook for his domestic and professional situation:

> I am glad to say that things are very much better on a personal front – if all goes well, there should be another Wilks in early January!
>
> If it is not too impertinent mentioning this, I should very much like to offer something else from Russian (possibly less morbid subject-matter – memoirs/biography, etc.). Perhaps you could let me know if you would like some details. (9 November 1976)

Wilks's subsequent recommendations for 'less morbid subject-matter' included Russian authors such as Leskov, Saltykov-Shchedrin, Zamiatin, Andreev, Pomialovskii, more Gorkii (rather surprisingly), and a Puffin children's book of selected Russian fairy tales. In spite of his expressed desire in 1972 to move away from translation and to take up editing or proofreading roles at Penguin instead, Wilks went on to translate seven collections of Chekhov's short stories and novels by several other authors too for three more decades. For such a long career with so many translations, there are very few reviews of Wilks's work. However, some measure of success can be gauged in a letter from 1972 when Wilks expressed astonishment at how well his translation of Gorkii's *My Childhood* was selling: nearly 100,000 copies sold in the space of six years, and his translation of Gorkii's *My Apprenticeship* is described in *The Evening Standard* as 'excellent, and conveys the exact feeling of a born writer who could say, "I was there"' (24 August 1974). More recently, Sibelan Forrester reviewed Wilks's 2009 Penguin translation of Dostoevskii's *Notes from Underground* and *The Double* for *Translation Review* and notes that 'Wilks does an excellent job of rendering peculiarities of the characters' speech and establishing an overall Victorian tone' (2010, p. 92). Forrester's review returns to the same debate about US- vs. UK-English, as previously raised by Richard D. Mical with regard to Magarshack's Britishisms in 1966. This time, though, Forrester is more accepting of Wilks's Britishisms; she writes that 'A North American reader will note and probably appreciate the British color of the colloquial language' (ibid.).

Wilks's Chekhov translations were broadcast eight times between 1981 and 1987 for BBC radio, and his translation of *Diary of a Madman* was adapted for Ireland's award-winning Focus Theatre and later used by Irish television (Moynihan, 2014, pp. 16–17).[9] After a sustained period of repeat commissions, robust Gorkii sales, and some broadcasting success, the sales figures for Wilks's Penguin translation of Saltykov-Shchedrin's *The Golovlyov Family* (1988) must, therefore, have come as something of a shock. With an intended print run of 6,000 copies (Keegan, 22 July 1987), only five were sold, which Wilks described as 'quite disastrous! Perhaps the ghost of the author is casting an evil spell, etc.!' (30 September 1989). This slump in figures might, however, be more indicative of a shift in reader interest away from traditional Russian Classics and towards the Penguin Twentieth Century Classics, which included newly discovered Soviet works.

Out with the old

Forty years on from the first Penguin Russian Classics translations, some were now deemed ready for re-translation. As Deane-Cox observes, 'Whereas the dominant agents will do what they can to preserve the configuration of the literary field as it stands, the newcomers will attempt to redraw the field, to bring about its re-configuration, by clearly differentiating themselves' (2014, p. 32). Magarshack's coveted position as Penguin's Dostoevskii translator was passed on to David McDuff, who re-translated Dostoevskii's *Crime and Punishment*, *The Brothers Karamazov*, and *The Idiot* between 1994 and 2004. (He also re-translated *The House of the Dead*, as well as contributing brand new translations of Isaac Babel's *Collected Stories* (1994), Andrei Bely's *Petersburg* (1995), and Nikolai Leskov's *Lady Macbeth of Mtsensk* (1987).) Had Magarshack still been alive, this 're-configuration' would no doubt have caused him some consternation. The consternation he might predictably have felt cannot compete, however, with that caused by Penguin's decision to re-translate *Eugene Onegin*. Penguin had first published Babette Deutsch's and her husband Avrahm Yarmolinksii's *Onegin* co-translation in 1964. On receiving their manuscript, Radice wrote in a letter to her colleague Duguid that she and Rieu were 'impressed by this work':

> The short Introduction is apt and well written, and the verse moves easily through the intricate stanza-pattern. I have read it all with real enjoyment; I have been wanting to read Onegin for years, and it has been a revelation to discover the astringency and irony of Pushkin. (11 March 1963)

Fifteen years on, however, editorial opinion underwent a change. According to Penguin Classics editor Will Sulkin, it 'is poor stuff and has never sold as it deserves' (6 March 1978). Faced with an opportunity to procure world paperback rights to Sir Charles Johnston's new, 'sparkling, elegant, marvellous translation [of *Eugene Onegin*] which has received very enthusiastic reviews' (ibid.), Sulkin took the decision – under somewhat pressured time deadlines and causing some upset to his US counterparts in the process – to replace the Deutsch/Yarmolinskii version with Johnston's. Sulkin then requested that Viking Penguin pulp 'any remaining Babette Deutsch stock when the new translation becomes available in Penguin (in say 14 months [sic] time)' (17 February 1978). Keen to act before losing the deal to another (undisclosed) US publisher, Sulkin telexed Viking Penguin repeatedly, seeking their approval to go ahead. Viking Penguin's apparent indecision

– arising from the fact that decision-maker Dick Seaver was away on holiday – elicited the following telex response (even with the typographical errors, Sulkin's sentiment is emphatic):

> I must say that it still surprises and disturbs me to be faced that [sic] Viking Penguin caution with books of this fort [sic]. Perhaps you or Dick could take time to explain how it is that a country with a population four times the size of Britain and a population studying Russian at university probably six or eight times the size of Britain will doubtless contrive to sell fewer copies than we do. (28 February 1978)

Viking Penguin editor, Sue Zuckermann, acting in Seaver's absence, replied equally emphatically:

> It seems to me you are riding a very high horse. I am truly offended by your attitude and shocked that you would make this gratuitous remark [...]. I thought you had better manners. (2 March 1978)

Babette Deutsch (now acting on her own after Yarmolinskii's death in 1975) only realised that her version had been replaced when the new Johnston translation appeared in Spring 1979. On this discovery, she expressed her own views about Sulkin's decision in a letter to Viking Penguin director Michael Loeb. Deutsch stated that:

> [...] after reading the rave reviews on the jacket I opened it with some diffidence, wondering how far superior to my version I would find it. But I did not read far before my dismay increased [...]. The British translator is careless not only with his rhymes and his metres, but writes as if he were ignorant of English. (17 April 1979)

She evidenced her claims – ranging from 'bungle[d] syntax' to mispronounced Latin and improbable lexical choices – with numerous examples where she felt 'Mr. Johnston has done Pushkin a great disservice'. She concluded with the perceptive notion that Johnston's 'admirers were so impressed by his political importance and his wife's rank that they overlooked all his blunders'. Her overall tone expresses disappointment with her treatment by Penguin. Viking Penguin editor Elisabeth Sifton alerted director Michael Loeb to Deutsch's situation ('What a sad letter' (Sifton, April 1979)). In a bid to restore Rieu-like professionalism, Loeb took up her case with Sulkin's superior, John Rolfe, in the UK:

> Apparently no editor ever informed her [Deutsch] that we were putting hers [her translation] out of print. It's not a pleasant way to treat a highly respected member of the literary community, or anyone for that matter. [...] Will Sulkin may wish to write an appropriate letter to

Babette Deutsch, or he may wish to avoid further correspondence. If he does write her, I would appreciate a copy of his letter. (4 May 1979)

A chastened Sulkin did indeed write to Deutsch, but still maintained (albeit politely) that 'For right or wrong, Sir Charles Johnston's book attracted widespread critical attention on both sides of the Atlantic. Since your own translation had never sold as it deserves, this publicity provided us with an opportunity to reach a larger market with <u>Eugene Onegin</u>' (6 June 1979). Sulkin's rationale is indicative of an apparent commercial shift that took Penguin's Russian literature further away from Rieu's ideals of great literature for great literature's sake. Instead, the emphasis moved towards optimising lucrative or reputational publishing opportunities, as will become increasingly evident with Penguin's pursuit of Solzhenitsyn's works.

In with the new: in pursuit of Solzhenitsyn

In addition to commissioning re-translations, Penguin embarked on introducing contemporary Russian literature in its new Penguin Twentieth Century Classics series. They commissioned new translators like Ralph Parker, Michael Glenny, the co-translators David Burg and Lord Nicholas Bethell, and the late Jamey Gambrell to tackle Soviet authors. By the time Soviet literature started to arrive, paper had been superseded by telex and telephone; Penguin's folders reveal scant information about commissions for Mikhail Bulgakov's *Black Snow* (Glenny) and Tatyana Tolstaya's *Sleepwalker in a Fog and On the Golden Porch* (Gambrell). The same cannot be said, however, for Penguin's Alexander Solzhenitsyn commissions. In the early 1960s, there is one title in the Penguin archive's Russian folders which offers some degree of insight into Lane's personal view on Soviet literature: Solzhenitsyn's *One Day in the Life of Ivan Denisovich*. The first mention of the book comes from translator Ronald Hingley, who wrote to Penguin on 14 December 1962 to try to persuade Lane to publish his and Max Hayward's translation. Hingley described *One Day* as:

> [...] not just a document of considerable scandal value, but a literary work of lasting worth and great originality. It has the peculiarity of being written in Russian concentration camp argot, which has made translating it a fascinating task. It is certainly the most important new literary work to have appeared in Russia since before the war.

It took another six weeks (31 January 1963) for Penguin editor Tony Godwin to correspond with Lane over the merits of either procuring rights from Victor Gollancz to publish Ralph Parker's translation of *One Day* or take Hayward and Hingley up on their offered manuscript. According to Godwin's three-page summary of *One Day* as a business case, Parker's version was regarded as the '"official" translation approved by the author and presumably the Soviet authorities, for what it's worth' and was an 'extremely literal translation'. The Hayward-Hingley version was regarded as 'a very free translation, much more talented and one which gives, apparently, much more the feel of the literary quality of the book' (ibid.). Godwin shared Hingley's view, adding in his summary that *One Day* carried 'considerable literary merit, perhaps not up to the heights of Zhivago but in the same country' (ibid.). For Godwin, the deciding factor was not literary merit, however, but 'whether or not it's going to sell' (ibid.), a view shared by Lane. Whilst acknowledging that the novel 'is an important book in that it shows a change of thinking in Moscow' (Lane, 4 February 1963), the political or humanitarian currency associated with the novel was not sufficient for commercial commitment; Lane described the novel's potential in doubtful terms:

> [...] we doubt whether it has any real literary merit. We think that it may well be one of those books which have a large sale on publication caused by public curiosity, but this is soon satisfied and it may well become a dead duck quite soon. (Ibid.)

Lane was unable, therefore, to identify any lasting merit – literary, commercial, or topical – in funding a publication like Solzhenitsyn's. As the *Russian Review* venture had proven, his idealism in promoting a literary counterweight to Russophobic sentiment could only stretch as far as corporate finances would justify. (Throughout the 1950s–60s when Soviet relations with the West were referred to as the Red Scare (Brinson, 2004, pp. 2–5), there is no evidence in the archive to suggest that Penguin intended any deviation from Rieu's position – of transcending current political trends with the *belles-lettres* of high culture – by capitalising, instead, on Cold War zeitgeist through their sale of Penguin Russian Classics.) However, on this occasion, Lane had an unexpected change of mind and Penguin released Parker's translation later that same year. There are no supporting letters in the archive to explain the volte-face, but one assumes that a reasonable figure was successfully negotiated with Gollancz. As to whether Penguin procured the 'best' version of Solzhenitsyn's novel, May writes that 'Four separate English translations appeared within a few months of the work's publication in the Soviet Union in 1962. Yet all, to one degree or another, sacrificed the raw camp language, which had been the first thing to shock Russian readers, for something far more ordinary' (1994, p. 47). Harrison E. Salisbury's review of Parker's, and Hayward's and Hingley's translations for *The New York Times* (22 January 1963) largely concurs with May's view but adds, in terms which recall Magarshack's approach to idiomatic equivalence, that not enough salt had been added. Haste aside, Parker's translation gained the critical edge:

> Of the two translations neither comes close to reproducing the rough vigour of the author's concentration camp slang. Each has been done with

too much haste. Each relies on standard four-letter words rather than the author's salty idiom. However, Ralph Parker's version [...] is superior to the patchwork thrown together by Max Hayward and Ronald Hingley for Praeger. The most striking blooper of the Hayward-Hingley translation is to put in the mouths of the prisoners the phrase "Comrade Warder". The prisoners were forbidden, as Solzhenitsyn notes, to call the guards "comrade", which is the customary Soviet greeting. They had to address the guards as "Citizen", removing their hats five paces away and keeping it off two paces beyond the guard. (*The New York Times*, 1963)

Unconvinced, however, by Parker's version, general readers such as Mrs. J.M. Addington, of Dagenham, Essex, had more probing questions for Penguin in a letter dated 11 November 1974. She cited a passage from David Burg's and George Feifer's 1973 biography *Solzhenitsyn*, which criticises Parker for turning Solzhenitsyn's 'sharp, distinctive prose into thin porridge' with an 'abundance of distortions, dampenings, and out-right omissions, often of the most piercing images. His text is still in print' (pp. 177–178). Mrs. Addington drew Penguin's attention to the fact that 'Many people buy your books considering them to be reliable translations. If the above [Burg and Feifer] quote is well founded, then I consider a publishing company as widely available as Penguin has rendered the author and his public a gross disfavour' (11 November 1974). Penguin sent the following assured explanation by way of reply:

> Thank you for your comments about our editions of Solzhenitsyn's work. In our opinion, our translation is reliable and adequate and moreover has been authorised by the author. (12 December 1974)

The Khrushchev and Brezhnev years facilitated a bias in contemporary literature 'toward information and away from art' (May, 1994, p. 46), an 'informational attitude [which] took its toll on translations; not only were works selected according to political criteria, they were translated so as to highlight content at the expense of style' (ibid.). From this perspective, one could argue that Lane's initial dismissal of *One Day* (on the sole grounds that it lacked literary merit) might have been justified. Since its publication in the West, though, *One Day* has appealed to readers on account both of its literary and informational merit. Burg and Feifer identified a new reader category – 'politicians and intellectuals' (1973, p. 178) – with interests more specifically in the message driving such literature, irrespective of the 'flaws in translation' (ibid.). The decision to bring 'informative' writers like Solzhenitsyn to the fore not only positioned content over style and prioritised dissident writers over esteemed non-dissidents (like Valentin Rasputin, Chingiz Aitmatov, Fazil' Iskander, and Yuri Trifonov), but it also inflated the figures being negotiated for publishing rights. Publishers and translators worked 'more like Monte Carlo pit crews than with the decorum usually associated with literary endeavors' (ibid., p. 177). In the case of Bulgakov, for example, Penguin secured the rights to translate and publish *Black Snow*, but could not meet Collins's asking price in early 1968 of £2,500 against 10% royalties for *The Master and Margarita*. With reluctance, and only after a series of exchanges over several days, Penguin's Joint Chief Editor Oliver Caldecott sent his final word to Julia Rollason, 'I don't feel inclined to go up as high as you suggest' (n.d.); instead, the deal went to Fontana. This was not the only title lost to Fontana, however; while Penguin pursued and secured rights to *August 1914*, it failed to secure *The Gulag Archipelago*. Penguin editor Judith Burnley's memorandum of 12 January 1974 informs her editorial colleague Tony Mott, 'I have done my best and there doesn't seem to be a snowball's chance in a Soviet hell of getting THE GULAG ARCHIPELAGO. Collins have no intention of letting Fontana miss out on this one, it seems'. Whereas Penguin Classics editors Rieu and Glover had previously kept competitively abreast of which nineteenth-century Russian titles other publishers were publishing (Hamish Hamilton, for example), publishing rivalries became acute in the 1960s–1970s in the race to commission previously untranslated, sensationalist (and living) Soviet writers.

Beyond *One Day*

Unlike previous Penguin Russian Classic commissions – the domain of long-dead, great Russian authors – Solzhenitsyn was alive, and his forced departure from the Soviet Union in 1974 (followed by Voinovich in 1980) caused a literary sensation on which any bidding publisher would wish to capitalise. The economic and symbolic capital attached to Penguin's Solzhenitsyn book deals rested – for the first time since *Lady Chatterley's Lover* – in authorial sensationalism as much as in literary merit. After expressing an apparently lukewarm interest in Solzhenitsyn's works initially, Penguin's pursuit of publishing rights gathered momentum during the early- to mid-1970s, when opportunities arose to obtain British publishing rights to various Solzhenitsyn works. The race to make commercial and political capital out of a high-profile Soviet dissident now showed how far publishing practices had shifted from the days of the early Penguin Russian Classics, when editors were guided by the 'safe' literary merit of a tried-and-trusted nineteenth-century author. Whereas Lane and Godwin were not prepared to 'be panicked into a rushed decision' (Lane, 4 February 1963) over *One Day*, and would not entertain the idea of participating in a tender for *One Day*'s publishing rights (Godwin, 31 January 1963), the mood changed when negotiations began for rights to other works (*Cancer Ward*, *August 1914*, and *The Gulag Archipelago*).

There is a palpable sense of urgency in Penguin's correspondence as editors tried to head off competitors. Court proceedings during November 1971 between The Bodley Head (and therefore Penguin by affiliation) and small publishing house The Flegon Press brought a climate of publishing excitement reminiscent of the *Lady Chatterley* legal case in 1960. The Bodley Head and Solzhenitsyn brought to trial the émigré Romanian publisher Alec Flegon, who had argued that 'Solzhenitsyn had broken the copyright laws of the Soviet Union by publishing the book [*August 1914*] abroad, so the copyright "is not valid in any country which has diplomatic relations with the Soviet Union"' (*The Telegraph*, 21 May 2003). Fearful that Flegon would breach Solzhenitsyn's copyright in the West by publishing a pirated, English-language version of *August 1914* (*The Times*, 25 November 1971), The Bodley Head and Solzhenitsyn (represented by his Swiss lawyer Dr. Fritz Heeb) jointly sought and won an injunction to stop Flegon. The legal case highlighted the lengths publishers were prepared to go to in order to secure copyright. Penguin might have been busy striving for leverage over bona fide publishing competitors, but it was also seeking to block rogue traders like Flegon.

Longman Divisional Managing Director Michael Hoare's enthusiastic pursuit of British publishing rights to *August 1914* provides insight into the perceived canon-forming qualities of this new genre of Soviet fiction as it reached the West.[10] Hoare's letter to Dr. Otto F. Walter – of West German publishing house Hermann Luchterhand Verlag, which liaised directly with Solzhenitsyn's official literary representative Dr. Heeb – formally expressed Longman/Penguin's and Random House's interest in publishing *August 1914* (we 'are now even more enthusiastic about Alexander Solzhenitsyn's work than before' (21 June 1971)). Hoare also defined the Soviet canon by new, Solzhenitsyn-inspired benchmarks which are worth citing in full:

> Solzhenitsyn's moral integrity, the range and scope of his writing and powers of characterisation and description are magnificently demonstrated in this book. Also, of course, even if there was only one reason to read Solzhenitsyn it would be for his honesty in his handling of subjects which are quintessentially Russian, but are of the kind which Soviet novelists have barely touched, even were they to convey to them: in things like the portrayal of the self-made millionaire farmer Tomchak, on his mechanised estate, - the account of that day in the life of his family is a magnificent short story in itself, as rich in its characterisation as its information about society; or the bringing out of the religious element in Samsonov's character; or the depth of feeling in the description of the burial of Captain Kabanov. (Ibid.)

According to Hoare, Solzhenitsyn's works offered an insight into the Russian identity which had not yet been fully portrayed, one which came with a new, raw Soviet dimension. Whilst 'moral integrity' might not have been on display to the same extent with other, lesser-known Soviet writers (Trifonov, Aitmatov, Rasputin, Bitov, for example), there were writers who offered equally vivid and valid insight into quintessentially Russian/Soviet themes. The GULAG writer Varlam Shalamov, for example, could have fulfilled the same moral function for Penguin as Solzhenitsyn. Shalamov submitted his labour camp tales to *Novy mir* just after it had printed Solzhenitsyn's *One Day* and, although *Novy mir* did not print Shalamov's tales, his work found its way to France and Germany via *tamizdat* (Toker, 2008, p. 742). Shalamov's camp experiences were 'longer and more bitter' (Solzhenitsyn in Terras, 1985, p. 402) than Solzhenitsyn's, and yet *Kolyma Tales* did not appear in Anglophone translation until 1981 (translated by John Glad and published by Graphite) and not until 1994 as a Penguin publication (still in Glad's translation). Shalamov is described as having briefly been 'a peculiarly Moscow-unofficial version of a literary lion' (Scammell and Hayward, 1970, p. 18), but he did not boast the same levels of global publicity as Solzhenitsyn. He lacked, therefore, the prospective capital. The absence of sales-inducing sensationalism in his case might explain the Western publishers' preference for Solzhenitsyn, and serves to illustrate Bourdieu's musings on the subject:

> The question that must then be asked is how it comes about that a certain writer or editor becomes the importer of a certain thought? Why is writer X published by publisher Y? For it is obvious that there will always be some sort of profit involved. (1999, p. 223)

Hoare set the financial bar for a share in Solzhenitsyn's publicity, pitching a sum of £60,000 (21 June 1971) brokered between Longman/Penguin in the United Kingdom and Random House in the United States, for joint UK-US paperback publishing rights to *August 1914*. The vast difference between this figure and the much lower asking price for rights to *The Master and Margarita* just three years earlier is indicative of the perceived value and significance attached to Solzhenitsyn (and his anticipated book sales) compared to Bulgakov.

For the first time in the history of Penguin Russian Classics, the publisher-negotiator (Hoare, in this case) pitched Penguin's suitability to take on such a special commission based on its commitment and ability to secure not just a suitable translator – whose required skillset is also stipulated – but an appropriately qualified editor too in order to carry out the commission successfully. Hoare positioned the task of choosing the translator as a priority in which every key figure, especially the author's official representatives, involved in the deal must have a say. He wrote:

> All of the three companies [Longman/Penguin and Random House] concerned in this offer are genuinely enthusiastic about the possibility of publishing Alexander Solzhenitsyn's work; and we are agreed that, if we were fortunate enough to be given the opportunity of doing so, the greatest care and judgement should be exercised in the choice of a translator, and you and Dr Heeb may indeed feel that this choice should be

subject in any case to your final approval. Perhaps I might add that one of our Editors comes from Russian stock on his mother's side, and he speaks and reads the language fluently; and it is he who has pointed out that any translator may well need an expert adviser to help him with the military terms in the book, which might not be familiar to a translator who, however well qualified from a literary point of view, may not be familiar with these particular matters; we have such an adviser in mind and available should his services be thought necessary, and if we were fortunate enough to publish the book. (Ibid.)

The Russian-proficient editor remains unidentified, and the rights were eventually sold to Farrar, Straus, and The Bodley Head. According to *The New York Times*, at the time of the negotiations, Roger W. Straus, the head of US publishing house Farrar, Straus & Giroux, flew to Germany specially to place a counter-bid for US publishing rights of 'nearly $500,000, and the understanding that the book's publication would be carried out in conjunction with [Bodley] Head in like [sic] Straus's a firm noted for the literary distinction of its line. Farrar, Straus had been one of the few U.S. publishers to offer royalties on the two earlier Solzhenitsyn novels it published' (10 September 1972). *The New York Times* noted that most publishers paid no royalties on Solzhenitsyn's works 'on the ground that the books were not copyrighted', a condition which, as it infers, led to greatly varying translation quality.

The translator selected to produce *August 1914* was Michael Glenny, described in *The New York Times* as 'a 45-year-old Briton, Oxford graduate, sometime Army interpreter and businessman, at present a university lecturer on German and Russian subjects' (ibid.). On paper, Glenny's credentials match many of the new Penguin Russian translators' who replaced the first cohort: military-trained, practical yet scholarly linguists. Fen's and Magarshack's capital had rested in the fact that they were born Russian-speaking, had grown up with the Russian classics, but had also acquired an excellent level of English. Many of Penguin's next cohort, however – Foote, Freeborn, Wilks, Glenny, Bethell, and Cooper – acquired their Russian-language skills through the JSSL military linguists' training programme, which included translation (Elliott and Shukman, 2011, pp. 71–72), largely excluded women (ibid., p. 31), and demonstrated solid academic knowledge of classic Russian literature (ibid., p. 143–144). Having benefited from much the same immersive language teaching that Magarshack had recommended for literary translators, these linguists found themselves well placed to undertake Russian literary translation commissions. Magarshack may have speedily turned his *Crime and Punishment* manuscript around comfortably within Penguin's suggested deadline of a year, but he was, arguably, already familiar with the story; and if in doubt he could have consulted an earlier translation for guidance. This was not the case for Glenny and his translations of Solzhenitsyn and, indeed, Bulgakov, where time was of the essence. *The New York Times* drew attention to Glenny's feat, stating: 'He was allowed little more than eight months to get the 280,000 word "August 1914" in shape for his editors' (1972). There is admiration for his achievement in meeting a pressured deadline and praise for his preceding translations. There is, however, also some criticism of his style, 'objected to by Americans as "slack" and filled with irritating Anglicisms' (ibid.). The slackness of Glenny's translation approach has been widely observed – by May (1994, pp. 145–153) and also France (2000, p. 608) – but still, Glenny's flair for literary translation has earned him respect. France evaluates the essence of his practice:

> Glenny's translations are never less than highly readable. He has a great feel for language and is not afraid to take idiomatic risks. But he is prone to the occasional blunder. Thus, for example, his *Black Snow* is extremely readable, bringing out very well Bulgakov's sardonic humour, but includes one extraordinary blunder, when he renders *Osenilo! Osenilo!* ('It suddenly struck me') as 'The autumn drew on'. He also misreads '*gostinaya*', 'drawing-room' as '*gostinitsa*', 'hotel', thus spoiling the point of the anecdote. But no translator is perfect, and Glenny deserves the highest praise for his efforts to bring Russian literature to the British public. (ibid.)

Contemporary critics were less forgiving of Glenny's shortcomings. In an academic article in *The Slavic and East European Journal* (Spring, 1971), New York University Professor Emerita Zoya Yurieff (1922–2000) evaluated Glenny's translations of *Black Snow* and *Heart of a Dog* by first defining the qualities of a good translator. She echoes Magarshack's sentiments:

> Translating is not easy. An ideal translator must know both languages perfectly, he must be an expert on the subject he translates, he must be endowed with an unerring aesthetic sense, and he must become so deeply involved in the original that he seems to metamorphose into the author in every way except in language. Neither man nor machine can be this ideal translator; however, approximations of this ideal are possible. A great deal depends on luck. The translator must be lucky. He must also realize that some things cannot be translated. The author too must be lucky. He has to find a translator who comes as close as possible to the above-mentioned qualifications. (p. 73)

Yurieff, inferring that Glenny falls short of an 'ideal translator', proceeds to criticise him; he 'handles Russian words inattentively, and disregards their lexical and stylistic colouring. He allows himself to edit, paraphrase, and add and omit words and phrases without regard for the intended meaning. He destroys [...] the "individual identity of the work of art"' (ibid., pp. 73–74). Yurieff cites more examples than France of Glenny's lexical miscoding and, as Magarshack before her about his translator peers and predecessors, conveys concern that these mistakes result in 'misinforming the Western reader' (ibid.).

Moral and ethical integrity

Even amidst high-paced negotiations, Solzhenitsyn's moral integrity permeated the commercial translation publishing debate, in a way not previously experienced in the Penguin Russian Classics division. During the period of negotiations for rights to publish *The Gulag Archipelago*, Penguin received a telegram from Solzhenitsyn in Switzerland. The message, typed in Cyrillic and appended with Penguin's subsequent gist translation in English in pencil immediately beneath, reveals the reach of Penguin's reputation as an accessible publisher, but admits that, according to Solzhenitsyn, there is scope for still more. Both messages appear as follows:

16.4.74
Издательство ПИНГВИН
директору Джеймсу Кокрану

многоуважаемый г. Кокран!
Я благодарен Вам за присланное. Я давно знаю и имею Ваши издания моих книг и отношусь к Вашему издательству с особой симпатией именно за то, что – оно народное, общедоступное. Я очень сочувствую целям Вашего издательства. С другой стороны я изумляюсь ненормальной цене книг на западе и очень бы хотел в отношении своих книг это положение изменить.

Если Ваше издательство желает обсудить со мной эту проблему и возможное наше сотрудничество, я готов принять Вашего представителя /говорящего по-русски, желательно, или уж по-немецки, в чем я сейчас вынужден упражняться/ на последней неделе апреля, т.е. с 22 апреля. Вы можете предварить меня письмом или телефонным звонком.

С уважением

Dear Mr C [Cochrane]
Thank you for your letter. I have long-known and possess your editions of my works and have particular feelings for your house because it is a popular one, accessible to all. I sympathise very much with your aims.

On the other hand, I am astonished at the abnormal prices of books in the West and wld [sic] very much like to change this as regards my own books.

If Penguin wld [sic] like to discuss this problem with me & our cooperation is possible, I am ready to receive yr [sic] representative (ideally speaking Russian or even German, which I must now practise) in the last week of April i.e. after 22 April. You can warn me by letter or phone.

Yrs [sic] sincerely
AS

At the foot of the page, as an aside to the original message and accompanying translation, someone (perhaps Cochrane himself) has added an asterisked point for further consideration 'It wld [sic] be interesting to relate Russian and Western book prices to income' (ibid.). In spite of Solzhenitsyn's appreciation of Penguin and willingness to discuss potential commissions, Penguin lost out on the rights to publish *The Gulag Archipelago*. It did, however, publish *Cancer Ward, August 1914, Matryona's House and Other Stories* in addition to *One Day*, but there is no archival evidence to suggest that Penguin pledged a commitment to reducing book prices further, as per Solzhenitsyn's telegram. Even without Penguin's assistance, the Solzhenitsyn Foundation, now known as 'The Aleksandr Solzhenitsyn Russian Social Fund' (Solzhenitsyna, 1997) – founded by Solzhenitsyn 'in the immediate aftermath of his arrest and expulsion from the Soviet Union' (ibid.) – donated the copyright and royalties from sales in every language of *The Gulag Archipelago* to fund 'The Russian Social Fund for Persecuted Persons and their Families'. According to Solzhenitsyn's wife, Natalia, interviewed in 1997 by Aleksandr Shchuplov: 'The price should cover only the translator's work and printing expenses. If any royalties are left, they will be used to memorialise the perished, and to help Soviet political prisoners and their families. And I will appeal to the publishers to donate their profits to the same cause' (ibid.).

Compared to early Penguin Russian Classic commissions, where the (often high) volume of correspondence represents time spent on text-based queries between editor-translator, there is an absence of correspondence between editor and translator in the Solzhenitsyn commissions. This shift perhaps points to greater proficiency on the part of the translator and/or to Penguin's trust (rather than disinterest) in their translators' abilities. In contrast to the Penguin Classics series, paratextual material for Russian texts in the Penguin Twentieth Century Classics and Penguin International Writers series was kept to the bare minimum. Introductions were rarely included, a trend which May recognises and attributes to two key factors: namely that, during the Brezhnev era, 'questions of style have been overshadowed by more superficial political considerations' (1994, p. 47), but also that 'publishers want audiences to think they are getting "the real thing"' (ibid., p. 48). This paratextual development also indicates the extent to which Penguin's readership was perceived to have evolved since Penguin's Russian Classics when Cochrane was keen for the translator's introduction to 'sell' the book to Penguin's intelligent but uninitiated target reader, and when Rieu expressed concerns over the accessibility of Russian names to the general reader. Even with a target audience now relatively initiated in Russian cultural and literary matters, however, occasional Translator's Notes appear in Solzhenitsyn texts. Far from being a translator's confession of failure (as Magarshack had claimed, and Rieu and Chukovskii before him), these notes formed an essential vehicle for explaining foreignising, highly specific Soviet stump compounds, and camp jargon, which would otherwise bewilder even a readership familiar with Russian customs.

By this stage, there are fewer letters from readers stored in the archives. Those who did write sought answers about the care publishers should take with Soviet literature, and the journey of such texts into the Western literary canon. There is the aforementioned Mrs. Addington, for example, who sought reassurance about the quality of Parker's translation and Penguin's commitment to producing the best versions of such literature. There was also a sixth-form student, Roger Michell of Clifton College, Bristol, who wrote to Penguin on 20 January 1972 seeking information – 'background material of any kind on the author concernerned [sic], or a proposed reading list on the subject' – for an English project he was undertaking on Solzhenitsyn. Michell requested specifically 'details of how the texts of these books ever reach the western printers as your selves [sic]', a question still being asked about translation publishing today. (Penguin's response on 26 January 1972 signposted Michell to their recently published *Solzhenitsyn: A Documentary Record*, but skirted any mention of how works by Solzhenitsyn and similar writers would generally reach the publisher.)

In spite of Hoare's expressed appreciation of the skills which a Solzhenitsyn translator must embody, the role of the translator in practice appears to have become of secondary importance at this stage, a development which led to a one-off episode of ethical embarrassment for Penguin. By now, there are no translator biographies, and translators' names are only included on the title-page. In the case of *Cancer Ward*, first published by The Bodley Head in 1968 and Penguin in 1971, the co-translators Lord Nicholas Bethell (former JSSL *kursant*)[11] and Russian-born David Burg (co-author with Feifer of the 1973 biography *Solzhenitsyn*, as cited by Mrs. Addington) do not receive this courtesy. There are no letters in the archive to explain how Bethell and Burg were commissioned and no correspondence relating to the actual process of translating Solzhenitsyn's novel, but the archive does contain a series of letters from early 1971 relating to this printing omission. Alarm is first raised by The Bodley Head's Guido Waldman in a letter to Penguin's Oliver Caldecott on 2 February 1971, but only after *Cancer Ward* has already been printed, widely sold, and was due a re-print. Waldman wrote:

> [...] in view of what she [your assistant] says about the imminence of a re-print (congratulations!), we'd better advise you quickly of a few mistakes which ought to be rectified.
>
> The major error is that of omitting all mention of the translators of the English edition. Their names ought to appear with suitable prominence on the title-page: Nicholas Bethell and David Burg.

The next letter that Caldecott received on the matter came from Burg himself on 16 April 1971, in which Burg made clear his views:

> I have spent several months away from England, and have only just learned from the press that you have omitted the names of the translators from your edition of Cancer Ward. The news was frankly a bit of a shock.

I note that it was a mistake and that you regret it. But I should like to ask you formally under the terms of my contract with the Bodley Head that you should not distribute any more copies of your edition without at least rubber stamping the names of the translators. I should also like to know how many books omitting the translators' names you have in fact distributed. I assume that all future printings will include the translators' names.

In his reply on 19 April 1971, Caldecott apologised emphatically, explaining the extensive measures Penguin had taken to rectify the error with haste; given the rarity of such exchanges, the majority of Caldecott's letter follows:

Yes, indeed, there was a slip, and the translators' names were omitted from our edition of CANCER WARD – a mistake which has caused us much distress. What is even more distressing is that the entire edition was over-subscribed and distributed before the mistake was spotted and it had been impossible to include an erratum slip or to over-pring [sic] the title page which, of course, we would have done if the omission had been discovered before the copies went out.

The new edition has gone to press and indeed should now be reaching the shops at any moment, if it has not already been done. I can only reiterate that we are extremely sorry about this mistake and we know it has caused both you and your fellow translator a great deal of embarrassment and irritation. I am afraid, however, there is nothing more we can do.

As you may have seen, there was an interview with myself in the "Evening Standard" in which the matter was explained.

Even though Penguin was prepared to go to significant lengths in order to restore goodwill between publisher and freelancer – an indication of how far professional relations have moved since Heinemann's dogged refusal to acknowledge Garnett's right to fair pay and royalties – Penguin's omission of Bethell's and Burg's names would, today, prompt comment under the Twitter hashtag '#namethetranslator', a campaign founded in order 'to ensure the contribution of translators is recognised' (The Society of Authors, 2008–2019). The Society of Authors' campaign page credits Helen Wang with helping to start the campaign, highlighting:

[...] the tendency amongst reviewers and marketers of translated works to omit the name of the translator. Often a translated work will mention only the name of the original author.

An author's name is their brand, and failure to properly credit any author lessens their ability to make a living from their work. (Ibid.)

The campaign is a modern response, therefore, to an old problem, as evidenced by Bethell and Burg. Compared to Penguin's Black Cover series, where translators received a biographical paragraph beneath the author's in the opening pages of the book, in which professional credentials were cited, the absence of such detail in the Twentieth Century Classics, Modern Penguin, and Penguin International Writers series was a regressive step in terms of translator visibility. Penguin was not alone, however, with US-based publisher Ardis making no mention of translators in their anthology, *Contemporary Russian Prose* (1982), and scarcely any mention in their follow-up anthology *The Barsukov Triangle* in 1984 (May, 1994, pp. 48–49). May acknowledges that 'in the century and a half since the early pirated editions of Gogol, Lermontov, and Turgenev, translation from the Russian seemed to have come full circle: the new efforts were more legitimate, more scholarly, but primarily a means for readers to find out more about Russia rather than a literary force in themselves' (1994, p. 49).

Conclusion

This chapter follows the shifting norms in translation publishing, from the Classic titles pursued by Rieu and Glover in the early Medallion phase to a new, post-Rieu phase. Russian literature fragmented into three different categories: commissions of lesser-known Classics by nineteenth-century Russian writers; re-translations of the key works by great Russian authors; and contemporary Soviet literature produced by living authors and sensationalised by their dissidence. The transition from Rieu to Radice included an overhaul of freelancing translators: the de-commissioning of early free-lancers and the commissioning of a new cohort of well-drilled, linguistically capable, creative practitioners, meeting their deadlines with ease and taking up little of their editors' time with text-based enquiries. Where the new cohort's language-based queries decrease in relative frequency, archived correspondence for this phase reveals more of the personal joys and professional woes typically afflicting the Penguin freelancer's personal life (Wilks); letters between Deutsch and her editors serve to illustrate the sensitivity and defensiveness described by Wolff (1968, p. 165) – understandably so in Deutsch's case – which form part of the freelancer's *hexis*; and Penguin's commercial pursuit of Soviet commissions exposes the paradox of the translator's position: essential to securing the commission in the first place, but forgettable and overlooked thereafter.

During this period, Penguin did not ask translators of Soviet literature to provide an introduction to the text; instead, these translators increasingly faded into the background. Their previous gatekeeping role, which had normally included writing an introduction to the text they had translated, became obsolete at Penguin Twentieth Century Classics and Penguin International Writers. Perhaps the role fell victim to Penguin's increasingly initiated, self-reliant readership, keen by now to feel like they were 'getting the real thing'. (This trend persists today; indeed, with the advent of the internet, every enquiring reader has the means to research the background to any text themselves.) Penguin's decision to remove paratextual material from translations of modern (as opposed to classic) Russian novels – paring the product down to the text alone – suggests a perception on the publisher's part that readers are more knowledgeable about living or recent authors and events, than they are about distant historical authors and events. The weighty paratextual material accompanying a classic Russian novel continues to be included, as evidenced by all recent translations of, for example, *Crime and Punishment*: Michael Katz's version for Liveright, Pasternak Slater's version for Oxford University Press, Ready's version for Penguin, and Pevear's and Volokhonskaia's Vintage version. The extensive front- and end-matter in these examples perform two roles. First, to provide a guide – often scholarly and consecrated by an established or rising name in the field (Bourdieu, 1993, p. 77) – designed to enhance the reader's understanding (and appreciation) of a remote literary era (Genette, 1997, p. 209). Secondly, to lend a competitive or informative edge to the text by providing any insight (historical, geographical, literary, or cultural) which previous versions might have overlooked. The more detailed the analysis which a text appears to require, the more positively it reflects on the translator's overall achievement in interpreting complex nineteenth-century subtleties for the modern reader. By contrast, the publisher's well-intentioned attempt to connect the reader more directly to Soviet (and now modern Russian) translations by removing explanatory material, removes vital visible markers of a translator's participation in the process and, consequently, risks diminishing their role.

As already seen with Magarshack and Garnett, the publisher and translator enjoy mutual benefit from the latter's paratextual presence (introductions, advertisements, and biographical notes). Translators gain visibility and prestige 'by the inclusion of a biographical note which outlines [his] credentials' (Deane-Cox, 2014, p. 75), and the translator's capital 'is, in turn, reflected back on to the publishers given their monopoly on the translator's proposed skill' (ibid.). It is inconceivable that Penguin Classics translators like Magarshack, Fen, and Edmonds – who engaged frequently with Rieu and Glover, reminding them of their existence, and who did not shy away from confrontations during the translation process – would allow themselves to be overlooked by their editors for long. Arguably, however, these translators' positions were strengthened during the early Penguin Classics years by not having to compete with a living Soviet cause célèbre vested with capital and power of their own. The existence of significant authorial capital (enhanced by political currency) during Penguin's Soviet phase eclipses the translator's capital, on which Penguin might previously have relied as a lever for sales. The translator's comparative lack of leverage and their absence from the paratext is to their own detriment, therefore, not to the author's or the publisher's. Soviet literature, published in haste between the 1960s–80s, could have been the making of several translators; it could have been their chance to capitalise on the craze of the moment and to become near-household names, following in the footsteps of Magarshack and Edmonds. It is ironic that the displacement of translators occurred during a period when Penguin editors were being actively considerate of them. In practice, translators became increasingly invisible, reduced to a name on the title page; and, on occasion, they did not even manage that, hence the rise of the hashtag on social media '#namethetranslator' (in which many translators, due to the computer-based nature of their work, actively participate).

Notes

1. 'I consider it an excellent translation which reads very well indeed.' Baldick, quoted in an internal memorandum from Jim C (James Cochrane) to AG (Tony Godwin), 14 May 1965.
2. The language of Baldick's report to Mr Duguid (21 November 1963) reveals the growing tension in his (and Penguin's) relationship with Magarshack.
3. '[...] Rieu's lead could work magic, the magic of pure, new, unfusty language, of the rediscovery of classical literature too long buried in school-books, that was almost Miranda-like in its innocence and delight' (Radice and Reynolds, 1987, p. 14).
4. In 'A History of Penguin Classics' (2008), Steve Hare identifies the 1960s as the decade of transition in Penguin's scholarly focus, attributing the new trend to 'the importance of the academic market, particularly in the United States' (p. 29).
5. Miss Jean Ollington (Penguin) replied to Edmonds's impassioned letter of complaint (dated 20 July 1961) with a letter clearly designed to pacify: 'I apologize for not acknowledging earlier receipt of the galleys [...] I am so sorry the galleys arrived without announcement in your absence. This letter seems to be a list of excuses, and I must apologize for the changes that were made in your manuscript [...].' (1 August 1961)
6. Ronald Wilks is cited as one of the company directors (see letter from Wilks dated 21 September 1971).
7. It is unclear whether this remained the case throughout his Penguin commissions but, by 1976, Wilks's letters no longer appear on company headed paper and he has moved to Mill Hill, London.
8. According to the biographical paragraph included on the title page of Wilks's 1972 Penguin translation of Gogol's *Diary of a Madman*, Wilks successfully defended his thesis on Russian literature at London University.
9. See: Ronald Wilks translations, BBC <https://genome.ch.bbc.co.uk/search/0/20?q=ronald+wilks#search> [Accessed 13 May 2019].
10. Like Penguin, Longman was gradually 'submerged' into the Pearson Group publishing house (Feather, 2006, p. 223).
11. The term for 'language cadets' enrolled on JSSL courses; according to Elliott and Shukman 'the Russian equivalent is *kursant* or in the plural *kursanty*' (2011, p. 30).

References

Anon., 1972. Solzhenitsyn: Writer Caught Between, 10 September, [online] Available at: *The New York Times Archive*, [Accessed 13 June 2019].

Anon., 1972. Obituary, Dr Robert Baldick, [online] Available at: *The Times Digital Archive*, [Accessed 04 October 2016].

Anon., 2008–2019. Name the Translator, [online] Available at: *The Society of Authors*, [Accessed 13 June 2019].

Anon., 2016. Ronald Wilks (1933–2016), Translator of Russian Literature, *Trinity College Cambridge Unpublished Obituaries*, [online] Available at: <https://share.trin.cam.ac.uk/sites/public/Alumni/obituaries/Ronald_Wilks.pdf> [Accessed 19 June 2019].

Anon., 2018. Genome Radio Times 1923–2009, *BBC*, [online] Available at: <http://genome.ch.bbc.co.uk> [Accessed 17 May 2019].

Bourdieu, P., 1993. *The Field of Cultural Production*. Cambridge: Polity Press.

• 1999. The Social Conditions of the International Circulation of Ideas. In: R. Shusterman, ed. *Bourdieu: A Critical Reader*. Oxford: Wiley-Blackwell, pp. 220–228.

Brinson, S.L., 2004. *The Red Scare, Politics, and the Federal Communications Commission, 1941–1960*. Westport: Praeger Publishers.

Burg, D., and Feifer, G., 1973. *Solzhenitsyn*. London: Hodder and Stoughton.

Deane-Cox, S., 2014. *Retranslation: Translation, Literature and Reinterpretation*. London and New York: Bloomsbury Academic.

Elliott, G., and Shukman, H., 2011. *Secret Classrooms, An Untold Story of the Cold War*. London: Faber & Faber.

Eliot, H., 2018. *The Penguin Classics Book*. London: Particular Books.

Feather, J., 2006. *A History of British Publishing*. 2nd ed. Abingdon and New York: Routledge.

Forrester, S., 2010. Review. *Notes from Underground and The Double*. Translated by Ronald Wilks, *Translation Review*, 80(1).

France, P., 2000. *The Oxford Guide to Literature in English Translation*. Oxford and New York: Oxford University Press.

Genette, G., 1997. *Paratexts*. Translated by Jane E. Lewin. Cambridge: Cambridge University Press.

Hare, S., 1995. *Penguin Portrait: Allen Lane and the Penguin Editors, 1935–1970*. London and New York: Penguin.

May, R., 1994. *The Translator in the Text: On Reading Russian Literature in English*. Evanston, IL: Northwestern University Press.

Moynihan, M., 2014. Loving the Art in Yourself, *Technological University Dublin*, [online] Available at: <https://arrow.dit.ie/cgi/viewcontent.cgi?article=1009&context=aaconmusbk> [Accessed 02 July 2019].

Oxford English Dictionary, 2018. OED editors of the 1920s: Jessie Coulson and James Wyllie, [online] Oxford: *Oxford University Press*. Available at: <https://public.oed.com/blog/oed-editors-1920s-jessie-coulson-and-james-wyllie/> [Accessed 3 June 2019].

Platt, B., 2008. Founding Father: E.V. Rieu. In: R. Edwards, S. Hare, and J. Robinson, eds. 2008. *Penguin Classics*. Revised ed. Exeter: Short Run Press, pp. 8.15.

Penguin Archive, Bristol: Bristol University Arts Library, Special Collections.

• Letter Edmonds to Miss Jean Ollington, 20 July 1961, DM1107/L119.

• Letter Miss Jean Ollington to Edmonds, 1 August 1961.

• Letter from Baldick to Mr Duguid, 21 November 1963, DM1107/L143.

• Letter from Cochrane to Duguid, 24 January 1964.

- Memo Betty Radice re. *Eugene Onegin* Translation, 11 March 1963, DM1107/L151.

  - Telex Sulkin to Dick Seaver, Viking Penguin Inc., 17 February 1978.
  - Telex Sulkin to Sue Zuckermann, Viking Penguin Inc., 28 February 1978.
  - Telex Zuckermann to Sulkin, 2 March 1978.
  - Letter Sulkin to Elisabeth Sifton, Viking Penguin Inc., 6 March 1978.
  - Letter Babette Deutsch to Michael Loeb, Viking Penguin Inc., 17 April 1979.
  - Memo Elisabeth Sifton to Michael Loeb, April 1979.
  - Letter Michael Loeb to John Rolfe, Penguin Classics, 4 May 1979.
  - Letter Sulkin to Deutsch, 6 June 1979.

- Memo Jim C [James Cochrane] to AG [Tony Godwin], 14 May 1965.
- Radice, B., 1984. A Classic Education (Betty Radice Remembers E.V. Rieu), *The Times Higher Education Supplement*, 19 October 1984, DM1187/3.
- Letter Miss Margaret Walsh, 29 December 1962, DM1107/D69.
- Letter Ronald Hingley to Penguin, 14 December 1962, DM1107/2053.

  - Memo Tony Godwin to Lane, 31 January 1963.
  - Memo AL to AG, 4 February 1963.

- Letter Mrs J.M. Addington to Penguin, 11 November 1974, DM1107/2053.

  - Letter Penguin to Mrs J.M. Addington, 12 December 1974.

- Letter Wilks to Miss Gill Woodeson, 16 Sept 1971, DM1952/329/044 L273.

  - Letter Wilks to Miss Gill Woodeson, 21 Sept 1971.
  - Letter Wilks to Cochrane, 26 October 1972.

- Memo Cochrane to Fred Plaat, 8 May 1972, DM1952/330/044/L291.
- Newspaper Cutting. 1974. Gorky (Review), *The Evening Standard*, 24 August., DM1952/331/044.3029.
- Memo from Helen Johns to Sulkin, 15 July 1975, DM1952/331/044.3029.

  - Letter Wilks to Sulkin, 21 April 1976.
  - Letter Sulkin to Wilks, 4 May 1976.
  - Letter Wilks to Sulkin, 9 November 1976.

- Letter Paul Keegan (Penguin) to Chatto & Windus, 22 July 1987, DM1952/334/044.490 4.

  - Letter Wilks to Keegan, 30 September 1989.

- Letter Penguin Joint Chief Editor Oliver Caldecott to Julia Rollason, Collins, re. *The Master and Margarita*, [n.d.] 1968, DM1952/676.
- Letter Guido Waldman (The Bodley Head) to Oliver Caldecott on 2 February 1971, DM1952/687.
- Letter Burg to Caldecott, 16 April 1971.
- Letter Caldecott to Burg, 19 April 1971.
- Letter Michael Hoare, Longman, to Dr. Walter, Luchterhand, 21 June 1971.
- Letter Roger Michell, Clifton College, Bristol, to Penguin, 20 January 1972.
- Letter Penguin to Roger Michell, 26 January 1972.
- Memo Judith Burnley to Tony Mott, 12 January 1974.
- Telegram A. Solzhenitsyn to Mr. James Cochrane, 16 April 1974.

Radice, W., and Reynolds, B. eds., 1987. *The Translator's Art*. Harmondsworth: Penguin.

Robinson, D., 2008. Becoming a Translator. 2nd ed. *London and* New York: Routledge.

Salisbury, H., 1963. One Day in the Life of Ivan Denisovich, *The New York Times*, [online]. Available at: <https://archive.nytimes.com/www.nytimes.com/books/98/03/01/home/solz-ivan.html> [Accessed 24 June 2019].

Scammell, M., and Hayward, M., 1970. *Russia's Other Writers*. London: Longman.

Solzhenitsyna, N., 1997. The Aleksandr Solzhenitsyn Prize is here for the Long Run. Interviewed by Aleksandr Shchuplov. [journal] *Knizhnoe obozrenie* [The Book Review] 21 October 1997. Translated from the Russian by S. Phillips. Available at: <https://www.solzhenitsyncenter.org/natalya-solzhenitsyn-interview-about-the-solzhenitsyn-prize> [Accessed 19 June 2019].

Speller, J., 2011. *Bourdieu and Literature*. New edition, [online] Cambridge: Open Book Publishers. Available at: <https://books.openedition.org/obp/481> [Accessed 22 May 2019].

Terras, V. ed., 1985. *Handbook of Russian Literature*. New York: Yale University Press.

Tilby, M., 2010. Baldick, Robert André Éduard (1927–1972), Oxford Dictionary of National Biography, [online] Available at: <http://www.oxforddnb.com/view/article/98382> [Accessed 04 October 2016].

Toker, L., 2008. Samizdat and the Problem of Authorial Control: The Case of Varlam Shalamov, *Poetics Today*, 29(4), pp. 735.758.

Wolff, H., 1968. Translation and the Editor. *Delos: A Journal On and Of Translation*, 1, Austin, TX: National Translation Center.

Yurieff, Z., 1971. Reviewed Works: *Black Snow* by Mikhail Bulgakov, Michael Glenny; *The Heart of a Dog* by Mikhail Bulgakov, Michael Glenny; *Heart of a Dog* by Mikhail Bulgakov, Mirra Ginsburg, *The Slavic and East European Journal*, 15(1), pp. 73–75.

Conclusion

This book has set out to analyse for the first time the people and the processes behind Penguin's Russian Classics. I have examined key agents involved in the series both in isolation within their socio-cultural settings, and as part of larger networks in order to understand the diverse, multidirectional forces, personalities, and influences that have shaped this modern phase of Russo-British literary history. This book has applied three methodological approaches: sociological, historical/archival, and textual. I have used them to analyse and develop two specific areas of study that have been identified as wanting by previous scholars: the need to fill gaps that still exist in our knowledge of Russian literature in English translation and the need for enhanced focus on publishers and translators as valued agents in the field in their own right.

Assimilation of Bourdieu's sociological concepts has afforded an appropriate structure and sharper focus upon the mechanics of the publishing business. This focus has in turn usefully illuminated my account of the development of Penguin's Russian Classics. Bourdieusian factors such as the convergence of internal (corporate) and external (market and socio-cultural) forces, the dispositions of agents, and the exchange of capital in the construction of this literary field, all provide a basic framework for this book. They enable the creation of a more meaningful picture of the complex dynamics operating within Penguin, both collaboratively and independently. Rather than drawing deterministic links between theory and practice, I have used Bourdieu's notion of *hexis* to unpack and foreground deeper complexities and contradictions in the field, including differently interpreting translators' attitudes and activities, since translators' dispositions are – as demonstrated by Magarshack, Wilks, and Deutsch – intrinsically complex.

This book explains why it is important to combine Bourdieu's sociological model of agent-analysis with historical/archival and close textual analysis in order to conduct a holistic investigation. For example, the combined study of Magarshack's private papers, his Penguin correspondence and his published translations has provided an in-depth knowledge of this particular phase of Russian literature publishing in the United Kingdom and an opportunity to explore the preoccupations of twentieth-century literary translation theory and practice, using my findings as an exemplar for twenty-first-century practices. On a more personal level, it has also provided valuable insight into this Penguin Classic translator's biography and opinions. My case study of Penguin has made a contribution to translation sociology by showing how detailed information found in archived material and translated texts may be pieced together and interpreted to illustrate dynamics in translating and publishing practices, which are relevant to Translation Studies research. These dynamics might, otherwise, be overlooked or misinterpreted. The Penguin case study has involved historical analysis of Western and Soviet literary translation trends during the Penguin era, a phase in Translation Studies that has itself been hitherto relatively understudied. In approaching this phase, I have demonstrated how Magarshack's theory and practice (unconventional in its time for incorporating elements from both Western and Soviet traditions) reflect the Russo-British influences in his own biography. The Magarshack microhistory also provides an essential point of comparison between the earliest Penguin translation expectations and practices under E.V. Rieu and those implemented later, when Penguin was commissioning translations of Soviet dissident literature.

My research shows that instances of theoretical flimsiness and even narcissism occur in Magarshack's own reflections; despite this, his theories always seek to validate the translator's contribution. Magarshack wanted the literary translation profession to recognise its own worth; he urged translation practitioners to demand both financial and reputational recognition from their commissioners. The salience of Magarshack's plea was shown in Chapter Four with Penguin's lamentable omission of the *Cancer Ward* co-translators Burg and Bethell. One further outcome from my case study, therefore, has been Magarshack's rehabilitation as a translator and as a theorist who should be celebrated for contributing to our modern appreciation of translators, who began to be overlooked during Penguin's Solzhenitsyn phase. Magarshack demonstrates a proactive mindset of 'defiant, honour-seeking' (Charlston, 2013, p. 55) self-assertion which is relevant and necessary to the profession even now. This aspect of my case study reaffirms Sela-Sheffy's and Charlston's arguments, therefore, that, far from being mutely submissive, some translators seek, hone, and believe in their own intellectual and professional prestige. In this respect, Magarshack's practice reflects the persona which he reveals in his letters and notes: he was a man of complexity, of competing and conflicting personal influences, but also a man of intense self-belief. This blend of attributes did not always make it easy for him to follow prescriptive rules and formulae in practice. For example, Magarshack's notes comment in general terms on the need to domesticate Russian texts for a British audience, but there are text-based specifics, as we have seen, which he treated inconsistently: the glossing over of Russian diminutives; the paraphrasing of idioms; and the Anglicising or omission of culture-specific references. As Charlston observes, bodily *hexis* extends 'into the body of the text' (ibid., p. 56) and the analysis of both – translatorial *hexis* and translated text – 'reveals something about the complex, decision-making processes involved in the translation' (ibid., p. 57). Once Penguin questioned Magarshack's practice in his last commission and tried to pin him down to translation minutiae, Magarshack adopted an attitude of resistance. This aspect of Magarshack's personal disposition, which illustrates Wolff's (1968, p. 165) evaluation of the translator as 'very sensitive' and 'defensive', has been spotlighted by my analysis of his archived papers and published texts. By contrast, Magarshack's successors – including Wilks, Freeborn, Foote, Glenny – do not exhibit prickliness in their correspondence. This development could be interpreted as a testimony to their confidence as native-speaker practitioners who also benefitted from the JSSL programme.

This book has provided the impetus to search archives for new material with a view to consolidating previously under-documented biographies, in particular Magarshack's. It has also re-examined previously documented biographies (Garnett's and Lane's, for example), but through a new lens. Even with its recognised limitations (occasional ambiguity, one-sided exchanges, and potential bias), an archive-based methodology for constructing microhistories has produced unexpected outcomes, namely the uncovering of Magarshack's previously unpublished papers on translation theory. There is scope to (re-)visit and scrutinise more fully other translators' archives, both in the United Kingdom[1] and in Russia[2] and the United States,[3] and to analyse what else can be learned from them and corresponding translations in terms of producing Russian literature in English translation. I hope that this archive- and text-based analysis will provide a scholarly model for future researchers wishing to conduct research into other Penguin series, translators, or, indeed, other publishing houses.

While there is a pre-Penguin history of publishers and translators of Russian literature, I have created the first, useful diachronic picture of Penguin's working practices. Penguin's approach to publishing translations – its mission, dynamics, and practices – offers rich material about practitioners and processes for Translation Studies research. In every publishing phase (Medallion, Black Cover, Twentieth Century Classics), Penguin's achievements have come about by devolving power to networks of carefully selected enthusiasts, experts, and advisors. Passionate about their subjects, dedicated to their own contributions for a range of personal and professional motivations, and galvanised by Lane's (and Rieu's) leadership, these individuals collaborated with Penguin's internal hierarchy to pursue a joint mission. This assertion challenges Bourdieu's over-generalised opinion that 'the intellectuals, rich in cultural capital and (relatively) poor in economic capital, and the owners of industry and business, rich in economic capital and (relatively) poor in cultural capital, are in opposition' (1993, p. 185). In a way that was previously lacking in translation publishing (as seen with Heinemann and Garnett, for example), the bonds of mutual reliance and the exchange of capital between agents appear to reach appropriate proportions under Rieu's editorship, assisted by dynamic market demand for their product. Bourdieu's claim, therefore, that '"pure art" and "commercial art" exist in a constant state of opposition' (ibid.) does not apply to the Penguin Classics series. With only a few exceptions (most notably Glover, but only after his long tenure at Penguin, and later Deutsch), agents felt sufficiently rewarded to dedicate time and energy to complete a Penguin commission well and on time. Many were motivated, no doubt, by the prospect of repeat print runs and the likelihood of ongoing royalties.

Lane and his agents looked outwards as well as inwards, keeping a careful note of changes in the social environment, shifts in the market, socio-political moods, and readership expectations, which would play to their advantage. They particularly noted changes to wages, the arrival of disposable income, post-war appreciation of books and aspirations for self-improvement, and post-war views on Russia. In response, Penguin maximised market opportunities and harnessed advancements in print technology, commissioning large print runs and stocking books more widely and accessibly than ever. Lane and his agents reinforced the reader's trust in the Penguin brand through advertising campaigns, both within the peritext of their books (end-cover book suggestions and lists of related titles) and beyond (in newspaper advertisements, articles, and reviews). The Penguin team also consciously cultivated the reader's affinity for the Penguin paperback through an inspired combination of value for money, user-friendly size, attractive and recognisable cover and logo design, collectability, and, in the case of Penguin Classics, informative introductions, accompanying notes and an accessible translation style.

The Penguin Classics series, operating under the auspices of the Penguin brand, benefitted from the company's established reputation and already wide recognition. On the back of Penguin's early success, and cashing in on the general reader's eagerness to acquire a thorough grounding, at affordable prices, in the sort of world literature that the educated elite would deem rudimentary, foreign-language literary canons found safety and publicity in numbers in the Penguin Classics series. Penguin fuelled mass interest by broadening the series across literary canons from several countries and cultures; they collectively pieced together a pan-European literary landscape in readable English. Penguin correctly anticipated human inquisitiveness: whilst it would be perfectly possible and acceptable to focus, for example, on only the French novels, in reality, the new type of dedicated and enthusiastic autodidacts, forged in Penguin's image, would be drawn to broaden their literary scope and consult other national literatures too. Acting upon this dependable level of reader curiosity, Penguin maintained its book sales. Translation commissions kept coming, often faster than the Penguin team could process them (as indicated at peak times in memoranda between editors and in their letters to enquiring translators). Later still, and after a somewhat hesitant start, Penguin realised the sensation that would accompany all of Solzhenitsyn's works if they could secure the rights to them.

Penguin diverted its attention away from other, lesser-known Soviet writers in order to pursue (competitively) as many of these zeitgeist publications as their budget would allow. The successful publication of key works by Solzhenitsyn enabled Penguin to maintain a high publishing profile and to broaden their existing customer base to include intellectuals and politicians. However, it also forced them to rush translations more than before, sometimes at the expense of the translator's convenience, sometimes at the expense of the source text's accurate transmission.

By commissioning talented freelance translators, paying them fair rates with negotiable deadlines and offering the prospect of repeat business, royalties, and even the potential, in some cases, to acquire a household reputation, Penguin secured a commitment to high-quality work and punctual delivery. This is the kind of mutually beneficial arrangement that Garnett ultimately found lacking from her own agreement with Heinemann, but which Magarshack, by contrast, worked to his advantage. Penguin, therefore, created gains on all sides. Magarshack earned his living, became a trusted name among Penguin translators, and was able to apply his considerable reputational and cultural capital to obtain work with numerous publishers. Gardiner, Fen and Magarshack (as émigré Russians), and Edmonds as a wartime linguist, all had mastery of an otherwise largely inaccessible and mysterious language, a phenomenon that set them apart from translators of the more widely understood languages like French and German. The Russian translators from that period can be regarded as more than 'simple adapter[s] of a foreign product' (Bourdieu, 2017, p. 20). Rather, they are the gatekeepers of a language and culture deemed at that time to be more remote and enigmatic than anything Western Europe could offer, a perception further highlighted by Churchill's famous analogy that Russia is 'a riddle, wrapped in a mystery, inside an enigma'. However, the gatekeeper role takes on a new, arguably more demanding dimension once the translator is required to convey – with speed and skill – niche Soviet lexis, as encountered, for example, in Solzhenitsyn's works.

The Russian literature that emerged in Anglophone translation during the twentieth-century was thus a product of two major groups. First, the translators, who brought their various professional backgrounds, skill-sets, and/or personal aesthetic, which could be adapted, or maybe, specialised, if required, to suit Penguin's specific needs and those of Penguin's readers. Secondly, the editors, who guaranteed the core Penguin values: the principles of equivalent effect and accessible literature in good modern English. This book has studied in depth these particular Penguin values that emanate, as I have argued, from Rieu's own carefully considered translation practice (in itself supportive of Lane's wider mission of democratising literature). However, apart from the brief mention of sample translations (which were supplied before Rieu would commission any translators to work with Penguin Classics), there is little evidence in the archive of Penguin making subsequent checks of the faithfulness and accuracy of translation manuscripts compared to the original text. The checks were generally provided gratis by readers, whether or not they had academic expertise. Penguin's usual trust in the translator facilitated considerable autonomy for the latter. While this was undoubtedly appealing to many, it also risked occasional flaws in practice. Take, for example, Magarshack's personal insistence on last-minute, costly corrections and, more significantly, his unexplained omissions of the Lazarus lines in *Crime and Punishment*. My research has also identified the emotional and psychological risks attached to working continuously in isolation, as experienced by Wilks.

Rieu honoured his commercial priorities and commitment to Allen Lane, but he also addressed the needs of his intelligent, if relatively uninitiated target readers. He hoped that the series would encourage them to form a lasting love of classic literature. He insisted that translations were composed without condescension or too many compensatory allowances, a decision which flattered the original qualities of both source text and author. However, we must ask whether more could have been done to check the quality of the translation beyond the basic benchmarks of accessibility and equivalence. As already discussed, the classic Russian literature that Penguin launched so enthusiastically from 1950 with brand new translations has itself, for the most part, been re-translated now.[4] Subsequent translators have built on the efforts of these early Penguin translators, identifying (with the benefit of hindsight) exactly what 'corrective' action should be taken in their own translations, whether to restore the text's original, stylistic features or to bring the target audience closer to the source culture. An overhaul of the older texts has, therefore, been a key priority in most cases and, as we have seen, there has been a concerted departure from their predecessors' efforts. These re-translations have taken into account and balanced the perceived needs of both the source author and an evolving target audience. In an apparent attempt to counter Magarshack's occasionally smooth and free translation style, his successor McDuff, for example, 'carries [this] literalism the furthest of any of the translators' (France, 2000, p. 596). Ready's post-McDuff translation of *Crime and Punishment* (2015) has seen a still more refined handling of Dostoevskii's idiosyncratic nuances; A.N. Wilson (2014) in *The Spectator* describes this version as 'colloquial, compellingly modern and [...] much closer to the Russian'.

Far from undermining or devaluing the earliest efforts bestowed upon the original Medallion Titles, recent re-translations of these works are timely, rejuvenating refinements of Penguin's Medallion legacy. The 'perfect' translation for all time does not exist, but there are versions that suit their era and their readers' tastes and cultural capabilities. For this reason, Penguin and Penguin's Russian translators should be acknowledged and celebrated for playing a most significant part in relaunching Russian literature, for cultivating a national interest in Russian culture in the readers of their day, and for preparing the general reader for the era of Soviet literature that later followed. Penguin's Russian Classics mission – the existence of a shared vision executed by skilful individuals working in collaboration and backed up by a corporate infrastructure – was an essential, necessary, though ultimately superseded stage for Russian literature in English translation.

Notes

1. Special collections at Leeds Russian Archive and the University of Reading hold archives for Russian/English translators (for example, Kornei Chukovskii, Natalia Kodrianskaia, Louise and Aylmer Maude, Tuckton House) and UK publishers (The Bodley Head, A & C Black Ltd., Chatto & Windus, Heinemann), respectively.
2. The Russian State Archive of Literature and Arts (RGALI) holds translators' personal collections, including the Soviet translation theorist Ivan Kashkin.
3. Curtis Brown Archive (which holds archived material relating to Magarshack) at Columbia Rare Book and Manuscript Library, Columbia University; Ardis Records, University of Michigan Special Collections.
4. The only Penguin exceptions are Magarshack's translation of Goncharov's *Oblomov*, and Edmonds's translation of Pushkin's *The Queen of Spades and Other Stories*, which are still in print.

References

Bourdieu, P., 1993. *The Field of Cultural Production*. Cambridge: Polity Press.

- 2017. A Conservative Revolution in Publishing. Translated from French by Vlot, M., and Pym, A. Available at: <https://www.academia.edu/32257217/Pierre_Bourdieu_A_conservative_revolution_in_French_publishing> [Accessed 24 February 2020].

Charlston, D., 2013. Textual Embodiments of Bourdieusian Hexis, *The Translator*, 19(1), pp. 51–80, DOI: 10.1080/13556509.2013.10799519.
Dostoevskii, F., 1866. *Crime and Punishment*, Translated from Russian by O. Ready., 2015. London: Penguin Books Ltd.
France, P. ed., 2000. *The Oxford Guide to Literature in English Translation*. Oxford and New York: Oxford University Press.
Wilson, A.N., 2014. This New Translation of Crime and Punishment is a Masterpiece, *The Spectator*, 20 September. [online] Available at: <http://www.spectator.co.uk/2014/09/crime-and-punishment-by-fyodor-dostoevsky-book-review/> [Accessed 24 February 2020].
Wolff, H., 1968. Translation and the Editor. *Delos: A Journal On and Of Translation*, 1, Austin, TX: National Translation Center.

Appendix 1
Titles in Penguin's Russian Classics, 1950–1970

Medallion Series, 1950–1962

Title	Author	Translator	Year Published	Penguin Archive Folder Reference
On The Eve	Ivan Turgenev	Gilbert Gardiner	1950	DM1107/L9
Three Plays	Anton Chekhov	Elisaveta Fen	1951	DM1107/L19
Crime and Punishment	Fëdor Dostoevskii	David Magarshack	1951	DM1107/L23
The Devils	Fëdor Dostoevskii	David Magarshack	1953	DM1107/L35
The Seagull and Other Plays	Anton Chekhov	Elisaveta Fen	1954	DM1107/L38
Oblomov	Ivan Goncharov	David Magarshack	1954	DM1107/L40
Anna Karenin	Leo Tolstoi	Rosemary Edmonds	1954	DM1107/L41
The Idiot	Fëdor Dostoevskii	David Magarshack	1955	DM1107/L54
War and Peace, vols. I & II	Leo Tolstoi	Rosemary Edmonds	1957	DM1107/L62 DM1107/L63
The Brothers Karamazov, vols. I & II	Fëdor Dostoevskii	David Magarshack	1958	DM1107/L78 DM1107/L79
Plays	Anton Chekhov	Elisaveta Fen	1959	DM1107/L96
The Cossacks	Leo Tolstoi	Rosemary Edmonds	1960	DM1107/L109
Dead Souls	Nikolai Gogol	David Magarshack	1961	DM1107/L113
The Queen of Spades and Other Stories	Alexander Pushkin	Rosemary Edmonds	1962	DM1107/119

Black Cover Titles, 1963–1970

Childhood, Boyhood, Youth	Leo Tolstoi	Rosemary Edmonds	1964	DM1107/L139
Lady with Lapdog and Other Stories	Anton Chekhov	David Magarshack	1964	DM1107/L143
Eugene Onegin	Alexander Pushkin	Babette Deutsch and Avrahm Yarmolinskii	1964	DM1107/L151
Fathers and Sons	Ivan Turgenev	Rosemary Edmonds	1965	DM1107/L147
A Hero of Our Time	Mikhail Lermontov	Paul Foote	1966	DM1107/L176
The Gambler [Bobok/A Nasty Story]	Fëdor Dostoevskii	Jessie Coulson	1966	DM1107/L179
Resurrection	Leo Tolstoi	Rosemary Edmonds	1966	DM1107/L184
Sketches from a Hunter's Album	Ivan Turgenev	Richard Freeborn	1967	DM1107/L186
The Home of the Gentry	Ivan Turgenev	Richard Freeborn	1970	DM1107/L224

Appendix 2
Transcript of Magarshack's translation taxonomy

<u>General</u>

Perfect Knowledge of Language of Original[1] Complete Acquaintance with the Subject

Dead Languages: Instances of Very Delicate Shades of Distinction

Liberty to Add or Correct Where Sense of Author is Doubtful

Liberty to Correct Careless or Inaccurate Expression

Style and Manner of Writing Same as the Original

True Character of Author's Style

Imitation of Style Regulated by the Nature or Genius of the Languages of Original and Translation

Translator Must Figure to Himself in What Manner the Original Author would have expressed himself if he had Written in the language of the translation

Translation Must have all the Ease of the Original Composition

Perfect Transcript of Sentiments and Style and Manner

Translator must adopt the Very Soul of the Author which must speak through his own Organs

Ease must not degenerate into licentiousness

Preposterous to depart from Sense for the Sake of Imitating Manner

Translation of Idioms

Genius of Translator must be akin to that of Original Author

Translator must be Recognised as the Creator of a New Work

Must not attempt to translate slang or colloquialisms into current slang or colloquialism of England or America

Every Translation must be Done over again every 25 years?[2]

Best Translations result of collaboration between Master of his Mother Tongue and Philological Expert in Original Language?

Any Translation is Merely the Creation of an Approximation but there is a Limit of Such an Approximation when we can speak of the <u>untranslatability</u>[3] of a Work

Reproduction of Rhythm of Original Text is height of Perfection of a Translator[4]

Prose Works more Difficult to Render than Verse because of idiosyncratic style[5]

Faithfulness to Tone, Mood and Content of Original while thinking: How would original author have said this if he had been writing in English?[6]

Great Difference between translating Contemporary Works and Classics

Only Realism founded on <u>Solid and Firm Foundation of Life</u> and not on <u>Book</u> Knowledge results in fruitful and Active Method of Artistic Translation[7]

Not only Words but <u>Thought</u> must be translated

Translator must Translate what the Author has Written and for <u>the Sake of which</u> he has written it

<u>Deviations</u> from original sometimes harmful, sometimes acceptable but sometimes Excellent

Mistranslation of Single Word leading to Religious Dogma

<u>Translator must Serve Author more than himself</u>

Must Keep Perfect Equilibrium between Literalness and Total Freedom: Can only be Achieved by Translator [who is a good Writer or Poet in his own right][8]

Recognition of Translator's Art by Prizes

Impossible criticise translation from a language the <u>Critic is</u> only vaguely familiar with[9]

Importance of thorough knowledge of background

Translator must be able to imagine clearly and distinctly the inner portraits of the characters of the original

Main thing in artistic translation is <u>talent</u>: knowledge of language <u>is not enough</u>

Interlinear translation merely make it possible for writers without talent to obtain the widest possible chance of being published[10]

Importance of combination of sound and sense and exact sensuous semantic and social and historical nuances of every word

Parochialism of assigning review books to Professors of the language in question[11]

Dangers of Public Subsidies of Translations

Translation as an Art (Lyubimov)

Translator's Organic Contact with Life[12]

Study of Colloquial Speech must be Conducted Everywhere

Translator must Live in Country whose language is that of the Translation[13]

Problem of Creation of Literary Type: Characteristic Speech of [Any Character in Original has to be carefully re-created: translator therefore must possess flexible and versatile command of words]:[14] he has no right to impoverish original author's language

Translation of Dialects[15]

Use of Archaisms: Proverbs and Idioms, Puns
Long periods: Translator must not interrupt author's deep breath[16]
Indirect questions, exclammations [sic], etc.
Imitation of Sounds
Defects of Standard Translations: Failure to Suggest Author not merely Great Mind but Great Writer[17]

Notes

1. Magarshack's irregular capitalisation has been reproduced according to his original document.
2. The question mark has been added in pencil.
3. Underlined in pencil multiple times (hereafter all under-linings are in pencil and, presumably, done by Magarshack). This statement is also prefixed by a pencilled question mark.
4. Statement has been marked out by pencilled brackets.
5. Ibid.
6. Ibid.
7. Ibid.
8. This phrasing has been highlighted by a bold, pencilled bracket.
9. Statement has been marked out by pencilled brackets.
10. Ibid.
11. Ibid.
12. Ibid.
13. Ibid.
14. Ibid.
15. Statement has been asterisked in pencil.
16. Statement has been marked out by pencilled brackets.
17. Ibid.

Index

For Product Safety Concerns and Information please contact our EU
representative GPSR@taylorandfrancis.com
Taylor & Francis Verlag GmbH, Kaufingerstraße 24, 80331 München, Germany

www.ingramcontent.com/pod-product-compliance
Lightning Source LLC
Chambersburg PA
CBHW071114100726
47908CB00008B/2369